The Indian Army founded by the East India Company in the eighteenth century was unique among the armies of the world in that it had two groups of officers – British and Indian. The intention was that the Indian officers, coming from similar backgrounds as their men and naturally understanding their social and religious mores and customs, would form the crucial link between the British officers and the sepoys. It is surprising, therefore, that there has been very little written, by either British or Indian historians, regarding the role and experience of those officers. They were promoted from the ranks and served for many years in their units, embodying both the spirit and the traditions of their regiments. So who were these Indian officers who look out at us from photographs taken from the eighteen eighties onwards? What was their background, education and training? How did they, and their British officers, interpret their role? The present volume is a long overdue attempt to answer these questions and to pay due tribute to the men who served the Raj and their country so well in peace and war. A wide variety of sources have been drawn upon, including interviews with British officers who served with the Indian Army. A thread running through the book is provided by the diary of Amar Singh, a Rajput from Jaipur. He was one of the first members of the elite Imperial Cadet Corps and served in China, France, Mesopotamia and on the North-West Frontier. He ended his military career as Commandant of the Jaipur State forces.

Dr Michael Creese is a retired headteacher and educational consultant with a life-long interest in military history and uniforms. His interest in the Indian Army was sparked by a visit aged eleven to an exhibition of model soldiers at Hamleys in 1947. He now has his own collection of model soldiers which naturally includes a strong Indian contingent. His doctoral thesis at the University of Leicester focussed on the Indian officers in four cavalry regiments, drawing on material in Britain and India. The scope of this thesis has been widened in the present volume to include infantry officers together with a broad history of the Indian Army. He has written a history of the Jodhpur Lancers which is awaiting publication in India.

'SWORDS TREMBLING IN THEIR SCABBARDS'

# War and Military Culture in South Asia, 1757–1947

www.helion.co.uk/warandmilitarycultureinsouthasia

## Series Editors

Professor Emeritus Raymond Callahan, University of Delaware

Alan Jeffreys, Imperial War Museum

Professor Daniel Marston, Australian National University

## Editorial Advisory Board

Squadron Leader (Retired) Rana Chhina, Centre of Armed Forces Historical Research, United Service Institution of India

Professor Anirudh Deshpande, University of Delhi

Professor Ashley Jackson, King's College London

Dr Robert Johnson, Oxford University

Lieutenant Commander Kalesh Mohanan, Naval History Division, Ministry of Defence, India

Dr Tim Moreman

Dr David Omissi, University of Hull

Professor Peter Stanley, University of New South Wales, Canberra

Dr Chandar Sundaram, Department of Continuing Studies, University of Victoria

Dr Erica Wald, Goldsmiths, University of London

## Submissions

The publishers would be pleased to receive submissions for this series. Please contact us via email (info@helion.co.uk), or in writing to Helion & Company Limited, 26 Willow Road, Solihull, West Midlands, B91 1UE.

## Titles

# Swords Trembling In Their Scabbards

## The Changing Status of Indian Officers in the Indian Army 1757-1947

War and Military Culture in South Asia, 1757-1947 No. 1

Michael Creese

'Our swords are trembling in their scabbards,
but have not yet shown their glitter.'

Daffadar Abdul Jabha, serving in France in 1915
with the 18th Lancers in a letter home to India.

 Helion & Company Limited

Helion & Company Limited
26 Willow Road
Solihull
West Midlands
B91 1UE
England
Tel. 0121 705 3393
Fax 0121 711 4075
Email: info@helion.co.uk
Website: www.helion.co.uk
Twitter: @helionbooks
Visit our blog http://blog.helion.co.uk/

Published by Helion & Company 2015

Designed and typeset by Bookcraft Ltd, Stroud, Gloucestershire
Cover designed by Paul Hewitt, Battlefield Design (www.battlefield-design.co.uk)
Printed by Lightning Source Limited, Milton Keynes, Buckinghamshire

Text © Michael Creese 2015
Images © as individually credited
Cover: Indian Army Officers and Non-Commissioned Officers, 2nd Regiment
of Cavalry, Punjab Frontier Force, c.1863. Oil on canvas by Gordon Hayward,
c.1890. © National Army Museum. A group of Indian Army Officers and Non-
Commissioned Officers, all holders of the Indian Order of Merit, seated and
standing under an exterior archway. The painting was based on photograph taken
as early as 1859 of eight officers and NCOs awarded the IOM for gallantry in
action during the Indian Mutiny (1857-1859). However, alongside the IOM stars,
the artist has added Indian Mutiny medals which were not distributed until 1863.
(Courtesy of the Council of the National Army Museum, London).

ISBN 978-1-909982-81-9

British Library Cataloguing-in-Publication Data.
A catalogue record for this book is available from the British Library.

For details of other military history titles published by Helion & Company
Limited contact the above address, or visit our website: http://www.helion.co.uk.

We always welcome receiving book proposals from prospective authors.

To the Indian officers, non-commissioned officers and men of the Indian Army who served the Raj and their country with fidelity and honour

# Contents

# List of Illustrations

# War and Military Culture in South Asia, 1757-1947
## Series Editor's Preface

The aim of this new academic historical series is to produce well-researched mono-graphs on the armed forces of South Asia, concentrating mainly on the East India Company and the Indian armed forces from 1757 until 1947. Books in the series will examine the military history of the period as well as social, cultural, political and economic factors, although inevitably the armies of the East India Company and the Indian Army will dominate the series. In addition, edited volumes of conference papers, memoirs and campaign histories will also be published. It is hoped this series will be of interest to both serious historians and the general military history reader.

The foundation of the series coincides with the rise of academic interest in Indian military history over the last few years. In particular the series will contribute to the 'new military history' of South Asia. This came to prominence at an academic confer-ence held in Cambridge in 1997 that was re-invigorated at two recent conferences held at the University of Greenwich and Jadavpur University, Kolkata in 2013-2014 with aim of 'Re-newing the Military History of Colonial South Asia'. The aim of this series is to harness this explosion of interest and channel it into a series of ground-breaking volumes that add to the growing historiography of the period. For example in the field of Second World War studies and the period until Partition, Daniel Marston and Tim Moreman have spearheaded this historical research with their volumes: *Phoenix from the Ashes: The Indian Army in the Burma Campaign* (2003) and *The Jungle, the Japanese and the Commonwealth Armies at War* (2005). These are complemented by Raymond Callahan's *Churchill and His Generals* (2007), a seminal work published in the United States that should be better known in the United Kingdom, and the wider study by Ashley Jackson on *The British Empire and the Second World War* (2006). Similarly there have been a number of relevant conferences such as one held at the Imperial War Museum in 2009, the papers of which were published as *The Indian Army, 1939-1947: Experience and Development* (2012). Daniel Marston's *The Indian Army and the End of the Raj* (2014) has also recently been published.

This interest has been mirrored in India as eight volumes of the official histories of the Indian Armed Forces during the Second World War were reprinted in India in 2012 and another four in 2014. They were originally published between 1954 and 1960. As Squadron Leader Rana Chhina stated at the launch of the reprints: 'As a resurgent India seeks to be a major player on the world stage, it behoves it to discard its narrow post-colonial world view, and to step up to reclaim the role that its armed forces played out on a global scale' during the Second World War. Anirudh Deshpande's *A Spring of Despair: Mutiny, Rebellion and Death in India, 1946* will be published in 2015. Similarly Rana Chhina and the United Service Institution of India are organising a number of events for the centenary of 'India and the Great War', including a number of detailed academic studies in partnership with this series. It is envisaged that monographs will be published on the role of the Indian Army in all the major First World War theatres as well as other aspects of the war such as the Indian State Forces and an edited volume of essays.

The series editors, members of the editorial advisory board and our publisher, Duncan Rogers of Helion, are all delighted to be involved in this series and we hope it will be of interest not only in the UK and India but globally, too.

Alan Jeffreys

# Acknowledgments

Any study of this nature depends very heavily upon the assistance and goodwill of many people. This book has its origins in a thesis written for the degree of Doctor of Philosophy at the University of Leicester and I am grateful to my supervisors in the School of Historical Studies. Dr Clive Dewey started me on the road, guided my faltering footsteps and suggested the role of Indian officers as a suitable one for study. When he left Leicester, Dr Peter Musgrave saw the thesis through to completion. I owe a considerable debt to Alan Jeffreys of the Imperial War Museum who has acted with great patience and forbearance as my editor for this volume and has helped me to avoid some of the more egregious errors. As always, however, the final responsibility for any faults rests with the author.

I am most deeply indebted to the late Mohan Singhji of Kanota, nephew of Amar Singh. for so freely providing access to the latter's diaries and for permission to quote from them. My wife and I spent a most delightful week with him at Narain Niwas, Amar Singh's home in Jaipur (now a hotel), and were also invited to see the diaries in situ in Amar Singh's library at Kanota. Sadly, Mohan Singhji died in February 2005 before my thesis was completed but Mohan's sons, Man Singh and Prithvi Singh, have been equally enthusiastic in their support.

Dhananajaya Singh hosted our visit to Jodhpur and helped enormously in my search for material on the Jodhpur Lancers. Colonel Karen Singh, late Poona Horse, generously gave me a copy of the latest version of his regiment's history and entertained my wife and I to a very pleasant evening in the Divisional Officers' Mess, Jodhpur, once the Officers' Mess of the Jodhpur Lancers.

The late Lt Col Emerson, Secretary of the Indian Army Officers' Association, very kindly put me in touch with a number of ex-Indian Army officers and they in their turn were most helpful in being prepared to share their experiences of working with Indian officers during and immediately after the Second World War. Paul Vickers, IT Director for the Army Library Service, assisted by providing me with references to the curriculum at Sandhurst in 1900 from the Prince Consort's Library, Aldershot.

I am most grateful to Gavin Edgerley-Harris, the Curator of the Gurkha Regimental Museum at Winchester for his assistance in providing material from the archives. I am also most grateful to the staff of the India and Oriental Library within the British Library, the staff of the Libraries of the National Army Museum, of the Imperial War

Museum, of the University of Cambridge Library and the National Archive of India for their unfailing patience and assistance in producing the material which I needed. The translations of letters to and from Indian officers soldiers serving in France and contained in the Reports of the Chief Censor offer fascinating comments on their feelings and concerns. I am most grateful to the British Library (Indian and Oriental Collections) for permission to quote from them. Dr Chandar S. Sundaram kindly read a late draft of my manuscript and made a number of helpful and perceptive comments from the Indian perspective. I am also grateful to him for allowing me quote from his, as yet, unpublished PhD thesis *A Grudging Concession: The Origins of the Indianization of the Indian Army's Officer Corps., 1817-1917*. This is a masterly and comphrensive survey of the topic and provided me with many fresh insights.

I am grateful to all of the following publishers/copyright holders for permission to quote from the books listed below and for which they hold the copyright.

*A Matter of Honour* by Philip Mason, copyright Sheil Land Associates Ltd.
*Between Two Worlds: The Diary of a Rajput Officer* by DeWitt C. Ellinwood Jr., copyright The Rowman and Littlefield Publishing Group.
*Sepoys in the Trenches* by Gordon Corrigan, copyright The History Press.
*The Road past Mandalay* by John Masters, copyright Pollinger Ltd.

Historians of the Indian army are deeply indepted to the Naval and Military Press of Uckfield for their programme of reprinting scarce regimental histories of the Indian Army and I am most grateful for permission to quote from a number of these. Efforts have been made to contact the other copyright holders of material quoted but without success.

Last but by no means least, I am happy to pay tribute to my wife, Lesley for her constant encouragement and enthusiasm. Together we have explored the battlefields and war cemeteries which hold the final resting place of so many Indian soldiers in Northern France. It was at her suggestion that I contacted HH the Maharaja of Jodhpur for information about the Jodhpur Lancers. That enquiry led to a visit to Jodhpur to write the history of the Jodhpur Lancers and to the making of many friendships and subsequent visits.

# Ranks and Decorations in the Indian Army

| Cavalry | Infantry | Rank insignia | British equivalent |
|---|---|---|---|
| Risaldar-Major | Subedar-Major | Crown | |
| Risaldar | Subedar | Two stars | |
| Jemadar | Jemadar | One star | |
| Daffadar | Havildar | Three stripes | Sergeant |
| Lance-Daffadar | Naik | Two stripes | Corporal |
| Acting Lance-Daffadar | Lance-Naik | One Stripe | Lance-Corporal |
| Sowar | Sepoy | | Trooper/Private |

In more modern times, the word 'sepoy' (from sipahi, the Persian word for army) is usually replaced by 'jawan' – 'young man'. One Indian officer usually served as assistant quartermaster and another as assistant adjutant; the latter was known as the Woordy-Major. In the cavalry there was, for a period, the rank of ressaider, intermediate between the risaldar and the jemadar. The ranks of Risaldar-Major and Subedar-Major having been first introduced in 1818 were re-instituted in 1866.

The titles of the Indian infantry regiments went through a bewildering series of changes in their history. For example, the 7th Madras Infantry, having been re-constituted in 1902, became the 67th Punjabis in 1903 who in turn metamorphosed into the 1st Battalion of the 2nd Punjab regiment in 1923. The 40th Bengal Infantry originated in the Shajahapur Levy raised in 1858. In 1861 it became the 44th but returned to the original number when the Gurkha battalions were removed from the line. By 1890, it was recruiting from further west and so became the 40th (Baluch) Regiment. Two years later it was known as the 40th (Pathan) Begal Infantry. It became the 40th Punjab in 1901 before reverting to the title of 40th Pathans in 1903 and finally becoming the 5th Battalion, 14th Punjab Regiment in 1922.[1]

---

1    Michael Glover, *An Assemblage of Indian Soldiers and Uniforms*, (London: Perpetua Press, 1973), p. 22.

**Indian Decorations**

The highest ranking award specific to the Indian Empire was the Most Exalted Order of the Star of India, established in 1861 and restricted to the very highest of the nobility. The Order of British India (OBI) was instituted in 1837 and consisted of two classes. The First Class, restricted to risaldars (subedars in the infantry) and above carried with it the title 'Sardar Bahadur' – literally 'The Brave One' or 'Chief'. The Second Class, open to jemadars, carried the title 'Bahadur'. Both awards brought with them a small increase in pay. The Indian Order of Merit (IOM), also instituted in 1837 and consisting of three classes, was open to any Indian officer or soldier, regardless of rank and was awarded for an act of conspicuous gallantry in the face of the enemy. This is the oldest award for gallantry in the British Empire, pre-dating the Victoria Cross by nineteen years. A first act of bravery gave admission to the Third Class, a second act by the same man to the Second and, extremely rarely, a third act gained the First Class award. All three classes included an increase in pay. In 1911, Indian officers and other ranks became eligible for the award of the Victoria Cross (VC), the highest British award for gallantry, and accordingly the First Class IOM was abolished. In 1917, Indian officers became eligible for the Military Cross (MC).

The Indian Distinguished Service Medal (IDSM) was introduced in 1907 as an award to recognise distinguished service by officers, non-commissioned officers and men of the Indian land forces. The Indian Meritorious Service Medal (IMSM) was established in 1888 and was granted, with a small annuity, to soldiers with eighteen or more years of meritorious service. Very few were awarded before 1914. In addition to all of the above awards, Indian soldiers were entitled to the appropriate campaign medals.

Current decorations in the Indian Armed Forces include the Param Veer Chakra (PVC) which is their highest award for gallantry – the equivalent of the VC. The Maha Veer Chakra (MVC) is the second highest gallantry award in India and the Param Vihist Seva Medal (PVSM) is awarded for distinguished service of the highest order. – the equivalent of the British Distinguished Service Order (DSO).

# Introduction

One of the unique features of the old Indian Army was the position and status of its Native Officers. For well over 150 years the title of Native Officer was honoured and greatly prized by the Indian Army. In no other army were there such men, having the social standing and prestige of officers together with the hard won experience of men who had learnt their trade in the ranks. Their influence could be, and frequently was, decisive. They upheld the authority of the commandant and at the same time upheld the interests and welfare of the rank and file.

These are the opening lines from a note describing the career of Subedar-Major Kharaksing Gurung Sirdar Bahadur, Order of British India 1st Class, Member of the Order of the British Empire, Indian Distinguished Service Medal, of the 6th Gurkha Rifles. He served in the regiment for 44 years including campaigns in Gallipoli, Mesopotamia, Waziristan and the Middle East.[1]

Throughout the period under discussion, Indian officers were a crucial link in the chain of command in the Indian Army. It is surprising, therefore, that there has been very little written, by either British or Indian historians, regarding the role and experience of those officers. They themselves have left very few records of their exploits and the regimental histories, written by British officers or historians, generally have very little to say about them. More general histories of the Indian Army usually make little reference to the importance of Indian officers although the issue of 'Indianisation', that is the admission of Indians to regimental command, has been addressed by a few historians such as David Omissi.[2] The Indian officers serving in their regiments were 'Men who had earned their commissions by brave and loyal service, of fighting stock, with martial traditions, ready to give their lives for the King-Emperor, proud of the profession of arms.'[3] They had served for many years in their units and embodied both the spirit and

---

1   Typewritten note in the papers collected by Lt-Col H. R. K. Gibbs, 6 G.R. now held in the archives of the Gurkha Regimental Museum, Winchester. Hereinafter 'The Gibbs Papers'.

2   See David Omissi, *The Sepoy and the Raj: The Indian Army 1860-1940* (Basingstoke: Macmillan, 1994).

3   Gen Sir J. Willcocks, *With the Indians in France* (London: Constable, 1920), p. 5.

the traditions of their regiments. They were looked up to by the sepoys who saw them as father figures. Lieutenant General Hanut Singh suggests that 'There can be no doubt that the efficiency for which the Indian army is justly famous, owes much to the Viceroy's Commissioned Officers.'[4] So who were the Indian officers who pose, rather stiffly, in paintings and photographs taken from the eighteen eighties onwards? What was their background, education and training? How did they, and their British officers, interpret their role? The present volume is a long overdue attempt to answer these questions and to pay due tribute to the men who served the Raj and their country so well in peace and war.

For almost two hundred years there were two armies in India. The first of these, the British Army, was made up of a number of regular units, infantry and cavalry, together with their supporting arms. These units were officered entirely by British officers, trained at the Military Academies at either Woolwich or Sandhurst. The second army was the Indian Army, reconstructed after the Great Mutiny/Rebellion (or The First War of Independence) of 1857-58 but still, until the turn of the century, organised into the three Presidency Armies of Bengal, Bombay and Madras. This Army, which was eventually to be divided between India and Pakistan in 1947, was unique among the armies of the world in that it had two groups of officers – British and Indian. The intention was that the Indian officers, coming from similar backgrounds as their men and naturally understanding their social and religious mores and customs, would form a link between the British officers and the sepoys.

The main Army was supplemented from time to time by various Auxiliary and Militia units, raised from Europeans and Anglo-Indians. These were volunteers who formed something in the nature of gentleman's clubs but they were from time to time called upon to act in some local crisis.[5] In particular, the various railway battalions were responsible for the protection of the 28,000 miles of railway in the sub-continent. They were also used to replace regular units on garrison duties. Auxiliary units were called out on a number of occasions between the two World Wars to guard installations and/or to deal with communal riots.[6] Organised in the same way as units of the British Army, each unit had an adjutant from the regular Army.[7]

In addition to the British and Indian Armies were the forces of the Princely States, which varied considerably in size and quality. The threat of a Russian invasion through Afghanistan in 1885 prompted the bringing together of the best of the State Forces under the Imperial Service Troops scheme. These would be part funded by the government, brought up to the same standard as the infantry and cavalry units of the Indian

---

4    Lieutenant General Hanut Singh, *Fakhr-i-Hind, The Story of the Poona Horse* (Dehra Dun: Agrim Publishers, 1993), p. 92.

5    See Carman, W.J., *Indian Army Uniforms (Cavalry)* (London: Leonard Hill Books, 1961), p. 198.

6    See Peter Boyden, 'The Indian Army and the Defence of India' in *Soldiers of the Raj*, eds Alan Guy and Peter Boyden (London: National Army Museum, 1997), p. 96.

7    See Major Donovan Jackson, *India's Army Vol III* (London: Sampson Low, Marston and Co, 1940), p. 205.

Army, and would be available in time of war to supplement the regulars. A number of these units, for instance the Jodhpur Lancers, were to fight with great distinction in a number of theatres of war. These units were officered entirely by Indians, with one or two attached British 'advisers'.

The British-led sepoys were to fight their first battles in India against Indian troops raised by the French, with a decisive battle at Plassey in 1757. Once the French had been defeated and the British had become the only European power with a major presence in India, they began to extend their influence across the sub-continent. At the end of the eighteenth century the British were involved in four wars in southern India against Hyder Ali and his son, the infamous Tippoo Sahib, known as the Tiger of Mysore.[8] During the same period they also had to contend in central India with the Maharatha Confederacy made up of several powerful polities. The Confederacy was only finally defeated in 1818. British and Indian units saw almost continuous service throughout the latter half of the nineteenth century, chiefly, but not exclusively, on the North-West Frontier. The first half of the nineteenth century saw the Indian Army fighting in Afghanistan, Burma, Sind and against the Sikhs. The Sikhs proved to be doughty fighters and so impressed were the British by their fighting qualities that they began to recruit them enthusiastically into the Indian Army, even to the extent of forming regiments composed entirely of Sikhs such as the Ludhiana Sikhs and Rattray's Sikhs. Similarly, following the defeat of the Gurkhas of Nepal in 1818, they too were recruited and they continue to serve with great distinction in the British and Indian armies. Regiments where the men all came from the same class, such as the Gurkhas and some other regiments, were known as class regiments. In other regiments the classes were divided into different companies. For instance, of the regiments which went to France in 1914, the 9th Bhopal infantry had one double company each of Sikhs, Punjabi Muslims, Rajputs and Brahmins. The 33rd Punjabis had two double companies of Punjabi Muslims and one each of Sikhs and Pathans.[9] These mixtures of classes could produce their own problems, with different languages, customs and dietary requirements among the companies.

The Second Afghan War (1878-80) revealed a number of defects in the Indian Army and in 1895 the three separate Presidency Armies were amalgamated and the Army divided into four commands.[10] When Lord Kitchener became Commander-in-Chief of the Indian Army in 1900 he set about a further series of reforms. He organised the Army into two Commands in which Northern Command had four divisions and the Southern Command five. A Staff College was established and the Army was re-equiped with a more modern rifle and the 2.75 inch Mountain Screw Gun. He produced an Army that was trained for warfare on the Frontier but it was never envisaged that the Indian Army would fight a large-scale war in Europe. Nevertheless,

8    See Philip Mason, *A Matter of Honour* (London: Jonathan Cape Ltd, 1994), p. 18.
9    See Gordon Corrigan, *Sepoys in the Trenches* (Staplehurst: Spellmount Ltd, 1999), p. 220.
10   See Boris Mollo, *The Indian Army* (Poole: The Blandford Press, 1981), p. 103.

a Corps from this unified Indian Army was to be the first reinforcement from the Empire to reach the hard-pressed British Expeditionary Force in Belgium in 1914.

Indian officers were initially referred to as 'native' officers. Officers in the infantry were known as 'subedars' and 'jemadars' with the cavalry equivalent of subedar being 'risaldar'. The word 'subedar' was derived from 'subah' meaning a province and 'dar' meaning a holder or keeper. From 1763 Indian officers received their commissions from the East India Company for which they had to pay a sum amounting to one week's wages.[11] It is important to distinguish clearly between those Indians who rose through the ranks to become jemadars and subedars and those who were commissioned after attending the Military Academies at Sandhurst or, later, Dehra Dun. From about 1935 those Indian officers who had followed the traditional route up through the ranks, were termed Viceroy's Commissioned Officers (VCOs) – indicating that they owed their commissions to the Viceroy rather than the Crown. After the First World War, Indian officers began to emerge from either the Royal Military Academy, Sandhurst or, later, it's Indian equivalent at Dehra Dun with King's Commissions. The former were termed King's Commissioned Officers (KCOs) and the latter King's Commissioned Indian officers (KCIOs). To add to the confusion, during the Second World war there were also Emergency Commissioned Indian Officers (ECIOs). The term 'Indian officer' has been used throughout this volume, adding the appropriate initials where necessary.[12]

To be a soldier in nineteenth century India was to be a member of an honourable profession and the Hindu warrior caste enjoyed high status; their standing within the population was very different from that of Wellington's 'scum of the earth'. Lord Kitchener, when Commander-in Chief in India, wrote:

> Soldiers of the Indian Army are of comparatively high social standing; many of them are of good birth. Some, poor as they may be, will take no other service except that of a soldier. They possess many sterling and admirable qualities and have proved themselves excellent fighting men and fit to stand shoulder to shoulder with the best. It follows that they are proud, and being sensitive, their susceptibilities are easily offended.[13]

The sowar (trooper) making his way back on horseback to his rural village on leave would be a respected member of the community. The East India Company, and later the British Government, took pains to ensure that this status was maintained and enhanced. Honours and awards, pensions and grants of land, privileges before

---

11  See Philip Mason, *A Matter of Honour*, p. 65.
12  The precise date on which the term VCO was introduced appears uncertain; see Rana China and Tony McClenaghan 'The VCO: Origin and Development' in *Durbar, The Journal of the Indian Army Historical Society*, Vol 28, No 3, Autumn 2011, pp. 134-142.
13  Lord Kitchener, Memorandum dated 1904, quoted in Sir G. Arthur, *Life of Lord Kitchener* (London: Macmillan and Co, 1920 Volume II, p. 183.

the courts, all helped to give dignity to serving and retired soldiers of the Indian Army. But these men were not mere mercenaries, serving the highest bidder for pay and pension only. Pandit Rambhaj Datt speaking at the 19th Session of the Indian National Congress at Madras in 1907 said 'We go to fight our battles not for 6 annas sake but for honour's sake, for duty's sake.'[14] The notion of *izzat* – of honour – was a crucial part of the Indian soldier's way of life: 'The Army works on izzat, born of pride – and the leader is the one who can get all the izzat the men need.'[15] The men recognised their obligation to fight, and if necessary to die, which service in the Army brought with it. Brigadier Bristow, who served for many years with the Dogra Regiment, wrote: 'According to his caste, a Dogra Rajput in the army believed that he was born into the world to be a soldier, and to fulfil his life he had to be a good soldier, with a clean conduct sheet and held in respect.'[16] Another Hindu concept is that of *dharma*, a code of conduct which may be translated as 'duty' – a sense of moral obligation.[17] The soldier's *dharma* is to fight and this, too, must surely have affected the sepoy's attitude towards their service: 'The Indian soldier, drawn from castes having their own martial traditions, was compelled by his *dharma* to soldierly virtue, which the all-encompassing life of the regiment did its best to reinforce.'[18] As Stephen Cohen points out, the concepts of honour and duty could be used by the British in order to further their own ends.[19]

In May 1915, Major Hira Singh serving with the State Forces in Kashmir wrote to two men, perhaps relations, serving with the Indian Corps in France:

> O dear friends, you know that for three or four generations we have been eating the salt of the British government. So that if we fulfil the obligation of this salt what shame is there in that? If you betray any cowardice, weakness or disloyalty you will be forever dishonoured and disgraced. The man who fears on the battle-field, who displays any pusillanimity, is sure to be killed. Dulce et decorum est pro patria mori.[20]

The use of the Latin quotation contrasts interestingly with Wilfred Owen's use of the same phrase in his well known poem about the effects of a gas attack – and, of

---

14   Report of the 19th Session of the Indian National Congress, quoted in Lt-Col Gautam Sharma, *The Nationalisation of the Indian Army, 1885-1947* (New Delhi: Allied Publishers Ltd, 1996), p. 36.
15   Brig H S Yadav, 'Tips from the Subedar Major', *JUSII*, Oct-Dec 1965, p. 249.
16   Brigadier R. C. B. Bristow, *Memories of the British Raj* (London: Johnson, 1974), p. 100.
17   See Gitanjali Kolanad, *Culture Shock, India* (London: Kuperard, 1994), p. 42.
18   J. Greenhut, 'Sahib and Sepoy', *Military Affairs*, Number 48, 1984, p. 18.
19   See Stephen Cohen, *The Indian Army: It's contribution to the development of a Nation* (New Delhi: Oxford University Press, 1990), p. 51.
20   Reports of the Chief Censor: Letters to and from Indian soldiers in the Great War, OIOC, L/MIL/5/826.

course, the country for which the Indian soldier was being asked to die for was not his own.[21]

In addition to sheer courage, there is a great sense of duty and honour summed up in the word '*izzat*'and as Philip Mason has pointed out: 'There was pride in caste, pride in family service, pride in the regiment.'[22] Future fame was also closely linked to *izzat*: 'A soldier who did great deeds would be spoken of and remembered even after his death. There would be reputation in the eyes of the world.'[23] This emerges in many of the letters written to and from Indian soldiers serving in France in 1914/15. For instance, Subedar Shad Muhammad Khan wrote from India to his brother Daffadar Faiz Mohammad Khan who was serving in France: 'Better a cairn in France than the noise of thy cowardice throughout the world!'[24] There was also a strong spirit of loyalty to the King-Emperor as well as honour and self-sacrifice among the Indian soldiers fighting in France. Sowar Tufazzal Husain Khan wrote to a friend in India in August 1915:

> I am a soldier whose business is to kill and fight and die. For men the battlefield is a place of enjoyment. One day we must all die, and if we die making a glorious reputation, 'Praise be to God' goes without saying.[25]

As George Jack points out, during the First World War the British continued to nurture the sepoys loyalty to the King-Emperor and his generals.[26] Indian officers met the King while they were on leave in London and had their gallantry medals presented by him. Lord Roberts (Bobs), the doyen of, and a great supporter of, the Indian Army, died shortly after reviewing Indian troops in France on a very cold day in 1915. His body was escorted back to England by a bodyguard of Indian troops.

European armies had been organised along regimental lines since the sixteenth century. Great stress was laid upon regimental identity in order to foster a communal loyalty and to strengthen morale. Distinctive uniforms, regimental colours, battle honours, all these combined to encourage a feeling of tradition and of a regimental community. The British recognised the significance of *izzat* and were quick to encourage the notion of regimental honour and traditions within the Indian Army.[27]

21  Wilfred Owen, 1917, *Dulce et Decorum est.*
22  Philip Mason, *A Matter of Honour*, p. 126.
23  Omissi, *The Sepoy and the Raj*, p. 79.
24  Reports of the Chief Censor, OIOC, L/MIL/5/826.
25  Ibid.
26  See George M. Jack, 'The Indian Army on the Western Front, 1914-15: A Portrait of Collaboration', in *War in History*, 13 (3), 2006, pp. 329-362.
27  See Kaushik Roy, *Brown Warriors of the Raj* (Delhi: Manohar Publishers Ltd,2008), pp. 202 et seq.

This was especially true in the case of Sikh and Gurkha regiments, which were rated particularly highly.[28] Lt-Gen Chibber wrote in 1984:

> The basis on which esprit-de-corps is promoted within the Indian army as a whole, continues to be what we inherited in 1947 – my unit/regiment/corps is the best and the noblest: I must do my utmost to ensure that it always stays at the very top; no sacrifice is too great to uphold its honour, tradition and good name.[29]

Increasingly throughout the nineteenth century the British recruited only from the so-called martial classes – Rajputs, Brahmans, Jats, Dogras, Gujars, Sikhs, Punjabi Muslims, Mahrattas, Pathans, Afghans and Gurkhas. This policy added to the soldier's status and their exclusivity and systematised the cultural and physiological differences between the classes. Stephen Cohen, writing on the martial races within the Indian Army, states that:

> The martial race theory, as well as the close connection of the (British) officer to his troops, enabled the British to strengthen the dependent relationship by going beyond it, giving the Indian Army a character that was unique among colonial armies.[30]

There was, however, a downside to this policy, as Tony Heathcote points out; it was the martial races which were the most backward in terms of western education and intellectual achievement.[31] Not only that, but by excluding educated Indians from recruitment as not being members of the so-called martial classes, the British justified their refusal to offer King's Commissions to Indians.[32] The vastly increased demand for manpower during the First and Second World Wars meant that recruits were taken from classes previously considered non-martial and it was found that they were perfectly able to perform as effectively as their previously favoured brethren. As Cohen puts it: 'For any who cared to examine the performance record it was clear that with adequate leadership and training virtually any group could be employed some-where in the military.'[33]

Although recruitment from the so-called martial races was encouraged, there was no suggestion during the nineteenth century that such men were fit to be officers on

---

28   See, for instance, Heather Streets, *Martial Races* (Manchester: Manchester University Press, 2004).
29   Lt Gen M.L. Chibber, 'Regimental System and Esprit-de-Corps in the Indian Army', *Indo-British Review,* 16 (1984), pp. 139-150.
30   Cohen, *The Indian Army*, (Delhi: Oxford University Press, 1990), pp. 49-50.
31   T. A. Heathcote, *The Indian Army: The Garrison of British Imperial India 1822-192.* (London: David and Charles, 1974), p. 94.
32   See J. Greenhut, 'Sahib and Sepoy', *Military Affairs*, Number 48, 1984, p. 16.
33   Stephen Cohen, *The Indian Army*, pp. 49-50.

the same footing as British officers. Right up to the start of the Second World War, the majority of British officers in the Indian Army agreed with the official doctrine that the military was best organised upon class lines and that recruitment should be from the martial races.[34] When it was found that the martial races were often too poorly educated to cope with the technical demands of a modern army, greater attention was paid to educating them in British-style schools. With the coming of Independence in 1947, it might have been thought that the ranks of subedar and jemadar would have been abolished as relics of the Raj. However, the two-tier system still remains within the Indian Army with what had been VCOs now referred to as Junior Commissioned officers (JCOs). Post-Independence, the bulk of India's and Pakistan's armies are still recruited from the martial classes and, as General Rajendra Nath points out: 'Unlike the officer-corps of most other former colonies, that of India has maintained or even surpassed colonial levels of professionalism.'[35]

This book will also tell the story of the military career of Amar Singh. He was born in Jaipur in 1878, the son of a court official and land owner. When he was ten he was sent to Jodhpur to be educated under the supervision of Sir Pratap Singh, three times regent of Jodhpur. Amar Singh attended the Powlett Nobles' School which had been established by Sir Pratap Singh and later acted as private secretary to him. As part of his education he was required to keep a daily diary in English. The first entry is dated September 3rd 1898 and the last, unfinished, entry is dated 3rd September 1942, the day of his death. In addition to the daily entries, Amar Singh from time to time wrote a series of longer 'Notes' on a wide variety of topics. He served as a squadron commander with the Jodhpur Lancers in China in 1900 and was one of the first intake of cadets into the Imperial Cadet Corps. Subsequently he served as an ADC to General Sir O'Moore Creagh before being posted to the Indian Corps in France in 1914. In 1919 he was on the North-West Frontier before leaving the Army and eventually becoming Commandant of the Jaipur State Forces. We thus have an eyewitness account, written from an Indian viewpoint, of many of the important events in the history of the Indian Army during the first half of the twentieth century. Amar Singh is a complex character. He was quite unlike the risaldars and jemadars who had come up through the ranks. He was of a higher (though not the highest) class, better educated and he received his commission in the Indian Land Forces following service in the Imperial Cadet Corps He was very conscious of his status and quick to take offence when he perceived that Indian officers were not being treated with proper respect. His service in China with the Jodhpur Lancers led him to admire the British officers whom he met but also increased his determination not to be 'a coolie of the

34  For s recent view of the martial race theory from the Indian perspective, see, for instance, Roy, *Brown Warriors of the Raj*.
35  Maj-Gen Rajendra Nath, *Military Leadership in India: The Vedik Period to the Indo-Pak wars* (Delhi: Lancer Books, 1990), p. 239.

British'.[36] Unfortunately, throughout his career this attitude was to lead to a number of conflicts with British officers. Ellinwood describes him as having class/caste prejudices which coincide with British prejudices. He empathizes with ordinary Indian soldiers but looks down on bourgeois individuals, both British and Indian.[37] The interested reader is referred to two volumes which have been published which cover Amar Singh's life in great detail. The first of these is *Reversing the Gaze*, edited by Susanne and Lloyd Rudolph together with Amar Singh's nephew, the late Mohan Singhji (Oxford and New Delhi: Oxford University Press, 2000) and the second *Between Two Worlds: A Rajput Officer in the Indian Army 1905-1921*, DeWitt Ellinwood (Lanham Maryland: Hamilton Books, 2005).

The thesis from which this book has been developed concentrated very much on four Indian cavalry regiments – one from each of the three Presidencies together with one State regiment. The scope has now been widened to give some account of the role of the Indian officers in the Infantry regiments. A more detailed account of some of the campaigns in which the Indian army fought has also been included for the benefit of the non-specialist reader.

---

36 DeWitt Ellinwood, *Between Two Worlds: A Rajput Officer in the Indian Army 1905-1921* (Lanham, Maryland: Hamilton Books, 2005), p. 599.

37 Ibid., p 48.

# 1

# The Early Years

---

The Indian Army began in a small, almost casual, way with the formation of forces to protect the East India Company's trading posts. The collapse of the Mughal Empire left a vacuum which the European powers were quick to exploit and the rivalry between the French and the British in India mirrored their campaigns for supremacy in Europe. The Indian Army thus grew to play its part in the successful struggle against the French which left the British as masters of India. The French, who had formed an alliance with the local nawab, captured Calcutta but, following its recapture by the British, Robert Clive defeated the nawab at the decisive battle of Plassey in 1757. The Treaty of Paris in 1763 ended French military power in India although they retained their trading posts for some years. Subsequently the British defeated Hyder Ali and his son Tippoo Sahib in a series of wars which lasted between 1767 and 1799 culminating in the battle of Seringapatam. (Hyder Ali was a Muslim adventurer who had seized Mysore 'He was a brave, determined and intelligent man and a fine soldier.'[1]) In western and central India the Maratha Confederacy, which consisted of several powerful States, also challenged British rule. They too were defeated in wars lasting between 1778 and 1818. After the Great Mutiny of 1857, the re-constituted Indian army fought most of its battles in Afghanistan and on the North-West Frontier, with occasional expeditions to Burma, China and elsewhere, until the Great War of 1914 made hitherto unforeseen demands upon it. In the Second World War the Indian Army became the largest volunteer army that the world has ever seen. Indian soldiers were to fight – and die – in North Africa and Italy and, after initial setbacks, were to rout the hitherto undefeated Japanese Army in Burma.

The East India Company, established in 1600, set up 'factories' or trading posts on the coast of India. The origin of the Indian Army, and of its Indian officers, can be traced back to the 'Chowdikars', a force raised to protect these factories. Major Stringer Lawrence, who arrived in India in 1747, is credited with being the first British

---

1   Mason, *A Matter of Honour*, p. 67.

officer to form a regiment of Indian soldiers on the European model.[2] Robert Clive, originally a civilian 'writer' in the Company's service, joined this battalion which was nicknamed the 'Lal Paltan' because of the soldiers' redcoats. The establishment of this unit, later designated the 1st Bengal Native Infantry, was fourteen British men and 862 Indians with a ratio of 3 British officers to 40 Indian though this remarkably low ratio of British to Indian officers was not to be maintained for long. It was Clive who began the policy of recruiting high-class Rajputs and peasant-farmers from Oudh to the Bengal army.[3] Two battalions similar to the 'Lal Paltan' were soon formed in Madras.

The first order prescribing the strength of an infantry company in the Indian Army is dated November 1755 and lays down that there shall be one subedar, four jemadars, 16 NCOs and 90 men. Mason points out that: 'It would be misleading to call a subedar a captain and a jemadar a lieutenant, but at that time men of those ranks did command a number of men we now regard as the command of a captain or a lieutenant'.[4] Companies were formed into battalions in 1758, each of which consisted of nine companies, each with 120 men The overall effect of the change was to reduce the number of Indian officers in a company while, at the same time, increasing the ratio of British officers to Indian officers who remained subordinate even to the British sergeant-majors. The Indian Commandant and the Adjutant formed the regimental headquarters with a staff made up of British officers and NCOs. The Indian Commandant and the senior British officer appeared side by side on parade. In 1818, a senior rank for Indian officers, subedar-major, or risaldar-major in the cavalry, was introduced in order to provide an ultimate goal for which the young soldier might aim. As Amiya Barat has stated:

> The early British rulers believed that they would secure the attachment as well as the obedience of natives of good character to enter their service as officers, and giving them ample authority in which their birth and habits of command fitted them to wield. The Indian commandant was indeed under the supervision of an English officer, but he was occasionally seen in command of a detachment of European soldiers.[5]

There were still relatively few British officers; in 1784 the 116,000 sepoys were commanded by just ten colonels and thirty lieutenant-colonels.[6] In addition to these regular units, so-called irregular regiments or Local Infantry, were raised. These units

2    See J. Lunt (ed) *From Sepoy to Subedar* (London: Military Book Society, 1970), p. xxii.
3    See Seema Alavi, *The Sepoys and the Company* (Delhi: Oxford University Press, 1998), p. 75 et seq.
4    Mason, *A Matter of Honour*, p. 62.
5    Amiya Barat, *The Bengal Native Infantry: its organisation and discipline* (Calcutta: Firma K.L. Mukhopadhway, 1990), pp. 123-126.
6    Stuart Reid, *Armies of the East India Company, 1750-1850* (Oxford: Osprey, 2009), p. 7.

were officered almost entirely by Indians with only a small staff of European officers.[7] One of the first of these was the Sirmoor Battalion formed from Gurkhas, which was eventually to become the 2nd King Edward VII's Own Gurkha Rifles. Initially they had only three British officers, a commandant, an adjutant and a medical officer, to ten companies of Gurkhas.[8]

Eventually each of the three settlements in Bengal, Madras and Bombay had their own army which developed very much independently of one another, largely because of the difficulties of communication. Different castes and cultures of Indians were recruited into the three armies. Initially the Company was glad to recruit anyone willing to serve, but eventually professional soldiers, who had served defeated or deposed local rulers, came into the ranks. These men came from the so-called martial races – Punjabi Muslims, Pathans, Mahrattas, Sikhs etc. The Bengal army recruited Hindus and Muslims from the Kingdom of Oudh, in particular high class Brahmins. The men were peasant farmers with little or no education; few could read or write their own name. The army had long been an attractive alternative to village life and groups of men, often led by the village headman, joined the army together. Amiya Barat gives a view of a typical recruit:

A representative Bengal sepoy recruit of c1800 was a Hindu of high caste, a resident of the Bihar and Oudh regions with Hindustani as his mother tongue. He was person of good physique and hailed from the peasantry and a station which possessed a social heritage. He was often of the landed gentry and enlisted to gain status. He remained a civilian at heart though a soldier by profession.[9]

Further re-organisation in 1796 brought an end to the old system and the numbers of British and Indian officers were now made almost equal. Battalions were grouped in pairs with a full Colonel in command of the pair. Each battalion now had twenty-two British officers; a Lt-Colonel, a Major, four Captains, eleven Lieutenants and five Ensigns.[10] It is not clear why this change was brought about although it certainly increased the prospects for promotion among the British officers. However the change had other very serious, though unintended, consequences. The very considerable increase in the number of British officers in a battalion meant that the role of the Indian officers was significantly down-graded. The subedar had previously been, in effect, a company commander and the jemadar a platoon commander but with many more British officers in the unit, the Indians lost the status that they had within the regiment. As an early historian of the Mutiny put it:

---

7    See ibid., p. 18.
8    See Mason, *A Matter of Honour*, p. 380.
9    Barat, *The Bengal Native Infantry*, p. 126.
10   See Notes on the History of the Indian Army, printed for the Indian Military Academy, 1933, p 6. Copy in the Gibbs Papers in the Gurkha Museum, Winchester.

Henceforward there was nothing to stimulate the ambition of a sepoy. Though he might give signs of the military genius of an Hyder, he knew that he could never attain the pay of a British subaltern.[11]

The regiment which eventually became the Royal Deccan Horse was raised in 1816 by the Nizam of Hyderabad. Until 1860 there were only three British officers in the regiment, the number being increased to four in that year. In 1888 the number was raised to six and to eight in 1892. According to the regimental historian:

> The paucity of British Officers has this advantage – that it throws more work, responsibility and independence upon the Indian officers, thus increasing their efficiency, which is liable to deteriorate when everything is done by the British officers.[12]

Indian officers were always promoted from the ranks and were usually elderly men who had spent their lives in a single regiment. Their grasp of English was uncertain, if they spoke it all. They were unlikely ever to aspire to equality with the British officers, as Byron Farwell stated: 'It was not men of this stamp who were expected to hold a King's Commission: they were unlikely to desire entrance to the British officer's mess as subalterns.'[13]

Study of the Regimental Histories of two infantry regiments, the 1st/2nd Punjab and the 1st/14th Punjab, enables us to build up a table to show the changes in the number of British and Indian officers over the eighteenth and nineteenth centuries.[14] What is most striking about this table is the huge increase in the number of British officers in the first half of the nineteenth century. Only with difficulty could the Indian officers make their status as officers felt either by the sepoys or by the European officers. They had emerged after long service as sepoys but still shared their life and were surrounded by men recruited from their own locality with ties of caste and even kinship. Elderly men with no prospects of further promotion or reward and deprived of incentives and status, the Indian officers came greatly to resent the harsh and contemptuous behaviour of the European officers towards them. Indeed the deterioration of this relationship overshadowed all other grievances and more than

---

11   S.L. Menezes, *Fidelity and Honour: The Indian Army from the Seventeenth to the Twenty-First Century* (New Delhi: Oxford University Press, 1999), p. 18.
12   Lt-Col E. Tennant, *The Royal Deccan Horse in the Great War* (Aldershot: Gale and Polden, 1939), p. 5.
13   B. Farwell, *Armies of the Raj from the Mutiny to Independence 1858 to 1947* (London: Viking, 1989), p. 30.
14   See Cols N. Ogle and H.W. Johnston, *History of the 1st Battalion, 2nd Punjab Regiment* (London: Straker and Co, c. 1923) and G.Pigot, *History of the 1st Battalion, 14th Punjab Regiment* (New Delhi: Roxy Printing Press, 1948).

| | 1st/2nd Punjab<br>Originally 7th Madras Infantry | | 1st/14th Punjab<br>Originally 5th Bengal Native Infantry | |
| --- | --- | --- | --- | --- |
| | British officers | Indian officers | British officers | Indian officers |
| Pre 1786 | 3 | 42 | 3 | 20 |
| | several British sergeants | | + 3 British sergeants | |
| 1786 | 3 | 20 | 10 + MO* | 16 |
| | + 10 British sergeants | | + 10 British NCOs | |
| 1804 | 22 | 20 | No information | |
| 1817 | Native commandant and native adjutant abolished<br>Subedar-major and colour-havildar ranks created | | | |
| 1824 | No information | | 23 | 17 |
| 1861 | No information | | 5 + MO | 17 |
| 1866 | No information | | 6 + MO | 17 |
| 1878 | No information | | 9 + MO | 15 |
| (2nd Afghan War) | | | | |
| 1914 | 12 + MO | 17 | 12 + MO | 17 |

* Medical Officer

anything else caused the native officers to lose all interest in their profession. Kaye, the first historian of the Indian Mutiny, suggested that:

> The native officers were aggrieved over the gradual curtailment of their authority. This trend had been visible in the Bengal army from 1786 onwards when a European subaltern was appointed to every company and the native officers collapsed into something little better than a name.[15]

In 1900 as part of a major re-organisation of the Indian Army the eight companies were grouped into four 'double-companies' which were commanded by British officers. Not only that, but the list of classes thought suitable for recruitment into the Army decreased significantly.[16] Men like General Roberts, Commander-in Chief in India 1885-93, believed that men from southern India had lost the martial characteristics of their forbears. He also was convinced that Indians could never replace the British officers because they did not possess the necessary qualities of leadership.[17]

15    J. W. Kaye, *The Sepoy War in India* (London: W H Allen, 1870-76), Vol I, p. 211.
16    See Mason, *A Matter of Honour*, p. 344.
17    See ibid., p. 401.

In contrast to the forces of the Indian princes, the East India Company took great care to pay its sepoys regularly and gave them a small pension when they retired. The families of soldiers killed in action were entitled to a pension and provision was made for disabled men. As pensions increased not only with rank but with length of service, there was every incentive for men to serve as long as possible – sometimes even for fifty years. General MacMunn illustrates the point thus: 'On the cross over the long trench graves on the battlefield of Chillianwalla are inscribed the names of two Brahmin subedars and against their names is recorded their ages, 65 and 70.'[18] Indian soldiers were given due respect by government departments and the civil authorities. Their prestige in society was further raised by the fact that they were given priority in the courts and as General Rajendra Nath points out:

> The English looked after the interests and welfare of the sepoys as well as the Indian officers holding the ranks of Jemadars and Subedars so well that even today after 42 years of independence we have not been able to match that.[19]

Good Conduct Pay was introduced in 1837; the longer a soldier served, the greater his additional pay. However, his commanding officer could remove the addition on the grounds of misconduct.[20] The Distinguished Service Medal was introduced in the seventeenth century and the Indian Order of Merit in 1837. Indian officers were offered greater financial incentives and honours as a means of setting them apart from the sepoys. The Order of British India, with a pension and the titles 'Bahadur or 'Sirdar Bahadur', was only awarded to Indian officers with long and exceptional service.[21]

The financial security and social respect contributed significantly to the fidelity and discipline of the Indian troops. Amiya Barat writing about the Bengal infantry points out that:

> The sepoys undoubtedly benefited from all these privileges (allowances, leave, pension, honours and decorations) but when considered in the proper perspective, they were really more interested in their immediate earnings and in their future promotion prospects. Their special interest in the latter may be explained by the fact that all the native officers in the Company's army rose from the ranks.[22]

---

18    Lt-Gen Sir G. MacMunn, *The Armies of India* (London: A.C. Black 1911), p. 13.
19    Nath, *Military Leadership in India*, p. 239.
20    Roy, *Brown Warriors of the Raj*, p. 157.
21    Ibid., pp. 161-162.
22    Barat, *The Bengal Native Infantry*, p. 151.

In *Sepoy to Subedar: The Life and Adventures of Sita Ram* we have a unique record of the service of a typical Indian soldier of the first half of the nineteenth century.[23] When Sita Ram retired he was encouraged to write his memoirs. The manuscript was translated into English from the original Urdu and published in Lahore in 1873. It was then used to help young British officers learn Urdu – the *lingua franca* of the Indian Army. Doubt has been cast upon the authenticity of the memoirs but there is a strong body of opinion in their favour.[24] Ram was encouraged to enlist, against his mother's wishes, in 1812 by his uncle who was already a jemadar in an infantry battalion. His uncle was wearing his bright red coat with gold buttons and a necklace of gold beads and it is no wonder that the young man's head was turned. He was to serve for a total of 48 years including seven major campaigns. He was wounded seven times, captured by Afghans (and escaped) and was awarded four campaign medals. He was promoted to jemadar after 35 years service and retired on a subedar's pension.

It was quite common for young men to follow their fathers or uncles into the Army – indeed at times it almost became a family business. For instance, three generations of the Muhiyal family served in Hodson's Horse.[25] The four sons of Mehta Divan Chand all served in the regiment. The eldest transferred to the Guides Cavalry and was killed at Delhi in 1857. His son – Mehta's grandson – received the family pension until he was old enough to enlist in the 2nd Punjab Cavalry. Mehta's second son, an expert swordsman, served for 34 years with Hodson's Horse and three of his four sons were also to serve in the regiment. Mehta's third son was severely wounded serving in the regiment as a daffadar, his son served from 1884 and took part in the Chitral and Tirah campaigns. Finally, Mehta Chand's fourth son served in the regiment for 28 years becoming regimental accountant and retiring with a jagir – a grant of a land.

Nor is this an isolated case. In the 2nd Punjab Cavalry, Risaldar-Major Bishan Singh (Indian Order of Merit, 1st Class) was to be followed by his son Jowahir Singh in the same office. Jawali Singh, the son of Risaldar-Major Singh Sirdar Bahadur (Order of British India and Indian Order of Merit 1st Class) succeeded him in command of the 3rd troop in the regiment and he too was eventually to rise to the rank of risaldar-major serving in that rank for over five years and being awarded the OBI.[26] Lieutenant Bhim Singh Thapa followed his father and grandfather into the Gurkhas, they having fought in the Mutiny, in Bhutan, Burma and in Afghanistan. Bhim Singh served in Waziristan, France, Sinai and Palestine. He was awarded the Military Cross, the Indian Order of Merit and mentioned in dispatches on four separate occasions. His

23   See J. Lunt (ed), *Sepoy to Subedar* (London,: Military Book Society 1977).
24   See Mason, *A Matter of Honour*, p. 207 et seq. and Col Sir P. Cadell, 'From Sepoy to Subedar – Fact or Fiction?', *JUSII*, Number 327, April 1947, pp. 265 -272.
25   Mehta Gyan Chan, *The Muhiyal Family of Hodson's Horse*. Pamphlet with no publisher or date. Unnumbered copy in the Library of the National Army Museum, London.
26   Anon, *History of the Second Panjab(sic) Cavalry* (London: Kegan, Paul, Trench and Co, 1888), p. 21.

sons all followed him into the regiment.[27] In 1857, Sir John Lawrence, Governor of the Punjab, invited Milkha Singh, who had fought against the British in the Second Sikh War, to form and command a troop of cavalry to serve the government. After the emergency was over, this troop formed part of the Deoli Irregular Force which was stationed on the frontier. There were only four British officers in the Force – the commandant, second-in-command, adjutant and medical officer. Milkha Singh was to rise to become risaldar-major. Twenty-five of his father's family had served in the unit by the nineteen thirties and thirteen members of his direct family served in other units within the Indian Army. Milkha Singh's great-grandson, Sirdar Thakur Singh MC, was to become subedar-major of the 47th Sikh Infantry.[28].

Nor was these family links confined to the Indian officers in the regiment. Generations of British men served in the Indian Army or Civil Service. For instance, three generations of the Jacob family were to serve in the Indian Army, beginning with William Jacob who joined the Bengal Artillery in 1817.[29] His great grandson, Claud William was the most successful member of the family. He joined the Baluch regiment which had been founded by his grandfather and was promoted to the rank of major after 19 years. He was promoted to Lt-Col when he was ordered to raise the 106th Hazara Pioneers. In 1914 he went to France as a Staff Officer to the Meerut Division and ended the war a well-respected Corps Commander. His final posting was as General commanding Northern Command in India. These family links meant that the young British officer, joining his father's regiment for the first time, would often find that the senior Indian officer had known him as a child.

The caste system was, and still is in many ways, central to the Hindu way of life. It governs every aspect of a man's life – such as what he may eat and drink and with whom he may do these things. If the strict rules governing the preparation of food are broken, the food must be thrown away. The British accepted and even encouraged caste practice, for instance allowing each man to have his own cooking pots and to prepare his own food. Such rules were to cause difficulties later on when the troops were on campaign, for example in Mesopotamia. As time went on, only high-caste men were recruited into the Bengal Army, which could cause significant problems. High caste men would not accept orders from officers or NCOs from a lower caste nor were they prepared to cross the sea.[30] Stuart Reid has commented that 'In the Bengal Army the victory of caste was complete.'[31] The high caste Hindus were horrified by

27    E.D.Smith, 'Valour': A History of the Gurkhas (Stroud: Spellmount, 2007), p. 68.
28    See General Sir O'Moore Creagh, Autobiography (London: Hutchinson and Co, 1925), p. 97.
29    See Raymond Callahan, 'Servants of the Raj: The Jacob Family in India 1817-1926', Journal of the Society for Army Historical Reserch, Vol. 56, No. 225, Spring 1978, pp. 4-24.
30    See Daniel Marston, Phoenix from the Ashes: The Indian Army in the Burma Campaign (Westport, Connecticut: Praeger Publishers, 2003), p. 11.
31    Reid, Armies of the East India Company, 1750-1850, p. 125.

the annexation of Oudh by the British in 1856 and they felt their loss of their status very keenly. As one soldier remarked 'I used to be a great man when I went home. The rest of the village rose when I approached. Now the lowest puff their pipes in my face.'[32] There was no such concern regarding caste in the Bombay and Madras Armies. A Madras subedar said 'We put our religion in our knapsacks when our colours are unfurled.'[33] A sepoy who transferred from the Bengal Army to the Bombay Army commented that whilst men in the Bengal army took pride in their religion, the men of the Bombay Army took pride in their regiment.[34]

When Lord Canning (Governor General of India 1856-62) tried to introduce a general service liability for the Bengal Army he met with opposition on religious grounds as to serve overseas entailed a loss of caste among the high-caste Hindus. As indicated above, this was especially acute in the Bengal Army where service had become very much a family affair with sons, brothers, cousins and nephews all serving in the same company, let alone regiment.[35] When Sita Ram enlisted he was taken by his uncle to be introduced to the Regimental Adjutant: 'To my surprise he spoke to him in his own language. He seemed glad to see him, asked after his welfare and 'touched his sword (a gesture of respect).'[36] Sita Ram found a changed situation in the Bengal Army when he returned from captivity in Afghanistan in 1845. The Sind War had been unpopular and the sepoys resented the loss of *batta* or extra field allowance. The best of the British officers soon tired of the dull routine of regimental employment and looked elsewhere for more interesting, and more profitable, employment. Those young officers who remained found themselves frustrated by their elderly colonels. A rather vague paternalism had replaced the ordered discipline to which the sepoys had been accustomed.[37] Sita Ram also commented on the increase in the number of Christian missionaries who told the Indians that their cherished religion was all false and exhorted them to become Christians.[38] The India Bill of 1813 obliged the East India Company to license missionaries to travel the country. Prior to the Great Mutiny of 1857 there had been previous, smaller, uprisings, for example in 1806 in Vellore where Madras sepoys mutinied against orders for them to trim their beards, shave off their moustaches and to relinquish their caste marks. They saw these orders as part of a move to convert them to Christianity.[39]

32    Quoted in Christopher Hibbert, *The Great Mutiny* (London: Penguin Books, 1978), p. 218.
33    Michael Barthorp, *Indian Infantry Regiments 1860-1914* (Oxford: Osprey.1979) p. 10.
34    Ibid., p 10.
35    See Menezes, *The Indian Army*, p. 156.
36    J. Lunt, (ed) *Sepoy to Subedar*, p. 13.
37    See ibid., p. 133.
38    See ibid., p. 165.
39    See William Dalrymple, *White Mughals* (London: Harper Collins, 2002), p. 433.

Philip Mason suggests that there are three elements which together are to be found in every outbreak of mutiny in India.[40] These are, firstly, some outside factor, such as in in the years preceding 1857, the Christian missionaries' attempts to convert the sepoys. Secondly, a failure among their British officers to know and understand their men. The third element was some military grievance such as the impact of the changes in the role and decline in the perceived authority of the Indian officers prior to 1857. These changes in status were undoubtedly a very significant factor which contributed to the Mutiny. In addition, there were a number of other organisational reasons which contributed to the discontent felt by Indian officers and sepoys. These factors included the increasing ages of both British and Indian officers together with the absence from their regiments of as many as half of the British officers. The pay of the Indian officers had not been increased although their duties had and they were no longer in close touch with their men. The training in peacetime was inevitably routine and not likely to foster enthusiasm among the sepoys.[41]

In the eighteenth and first half of the nineteenth centuries many European men, living alone, had accepted Indian culture and customs and taken Indian wives or mistresses. For instance, each evening Sir David Ochterlony, the British Resident at the Mughal Court, would process around Delhi followed by his thirteen Indian consorts each riding her own elephant. Sir James Kirkpatrick, the Resident in Hyderabad, married a high born lady from the Nizam's court. The French General Allard, who had fought in Napoleon's Army, commanded two regiments of dragoons and one of lancers for the Sikh leader Ranjit Singh and married a beautiful Kashmiri girl. The American William Gardner, who had chosen the losing side in the American War of Independence, married a Mughal princess and founded Gardner's Horse, the second most senior cavalry regiment in the Indian Army. Many European men at this time made provision in their wills for Indian wives or mistresses.[42]

But, as more and more Englishmen – and women – went out to India, attitudes towards the Indians began to change. No longer was it socially acceptable for an English officer to have an Indian mistress and the child of a mixed marriage, such as James Skinner (founder of Skinner's Horse, the most senior cavalry regiment), would have had little hope of advancement among English society. Amiya Barat commented that:

> The European officers of the Native infantry were not immune to this changing social environment and their behaviour towards the sepoys reflected the attitude of society in general and the manner in which they exercised command over the sepoys and native officers, the latter often far older than themselves.[43]

40    See Mason, *A Matter of Honour,* p. 236.
41    See Notes on the History of the Indian Army, printed for the Indian Military Academy, 1933, p. 10. Copy in the Gibbs Papers, Gurkha Museum, Winchester.
42    See Fanny Parkes (Introduction by William Dalrymple), *Begums, Thugs and White Mughals* (London: Sickle Moon Books, 2002), p. xiii.
43    Barat, *The Bengal Native Infantry,* p. 152.

Indifference and abuse became the order of the day and social contact with the sepoys and native officers was looked down upon. The reforms of 1796 had denuded the Indian officers of the remnants of authority that had rested with them. From being the leaders of men, they were reduced to playing the role of contact-men between the sepoys and the commanding officers of their regiments. They had virtually no effective authority and even as go-betweens were under the command of the most junior European subaltern. This feeling of frustration was aggravated when the Indian officers compared themselves with their civilian colleagues:

> In the early days the small number of British officers allotted to units – sometimes no more than three – gave rise to closer relations with the men and a greater degree of responsibility and, consequently, efficiency and initiative amongst the native officers. The steady increase in the number of British officers in units eroded all these desirable qualities and was contributory factors in the debacle of 1857.[44]

In the 1840s Colonel Briggs of the Madras Army expressed his concern at the manner in which the standing of the Indian officer was eroded by the attachment of more and more British officers to a battalion. The status of the Indian officers was further aggravated by the fact that inexperienced immature cadets were sent out from England. Briggs believed that many of those British officers were unsuitable for their role, writing:

> Youths without experience … without knowledge of the language, and ignorant of the habits and religious prejudices of the natives, to command these distinguished native officers created in the latter a disgust in the service.[45]

Briggs proposed a scheme by which native gentlemen would be eligible for 'volunteer' appointments. They would serve for six years in the ranks before becoming officers. He was also the first to argue for the establishment of a college for training young Indian officers.[46]

Saul David argues persuasively that an underlying cause of the uprising of 1857 was a financial one because as British rule extended further and further, the opportunities

44   Maj-Gen Shahid Hamid, *So They Rode and Fought* (Tunbridge Wells: Midas Books, 1983), p. 36.
45   Col John Briggs, *Letters to a Young Person in India* (London, no date, Reprinted Oxford 1922), p. 16.
46   See Chandar Sundaram, *A Grudging Concession: The Origins of the Indianization of the Indian Army's Officer Corps, 1817-1917*, Unpublished PhD thesis, McGill University, Montreal, 1996, p. 83.

for loot decreased.[47] The ringleaders were ambitious men who were united in their exasperation with the limitations of Company service. They wanted a government which would give them greater opportunities for advancement and better pay. Communications between the English officers and the sepoys broke down when either the Indian officers identified themselves too closely with the men or conversely when the sepoys saw the latter as hostile to their interests. Had the European officers been more closely in touch with the men, the weakness of the link between the Indian officers and the sepoys would not have been such a problem. However, the English officers did not bother to learn the language of their men and they were often inexperienced and/or absent from their regiments. Charles Allen pointed out that:

> Over the last decade, something had been lost from the relationship that bound officers and men together: more British officers were being allotted to each regiment, with a corresponding loss of responsibility for Native Officers.[48]

There had been warnings of impending trouble from some of the more prescient British officers. Sir Henry Lawrence wrote in 1844: ' Is it not absurd that the rank of Subedar and Russaldar (sic) Major is the highest that a native can attain in an army of nearly three hundred thousand men?'[49] When his advice was ignored, Sir Henry wrote a further essay in 1856; stating that 'The minds of Subedars and Risaldars, Sepoys and Sowars can no more with safety be forever cramped, trammelled and restricted as at present, than can a twenty-foot embankment restrain the Atlantic.'[50] He was concerned at the number of Indian officers and non-commissioned officers who were leaving the Company's service to join the forces of the Princely States, often attaining high rank within them. Like Briggs before him, Lawrence argued for a system of training for Indian officers.[51]

Whatever the underlying reasons for the Mutiny of 1857, the final ostensible cause was the issue of cartridges which were rumoured to be greased with a mixture of cow and pig fat and therefore unclean to both Hindus and Muslims, In spite of reassurances, the men refused to take the cartridges. On March 29th 1857 a sepoy named Mangal Pande, under the influence of drink or drugs, ran amok and attacked and wounded a British officer and sergeant major. He was captured, tried and sentenced to death. His regiment was to be disbanded in order to prevent further disturbances. Trouble soon followed in the 3rd Bengal Light Cavalry which was also stationed at Meerut. Following further refusals by the sepoys to accept the new cartridges, they

47    See Saul David, *The Indian Mutiny* (London: Viking, 2002), p. 28 et seq.
48    Charles Allen, *Soldier Sahibs: The Men who made the North-West Frontier* ( London: John Murray, 2000), p. 264.
49    Quoted in Menezes., *The Indian Army*, p. 25.
50    Ibid.
51    See Sir Henry Lawrence, *The Military Defence of our Empire* (London, Blackwood, 1859).

were sentenced to 10 years hard labour. The parade at which they were stripped of their uniforms and fettered took place amid scenes of much distress

On Sunday 10th May at Meerut when the British soldiers were at church parade (and therefore unarmed), men of the 3rd Light Cavalry together with the 11th and 20th Regiments of Native Infantry mutinied and killed a number of British soldiers and their families. They then set off for Delhi, which had only a small British garrison, where they massacred more Europeans. The aged and infirm King of Delhi, Bahadur Shah II, was declared Emperor and put upon the throne of his illustrious ancestors. Those Europeans who were able to escape gathered around the Flagstaff Tower on the ridge to the north of the City. As additional British troops arrived, supported by Gurkhas and Sikhs including some newly raised regiments from the Punjab, they settled down to besiege the city. Eventually a breach was made in the walls, an attack made at the Kashmir Gate and the city recaptured.

Meanwhile British garrisons at Cawnpore and Lucknow had been besieged by mutinous sepoys. At Cawnpore, General Wheeler was not able to choose a suitable stronghold and his forces eventually had to surrender, having been given assurances of safe conduct. The British were betrayed, many of the men being killed in boats on the River Ganges while the women and children were taken prisoner and later murdered, their bodies being thrown down a well. These murders, especially of the women and children, were to lead to some of the most horrific scenes of revenge by the British. The Residency at Lucknow proved to be a much stronger defensive position and held out for many days before eventually being relieved. As more and more British troops arrived in India, the last of the mutineers were eventually rounded up and executed.

When mutinies came, the Indian officers generally preferred to swim with the tide rather than against it. Sometimes they were implicated in the mutiny (the 47th in 1824) but more often they simply stood aside (the 64th in 1844, the 66th in 1850). In the mutiny of 1857, many Indian officers were to lead their men against the British whilst a minority in the mutinous regiments were to stay loyal and 'true to their salt.' According to Major O'Brien of the 6th Oudh Irregular Infantry, a large body of the Indian officers of his regiment were active instigators of the mutiny.[52] In very many cases the mutineers were able to persuade their officers to join them and the military hierarchy was maintained to the extent that those Indian officers took control of their regiments. They proved perfectly capable of exercising the higher command which had for so long been denied to them. For instance, Lal Khan, a Muslim subedar of the 3rd Light Cavalry is said to have been elected generalissimo of the Meerut Brigade with Bulcho Singh, a Hindu subedar from the 20th Native infantry as his second in command. Some Indian officers even set themselves up as de facto rulers. In the Fategarh district, Subedar Thakur Pandy of the 1st Native infantry assumed command of the eastern division. The Indian officer who rose highest was Subedar Bakht Khan of the 6/8th artillery who was made Commander-in-Chief of the rebel army by the

---

52   See Saul David, *The Indian Mutiny 1857*, p. 391.

King of Delhi[53] However, a significant proportion of Indian officers did not mutiny possibly because of their age and the proximity of their pension. The mutiny of 1857 was by no means the only mutiny to affect the Indian, or indeed the British Army, during the nineteenth and twentieth centuries. It was, however, by far the most significant, both in terms of the number of men involved and the wide geographical area over which the mutiny and its suppression took place.

53    See ibid.

**2**

# The Second Half of the Nineteenth Century

---

The old Bengal Army was almost completely swept away by the tragic events of 1857. Out of 74 infantry regiments, 45 mutinied and all but five of the remainder were either disarmed or disbanded.[1] All of the regular Bengal cavalry regiments mutinied. The Bombay and Madras Armies were scarcely affected – indeed fresh regiments were raised in the Punjab specifically in order to quell the mutiny. One group of British officers argued that during the Mutiny the Indian officers had failed to give forewarning nor had they assisted in putting down the revolt. It was suggested that about half of the Indian officers in the Bengal Army had supported the mutiny. On the other hand, it was argued that Sikh officers had remained loyal and there had been no mutiny in the Punjab Frontier Force. In the view of this group of British officers, the Indian officers had been carried away by the mutiny rather than leading it.[2] Sir James Outram commented on the difference between the Armies of Bengal and Bombay:

> The mutinous spirit displayed in the Bengal Army ... is the consequence of the faulty system of its organisation so different from that of Bombay. Our native officers are a loyal and efficient body, selected for their superior ability which naturally exercises a wholesome influence over the men. The seniority system of the Bengal Army supplies neither influential nor able officers – old imbeciles merely, possessing no control over the men.[3]

The events of the Great Mutiny were to cast a long shadow over the relationship between the British and the Indian officers and troops. The degree of trust which had

---

1    See Reid, *Armies of the East India Company 1750-1850*, p. 12.
2    See Roy, *Brown Warriors of the Raj*, pp. 247-248.
3    Quoted in Col W.G.P. Tugwell *History of the Bombay Pioneers 1777-1933* (Bedford: The Sydney Press, 1938 ), p. 103.

been established would take very many years to re-establish. As Byron Farwell has noted:

> The Mutiny swept away what little social intercourse was left between Briton and Indian. Friendliness and hospitality became unnaturally strained or non-existent. The knowledge of ways of life, ways of thinking which come from familiar daily intercourse disappeared. Even in the army, distrust, however slight, distanced officers and men in all but the Gurkha regiments.[4]

In particular, there was concern about giving the Indian officers too much responsibility and experience. As Major General Rajendra Nath points out:

> 'In the army, leadership plays a significant role. It was the British intention to make full use of the sepoys as cannon-fodder but ensure that they were given no opportunity to learn the art of command or leadership.'[5]

However, whether or not they were trusted by the British officers, the Indian officers would always have considerable influence upon the sepoys – influence which might be used for good or bad. A Memorandum submitted to the Secretary of State for India in 1876 pointed out that:

> Indian officers who are treated as mere fighting tools, entrusted with no real honour or responsibility and denied the opportunities for promotion found in other aspects of the British administration in India were unlikely to demonstrate their fidelity in time of temptation or trial.[6]

It was hardly surprising that after 1857 there should be a change in recruitment policy. Instead of recruiting Brahmins from Oudh, from whence the mutineers had come, there was a shift towards men, such as Sikhs and Gurkhas, who had remained loyal to the government during the crisis. The old Bengal Army was swept away and replaced by new regiments recruited from the Punjab and Nepal. There was, however, a further and more insidious development as the century wore on. A belief developed among influential British officers that men from southern India had lost their fighting spirit. Regiments from Madras were disbanded and replaced by even more regiments consisting of men recruited from the Punjab so that by the start of the First World War, about half of the Indian Army was made up by men from that area.[7] Three

---

4    Farwell, *Armies of the Raj from the Mutiny to Independence*, p. 64.
5    Nath, *Military Leadership in India*, p. 25.
6    Memorandum submitted to the Secretary of State for India 1876, OIOC, L/MIL/7/7240, p. 8.
7    See Menezes, *The Indian Army*, p. 300.

quarters of men of the Army were from the so-called 'martial races' – Sikhs, Jats, Rajputs, Gurkhas etc. In 1914, of the 552 infantry companies in the Indian Army, 211 were recruited from the Punjab and a further 121 from the North-West Frontier region.[8] By 1933 there was not one infantry regiment from Madras and this remained the case until the demands of the Second World War drove the recruiters to look once more in that direction.

The martial race theory was linked to the quasi-scientific ideas of racial superiority which were prevalent among Europeans at the end of the nineteenth century. It was unfortunate that Lord Roberts, who had been Commander in Chief of the Madras Army before becoming Commander in Chief of the newly united Indian Army from 1885 until 1893, should be one of the foremost proponents of the martial race theory and in a position to put his ideas into practice. In 1882, Roberts wrote to Major General Stewart, then Military Member of the Indian Council,: 'The fact is that the Madras sepoy has never met a formidable enemy, and nearly 100 years of peace have almost quenched any martial spirit there may have been in him.'[9]

Jeffrey Greenhut ascribes what he sees as the failure of the Indian infantry in France in 1914-15 to the martial race theory, bringing as it did into the army 'men whose backgrounds made them a poor choice to fight a modern war.'[10] This seems to be a rather unfair comment. Whether or not the Indian Corps 'failed' in France is a matter for debate and the fact that the troops came from the martial races is not usually adduced as a cause for the supposed failure. If the sepoys been led by Indian officers fully trained and holding the King's commission it is possible that there might have been an even greater chance of success. As late as 1932, General Sir George MacMunn could write:

> In India we speak of the martial races as a thing apart and because the mass of the people have neither martial aptitude not physical courage … the courage that we should talk of colloquially as 'guts.[11]

Mason points out that the idea that some people will make soldiers and some will not is much older than the Raj, being implicit in the Hindu caste system.[12] However, it was the British in India who, after the Mutiny, formulated and developed the theory to its fullest extent. Heather Streets argues that the exploits of Sikhs and Gurkhas in the Mutiny and afterwards were deliberately 'talked up' in the press, their deeds often

8   See Marston, *Phoenix from the Ashes*, p. 13.
9   Brian Robson (ed) *The Military Papers of Lord Roberts* (Stroud: Alan Sutton Publishing Co for the Army Records Society, 1993), p. 264.
10  Jeffrey. Greenhut, 'The Imperial Reserve: The Indian Corps on the Western Front 1914-15' *Journal of Imperial and Commonwealth History*, XII, 1983, p. 70.
11  Lt-Gen Sir G. MacMunn, *The Martial Races of India* (London: Sampson Low, Marston and Co, 1932.), p. 2.
12  Mason, *A Matter of Honour*, p. 349.

being linked with the 'glamorous' Highlanders of the period.[13] Chandar Sundaram points out that in the nineteenth century, Sir George Chesney compared the Indians who might be expected to become officers to the Highland Chiefs of the sixteenth and seventeenth centuries.[14] It took two World Wars to demonstrate that courage was not confined to the few. Charles Chenevix Trench tells of the behaviour of a Madras Sapper during an opposed river crossing in Mesopotamia:

> He was the last rower left alive in his boat and when his oar was smashed he jumped overboard, tied a rope around his waist and attempted to tow the boat by swimming before he too was killed. If ever a deed deserved the VC it was his; but there was no survivor to tell his name. He was just an anonymous, little, blackish, low-caste Madrassi.[15]

During the First World War, men from seventy-five classes previously considered 'non-martial' were now recruited into the Army. Some of these, such as the Mahars, Telegus and Moplahs had formerly been recruited but had gradually been excluded while men were also taken from classes, such as the Punjabi Christians, who had never previously served. At the end of the War, however, these men were gradually discharged and newly raised regiments disbanded. However, the even greater demands of the Second World War led to the re-raising of the Madras Regiment, the Mahar regiment and the Sikh Light infantry. Other regiments were made up of such apparently 'non-martial' classes as the Rawats, Minas and Assamese. A number of these regiments are still on the order of battle of the modern Indian Army.

Two interlinked questions concerning the re-organisation of the Indian Army aroused considerable debate in the mid-1870s. What was the appropriate ratio of British to Indian officers in a regiment and what were to be the duties and responsibilities of the Indian Officers? Following the Mutiny, the army of the East India Company was taken over by the Crown. Prior to the Mutiny there had sometimes been as many as 26 British officers in a unit which meant that, as a Departmental Minutes points out, their duties were often:

> light and insignificant while the Native officers were stamped as mere ciphers. The system under which they have been employed and treated has been such as to ensure as far as possible their degradation and inefficiency. They have been treated as private sepoys, with better coats and better pay, but they have studiously been denied all real official authority and influence. They have been treated

---

13   See Streets, *Martial Races*, pp. 137-150.

14   See Chandar Sundaram, 'Reviving a 'Dead Letter': Military Indianisation and the Ideology of Anglo-India 1885-91' in Partha Gupta and Antrudh Deshpande (eds) *The British Raj and Its Indian Armed Forces 1857-`1939* (New Delhi: Oxford University Press, 2002), p. 53.

15   Chenevix Trench, *The Indian Army and the King's Enemies*, p. 85.

as an entirely inferior class. It is simply impossible that the intelligence, independence and self respect which should characterise the officer should be developed among men under such a system.[16]

Sir George Chesney, Military Secretary and later a Member of the Military Department was one liberal British officer who, after the Mutiny, put forward a number of positive proposals regarding the status of Indian officers.

> The time has come when, on the grounds of justice no less than that of policy, it is right and proper to open a military career to the higher classes of native subjects of the Queen, including the native soldiers already in the army who are deserving of advancement.[17]

One of his ideas was the formation of a new regiment to be officered entirely by Indian 'gentlemen'. He was well aware of the lack of education among many Indian officers and he laid great stress upon the importance of an English education for them. He suggested that the Chief's Colleges might offer an appropriate curriculum or that a separate military college should be established as an alternative to Royal Military Academy at Sandhurst. He believed that:

> Giving selected native officers training at a military college and especially instructing them in English … would greatly increase their efficiency and it would be possible to select the most deserving for higher promotion.[18]

If the one regiment proved to be a success, then further regiments could be formed. The notion of a separate regiment was taken up by Sir Donald Stewart, the then Commander-in-Chief, who proposed that one such cavalry regiment be formed and one infantry regiment.[19] The officers for these regiments would come initially from among specially selected VCOs, until suitably trained candidates would emerge from among the Indian Princes and gentlemen. This suggestion avoided the potential difficulty which would occur if British officers were to come under the command of an Indian officer. The Army Department, while accepting Chesney's general idea, was not prepared to accept that Indians from 'good' families who had received direct commissions as VCOs were fit to hold the Queen's Commission. Nor did they believe that men of high social standing would be satisfied with honorary Queen's Commissions.

---

16   Departmental Minute No 438 of 1876, submitted to the Secretary of State 20.5.76, pp. 5, 6 and 7, OIOC, L/MIL/7/7240.

17   Lt-Gen Sir G. Chesney, Military Education for the Natives of India, OIOC, L/MIL/7/19019, and quoted in Chandar Sundaram, 'Reviving a 'Dead Letter', p. 45.

18   Chesney's Minute 23/1/1888 para 32,OIOC, L/MIL/17/5/2202, and see Chandar Sundaram, *Reviving a 'Dead Letter': Letter'*, p. 45.

19   GOI(AD) Despatch 47 of 1885,para 1, 21.3.1885,OIOC, L/MIL/3/133.

When the views of other senior officers were sought there were a surprising number of them in favour of the plan. Lord Napier, for instance, believed that the time had come to open the higher posts in the army to Indian gentlemen of a suitable character. He wrote:

> The prospect of rising to the command of a regiment will give stimulus and encouragement to the Native army which will be invaluable, and it would provide for the sons of loyal chiefs and heads of clans an opening in the Army that would secure their warm attachment and bind them to our service.[20]

However, opponents of the scheme argued that the scheme would decrease the efficiency of the army and questioned whether British soldiers would have confidence in the leadership of Indian officers.[21] In the end the scheme was defeated by the strong opposition of Lord Roberts, the new Commander-in Chief.[22] He stated that

> I cannot but think that one of the principal reasons why the Native Army has remained as loyal and contented as I believe it to be is that its true interests have been satisfied without elevating the more highly educated native officers to positions which they recognise as properly reserved for the governing race.[23]

Roberts came up with a scheme of his own which was to appoint a few of the best of the VCOs to the Frontier Levies currently operating in the Kyber pass. He named four VCOs as examples of the type of men that he had in mind. These were Ressaidar Mohammed Afzal Khan (11th Bengal Lancers), Subedar-Major Mouladad (20th Punjab Infantry), Subedar-Major Natha Singh (23rd Pioneers) and Risaldar-Major Hassan Ali Khan (13th Bengal Lancers). This arrangement would give an opportunity for VCOs who sought higher command and, at the same time, strengthen the frontier forces. Eventually the best of these levies might be formed into regiments.[24]

After the Mutiny, the Indian infantry regiments were reduced to a strength of 600 soldiers organised into eight companies each commanded by a subedar with a jemadar as second-in-command. There were only six British officers – the Commanding Officer, Second-in-Command, Adjutant, Quartermaster, Medical officer and a General Duties officer. Cavalry regiments had a strength of 420 sowars organised into six troops again with six British officers.[25] Later four of the infantry companies were grouped together as a 'wing' under a British officer, making eight British officers

---

20   Secret Memorandum by Lord Napier of Magdala, OIOC, L/MIL/3/950.
21   See Chandar Sundaram, Reviving a 'Dead Letter', p. 59.
22   See Pradeep Barua, *The Army Officer Corps and Military Modernisation in later Colonial India* (Hull: University of Hull Press, 1999), pp. 13-14.
23   Gen Sir F. Roberts, *Correspondence of General Sir Frederick Roberts* (Simla/Calcutta: 1890-1893), Part VI, p. 672.
24   Roberts' Memo 29/7/1886, para 14, OIOC, L/MIL/17/5/1615, ptbVI (i).
25   See Menezes, *The Indian Army*, p. 192.

in all. Experience in the Second Afghan War showed that this number of British officers was too small to allow for casualties and a British subaltern was allocated to each wing as a second-in-command. Finally, by 1900, the eight company organisation had been changed to four double-companies. Each of these had two British officers with possibly another young British officer under training. Of the four half-companies in a double company, two were commanded by subedars and two by jemadars. This gave the Indian officers more direct and obvious responsibilities than they were to have under the later platoon organisation.[26] By 1914, although the number of Indian officers was unchanged, there were now nearly twice as many British officers in the battalion as there had been in 1860 with a consequent diminution in the role and responsibility of the Indian officers.[27] The disciplinary powers of the Indian officers were limited and because of their long service in the ranks, they might not have the physical agility of a young British subaltern. Though they were brave and loyal, they usually lacked the education and training which would have fitted them for higher command, especially as warfare became more complex in matters such as logistics and inter-service co-operation.[28]

Following the Mutiny, the loyalty of the Indian troops, and especially of their officers who might, perhaps, lead the men in any future uprising, was a major concern. There was, however, a belief among at least some British officers that it was important to train the Indian officers properly and to give them a position of real authority. Sir Harry Norman's view was that:

> I do not conceive it possible to have a satisfactory Native army without thor-oughly good Native officers. We should have thoroughly efficient and, if possible, thoroughly loyal and contented Native officers; and I think we do our best to secure them under a system under which we give our Native officers responsible and honourable positions, with a suitable and adequate training.[29]

One of the changes introduced was that henceforth promotion would be on the basis of merit and capability rather than simply on length of service; there would be no more sixty- and seventy-year old native officers. In the Bombay Army, promotion had always been by merit and selection and this system was now applied in the other two Presidencies with a consequent improvement, not only in the promotion prospects of the most able soldiers, but also in the efficiency of the regiments. As General Shahid

---

26    See Anon, *History of the 5th Royal Gurkha Rifles (Frontier Force), 1858- 1928* (Aldershot: Gale and Polden, c 1928), p. 158.
27    See Michael Barthorp, *Indian Infantry Regiments 1860-1914* (Oxford: Osprey, 1979), p. 8.
28    See ibid., p. 11.
29    Sir Harry Norman, 1875 Notes on the organisation of the Indian Army, Chapter 1, para 15, OIOC, L/MIL/7/7240.

Hamid states: 'The return to the small establishment of British officers restored the authority and responsibility of the native officers.'[30] David Omissi adds that:

> The Indian officers warmed to their new responsibilities. They proved competent to command companies and troops and acquitted themselves well on detached duties. They developed and improved as a result of being given greater authority. Some regimental commanders came to prefer veteran Indian officers to inexperienced British subalterns because the former exercised more effective sway over the men.[31]

Mason points out that it is remarkable, in the immediate post-Mutiny period, that the idea of regiments based upon the irregular system, with considerable trust of, and responsibility given to, the Indian officers, should have received such a good hearing.[32] Irregular units, such as Hodson's Horse and the Scinde Horse raised by Sir John Jacob, were those which were raised in the first instance for specific service in specific areas. They differed from 'regular' units only in that they had only a few British officers – usually three and the lower costs of such units made them popular with the government. Jacob argued very strongly that there should be the smallest possible number of British officers and that they should be hand-picked.[33] The more British officers there are, the more the importance of the native officer was lessened. Omissi suggests that these British officers were better than average and also that the Indian officers in these regiments took a greater interest in their men. They were proud of their unit and of their rank.[34] However, as the century wore on, the number of British officers was gradually increased again with a consequent diminution in the role of the VCOs. Most Indian Army infantry regiments went into action in 1914 with 14 British and 16 Indian officers.

A few regimental Record Books survive from the nineteenth century. These were hand-written in English – perhaps by the adjutant. They vary in content. The least useful are little more than a record of successive inspections by various generals, noting their comments. Others, such as that of the 2nd Panjab (sic) Cavalry, give details of regimental orders, special events and outstanding actions by officers and men. The writer of the first regimental history of this regiment published in 1888 draws heavily upon this manuscript.[35] The book also contains two sets of photographs of the Indian officers, one dated 1859 and the other undated but probably 1886. One of the earlier photographs showing eight officers and NCOs of the regiment, all holders of the

30    Hamid, *They Rode and Fought*, p. 38.
31    Omissi, *The Sepoy and the Raj*, p. 158.
32    See Mason, *A Matter of Honour*, p. 325.
33    See ibid., p 320.
34    See Omissi, *The Sepoy and the Raj*, p. 157.
35    See Anon, *History of the 2nd Panjab Cavalry 1849-1866* (London: Kegan Paul Trench and Co, 1888).

Indian Order of Merit for their services during the Mutiny, was later used as a basis for a painting by the artist Gordon Hayward (see front cover). Pen portraits from sources such as these give us a picture of the men and their characters. For instance: Jemadar Jasmyat Singh (Indian Order of Merit, 1st Class) joined the regiment in 1853 and served with it for 25 years. At Lucknow he distinguished himself by, with the help of Daffadar Punjab Singh, recovering the body of Major Sandford under fire. Captain Probyn (1833-1924) described him as 'Brave as a lion, a great horseman and spearsman, he killed about a company of men in this campaign.' He was promoted to Jemadar in 1859 and advanced to the 1st Class Order of Merit following the campaign in Afghanistan. In 1873 he transferred to the 5th Punjab Cavalry as a Ressaidar as an excess of officers of his rank and class meant that further advancement in the 2nd was unlikely. He thus secured his troop after 25 years service. He had four sons; Amin Singh became a Risaldar in the 5th Punjab Cavalry, Bhagwan Singh, Risaldar-Major in the 7th Bombay Lancers, Natha Singh a Jemadar in the 5th Bombay Cavalry, and Daffadar Partak Singh who was killed at Ahmad Khal in 1880. When Jamyat Singh left the 2nd Punjab his commanding officer wrote: 'The officer commanding takes this opportunity of expressing the pleasure that he feels on the advancement of this native officer and at the same time his great regret at losing him from the regiment with which he has so long been connected.'[36]

Jemadar Sher Singh (Order of British India 2nd Class and Indian Order of Merit 3rd Class) joined the 2nd Punjab Cavalry in 1849, was promoted to Jemadar in 1859 and to Ressaidar in 1874. When he died in 1888, his commanding officer wrote;

> The late rissaldar's (sic) devotion and gallantry, signally displayed on numerous occasions during the mutiny campaign won him the 2nd Class Order of Merit as well as the admiration and respect of all soldiers English and native with whom he was associated. The late rissaldar's unswerving loyalty to the State and to the officers under whom he served, his general demeanour, his single hearted honesty and his untiring energy which the weight of 75 years had failed to impair, afford a bright example to his fellow soldiers which Colonel Lance trusts will be long remembered in the regiment.[37]

Risaldar-Major Gholam Hyder joined the 2nd Punjab Cavalry on the 15th March 1853 as a Jemadar, he was promoted to Ressaidar on the 21st January 1857 and to Risaldar on the 1st January 1859 when Panjab Singh transferred out of the regiment.[38] He was advanced from the 3rd to the 2nd class of Risaldar in 1867 and became Risaldar-Major on the 30th April 1874 when he was advanced a further grade. He was invalided out in 1879. According to the regimental history:

---

36   Ibid.
37   Ibid.
38   Bengal Army List 1877.

His high character, integrity and courteous and dignified manner earned him the respect of all with whom he served. When Woordie-Major of the Regiment he was especially marked for his strict impartiality to all classes in the Regiment and, by thorough knowledge of, and attention to, his difficult and important duties, he gave valuable assistance to the officers with whom he was associating in maintaining the order and discipline of the Regiment.[39]

Nor were these three examples from a single regiment exceptional. The Commanding Officer of the Poona Horse, Captain G K Erskine, wrote pen-portraits of the Indian officers (probably all from the same Risaldar) in 1840 and commented on one of them as follows:

Risaldar Dowlut Roa Ghorpana, Sirdar Bahadur (22 years and 8 months service). An officer of distinction and possessed of the most creditable testimonials: served throughout the Mahratta Wars and operations in Sind and Afghanistan with the Army of the Indus.[40]

In a Brigade Order of 30th November 1830, Captain Spiller had written of this officer:

Added to his being a soldier of the most distinguished bravery, his talents and conduct are such as to render him, on all occasions, an officer of the greatest use. His conduct to his men has always been marked by kindness and liberality: hence he is deservedly loved by them, and, from his rank and influence, he is no less respected by all classes of men not belonging to the army, and which he has, on many occasions, turned to account for the public service, and I look on him as one of the best soldiers I have ever seen.

When Major General Roberts, commanding the Punjab Frontier Force, inspected the regiment in 1878 he wrote in his report that he 'was particularly struck by the intelligent manner in which Rissaldar (sic) Major Gholam Hyder and Rissaldar (sic) Badawah Singh disposed of their squadrons for outpost duties.'[41]

The following tribute was paid to Risaldar-Major Lahrasaf Khan of the Poona Horse on his death by his commanding officer:

During the 29 years he served with the regiment his high character for justice and impartiality towards those under him, for conciliatory and courteous bearing to his equals, and for unswerving devotion to his duty won him the respect of

39   *History of the 2nd Panjab Cavalry,* pp. 40-41.
40   Typescript Notes on the History of the Poona Horse, NAM, London 6910-11.
41   Ibid., p. 54.

all ranks. During three years as rissaldar-major (sic) he rendered the highest service to the Regiment by assisting in the maintenance of soldierly feeling, and by setting a bright example to his brother native officers in keeping up that spirit of unity and friendship which is so essential to the well-being of the Regiment. On this melancholy occasion the Commanding officer calls on Native Officers severally and collectively to maintain that unanimity amongst themselves which has for so long been a privilege and an honour to the regiment.[42]

The comments made by their British colleagues clearly demonstrate that the Indian officers made a very significant contribution to the success of the regiment. Their courage and loyalty had been amply demonstrated through, for instance, the action of Hakdad Khan at Sissiah in January 1859, when he rallied a company of the 42nd Highlanders (The Black Watch). This would almost certainly have earned him a DSO in the British army and, at a time when the decoration was more freely awarded than in later years, possibly even a VC. In the comments quoted above, the quality most often noted by British officers when writing of Indian officers was their bravery, with integrity, impartiality, loyalty and professionalism also being frequently mentioned. Nor were the officers considered above exceptional. Between 1847 and 1876 Indian officers of the Scinde Horse were engaged by the enemy while in command of detachments in thirteen separate actions. General Jacob wrote of the 2nd Punjab Regiment in 1857 that 'its native officers are, as subalterns, equal to the best Europeans.'[43]

The average length of service of the Indian officers and therefore their age upon retirement seems to have declined during the second half of the nineteenth century. Though it took Jamyat Singh of the 2nd Punjab twenty-five years to secure command of a troop, Gholam Hyder retired after twenty-six years, Jiwan Singh after twenty-eight and Lahrasaf Khan after thirty. If we assume that they joined the regiment around age twenty, possibly younger, this would have them retiring at approximately fifty years old. Sarmukh Singh seems to have been the exception being over sixty when he retired. These officers, not unjustifiably, were well rewarded upon their retirement. In addition to the medals and awards which they had gained during their service (some of which carried with them a small pension) they all earned a basic pension which might well be supplemented. Risaldar Hakdad Khan who was discharged in 1863 as too old for further service was given a gratuity of nine month's full pay. Rewards were also extended to the widows and sons of ex-officers. The second son of Risaldar-Major Lahrasaf Khan, Arjasaf Khan, was promoted to Duffadar in recognition of his father's service. In recognition of the service of Ressaldar Bishan Singh Sirdar Bahadur, his widow was granted for her lifetime the share in the village of Kariala and his eldest

---

42    Permanent Order Book, Sam Browne's Cavalry, entry for 24.12.83. Handwritten, 1898. NAM, London.
43    Anon, *History of the 2nd Panjab Cavalry*.

legitimate heir the share, value 330 rupees, in the village of Samupura which Bishan Singh had enjoyed.

During the second half of the nineteenth century, Indian troops were to serve in Abyssinia, Burma, China, East Africa, Egypt and the Sudan and Tibet. The bulk of their fighting, however, took place on the North-West Frontier including the First and Second Afghan Wars. The First Afghan War (1839-1842) had resulted in the complete destruction of the British-Indian army which had been forced to retreat. The Second Afghan War (1878-1880) began equally inauspiciously with the murder of the British Resident in Kabul and his escort of Guides. British honour was restored by forces led by General (later Lord) Roberts who fought a number of battles culminating in Roberts' famous march from Kabul to Kandahar and the ensuing Battle of Kandahar.

In 1900 Indian troops found themselves in China for a second time. A secret society, known as the Boxers, massacred Chinese Christians and tortured and killed their missionaries. Now supported by regular Chinese troops, on June 20th they surrounded the Legation Quarter of Peking where the foreign embassies were concentrated. The countries whose Legations were besieged responded by assembling the first truly multi-national force in history, containing troops from France, Germany, Great Britain, India, Japan, Russia and the United States of America. The Indian contingent included State Forces from Alwar, Bikanir, Jodhpur and Malkerkotla and they were accompanied by the Maharajahs of Bikanir and Jodhpur.

Amar Singh was a risaldar (squadron commander) in the Jodhpur Lancers at the time and he also acted as regimental adjutant and secretary to Sir Pratap Singh, the Regent of Jodhpur, throughout the campaign. Sir Pratap, always keen to see action, was overjoyed at the news that the regiment had been selected for service overseas with himself as honorary commandant. The regiment was officered entirely by Indians with two British officers as advisers. They arrived in China after the Legations had been relieved. Having disembarked, they waited for a fortnight before they were assigned a task. On the 8th of October Amar Singh and his squadron were ordered to take part in a sweep around Shanghai. Amar Singh's reports from the reconnaissance were duly passed up to Brigade Headquarters and a staff officer, Captain Stewart, replied to Major Turner (Inspector of Imperial Service Troops, Jodhpur, who had accompanied the regiment) that the General:

> Would be glad if you would express to Sir Pratap his appreciation of the way the Jodhpur Lancers worked today. He is afraid they must have had a very long and trying day for both men and horses. The country he knew was a very bad one but he had every confidence, which has not been misplaced, that the Jodhpur cavalry would get over it if anyone could.[44]

44   Amar Singh diary, 10.10.1900.

On October 9th the regiment sailed for Shan-Hai-Kuan, northeast of Peking, arriving on the 12th. The Lancers were to remain in the area throughout the long cold winter – on the night of 31 January 1901 there were thirty-nine degrees of frost and the ink froze in the ink-stands. Amar Singh commented in his diary that the city was dirty, filthy and very smelly but that the regiment's quarters were good with warm stables for the horses.[45] The troops settled down to a routine of patrols searching for weapons in the surrounding villages. The regiment's only serious engagement with the enemy came on 12 January 1901 when shots were fired by a large body of Chinese armed brigands at a Jodhpur party which was out collecting wood about 5 miles northeast of Shan-Hai-Kuan. In the subsequent skirmish, two Lancers had been killed and six brigands. Daffadar Dool Singh was awarded the Indian Order of Merit.[46]

In Amar Singh's view the Jodhpur Lancers had done good work, given every satisfaction expected of the regiment and had undergone the winter most admirably with the men bearing all hardships equally well. He believed that the regiment was better than any of the other cavalry that he had seen in China, the men being more skilful horseman with higher quality horses, stating that "Rajpoots (sic) did and can stand much more hardships than others.'[47] Major General Richardson, Commanding the Cavalry Brigade of the Expeditionary Force, inspected the regiment in March 1901 and wrote in his report that 'The Jodhpur Lancers are a very fine regiment of Imperial Service troops, fit for service in every respect.'[48] It is important to remember that this was a unit officered entirely by Indians with two British 'advisers'. The success of such a unit showed that Indians were capable of command at all levels within the regiment and that it was only prejudice that prevented them from going further.

Amar Singh was disgusted by the way in which Indian troops were treated by the British.

> The Indians are looked on as inferior in the scale of humanity. The British are better treated, supplied, fed and clothed and paid than the Indians. No Indian can rise above the rank of rissaldar or subadar major, and no matter how young a British officer may be, he always looks down upon the other as an ignorant fellow, even though the Indian may be much more experienced. British sergeants and soldiers never salute Indian officers, not even Sir Pratap. They look as though they expect the Indian to salute them. It is a mark of great favour on the part of the soldier or sergeant if he even condescends to say 'Good morning'. If an Indian officer failed to salute a British officer there would be a hell of a row. The British

45   Ibid., 15. 10. 1900.
46   Ibid., 21. 1. 1901.
47   Amar Singh, 'Note' dated, 4. 7. 1901.
48   Ibid.

make a great row when they hear the foreigners calling Indian soldiers and officers 'coolies' though they do not mind treating them as such themselves.[49]

Amar Singh was only 22 when he served as a risaldar and squadron commander in China. In a regular Indian army regiment he might not have become a jemadar until he was in his thirties and the squadron commanders would have been English officers. However, in the regiments of the Imperial State Forces, the senior appointments were in the hands of the ruler of the State and Amar Singh presumably owed his position to the fact that he was a protégé of Sir Pratap Singh, commandant of the regiment. By his own account, Amar Singh seems to have acquitted himself well as an officer. He had a charming readiness to be truthful and even to record his own shortcomings. In his diary for 14 September 1899, he notes the perceptive comments on himself by Captain Patterson (Assistant Inspecting Officer, Jodhpur Lancers):

> This young officer has first-rate abilities, a good knowledge of English and is a fine horsemen. He however does not know his work and takes no trouble to learn it. It is a pity he is not made to.

Amar Singh commented: 'I think it was all right and much more than I expected.'[50] Unfortunately, this unwillingness to get down to serious work seems to be characteristic of Amar Singh throughout his military career and may account, in part at least, for some of the difficulties which he encountered later.

By the turn of the century most of the Indian officers had qualifications in musketry, use of the machine gun and equitation. Many, especially the younger men, had more than one qualification.[51] They were excellent troop and squadron leaders, who could probably have led their regiments in a charge, but what they lacked was any experience of, or training for, higher command. Accustomed over the years to look to their British officers for leadership, many of them found themselves unable to take over when those officers became casualties. Used to fighting tribesmen on the Frontier, none of the Indian officers, and it must said, few of the British officers, were ready for the conditions in which they found themselves fighting in Northern France against one of the most professional armies in the world. The Indian officers who went to war in 1914 were extremely experienced soldiers who knew all there was to know about low-level regimental soldiering. At this time the average length of service of jemadars, the most junior of the Indian officers, was around thirteen and a half years.[52] This may be compared with the average young British subaltern who might find himself in the trenches only a few weeks after leaving school. However, one disadvantage of this

---

49   Ibid.
50   Ibid.
51   See for example the Indian Army List 1914.
52   See ibid.

length of service of the Indian officers might be the unfitness of the older men to cope with the conditions in France. For instance Risaldar-Major Ram Singh of Hodson's Horse went home after less than twelve months in France, having collapsed in the trenches and he died at home one year later.[53]

---

53  See War Narrative of the 9th, Hodson's Horse. A Typescript in the National Army
    Museum London, entry for September 15th 1915.

**3**

## The Imperial Cadet Corps

Although the Imperial Cadet Corps failed to live up to its founder's expectations, it is nevertheless the first attempt to provide professional training for potential. Indian officers. It is the first official acknowledgment that it might be possible for Indians, albeit from a very limited class, to become officers on a par with their British counterparts. Chandar Sundaram points out that in the on-going debate regarding Indianisation in the Indian Army:

> It raised two questions: were Indians fit for command and leadership in the same class as Britons; and if they were, how were they to be fully integrated into the Army in a manner that did not endanger the Raj?[1]

As a protégé of Sir Pratap Singh, the Honorary Commandant of the new Corps, Amar Singh joined the initial intake of cadets. His diary provides a unique first-hand account of the training undertaken by the cadets.

Lord Curzon's (Viceroy 1899–1905) aim in founding the Corps was to provide a military education for young Indians and to turn them into 'officers and gentlemen', able to serve alongside British officers. He was against the policy of denying King's commissions to young Indians, especially to those from the princely classes who were linked to the British by ties of self-interest if not of loyalty.[2] He was keen to encourage suitable young men, ie of aristocratic birth, to join the Indian Army or, at least, to become officers in their own State Forces and entry was therefore restricted to the sons of princes and nobles. Membership would be by invitation only. He wished primarily

---

1  Chandar S. Sundaram 'The Imperial Cadet Corps and the Indianisation of the Indian Army's Officer Corps 1897- 1923'*Durbar: Journal of the Indian Military Historical Society*, Vol 27, No 2, Summer 2010, p. 53.
2  See Foreign Department Proceedings August 1900, Number 925-926B, quoted in Lt-Col Gautam Sharma, *The Nationalisation of the Indian Army 1885-1947* (New Delhi: Allied Publishers Ltd, 1996), p. 13.

to satisfy political aspirations rather than add to the country's military strength.[3] Between twenty and thirty students a year were expected and most of them would have attended one of the four Chiefs' Colleges at Ajmer, Lahore, Rajkot and Indore and would have had the equivalent of an English public school education. The preliminary course would last two years. Those students who seriously wished to pursue a military career would undergo a more sustained military education lasting another year and a half, broadly similar to the course at Sandhurst. They were provided with a richly embroidered white uniform with sky-blue facings and they rode on black horses with leopard skin saddlecloths as close escort to the Viceroy at the 1903 Durbar in Delhi and to the King-Emperor in 1911. DeWitt Ellinwood suggests that Curzon was always glad of an opportunity to show off the Corps on ceremonial occasions and that this was one reason for its creation.[4] What Curzon signally failed to do in setting out his ideas on the formation of the Corps was to state explicitly the precise nature of the commissions to be granted to successful graduates. This lack of clarity incorporated from the very beginning was the seed of the Corps' failure. A second underlying problem was that control of the Corps was vested in the Foreign Department and not in the Army Department. Political officers were not especially committed to the Corps and the Military Department could shrug their shoulders and claim that it was not their responsibility. After the departure of Curzon, his successors as Viceroy lacked his particular attachment to the Corps.

The staff of the Corps consisted of a British Commandant (Major Watson of the Central India Horse) and an Adjutant (Captain Cameron of the same regiment) together with a British drill-sergeant. Was it coincidence or by choice that the two officers should have come from the same regiment which was rather different from the mainstream of the Indian cavalry? In Mason's words, 'they admired reckless daring, were inclined to parade a light-hearted dislike of red tape and pipeclay, frequently showed an interest in Indian states and the ways of the country.'[5] If these two officers *were* chosen by the Viceroy, then it was certainly an interesting decision. Rao Bahadur Thakur Dip Singh, formerly commandant of the Bikaner Camel Corps was appointed as native Adjutant. The final member of the staff was Sergeant-Major Chapman of the Fifteenth Hussars. Amar Singh commented; 'He was a very good man all round. He knew his work very well and had the knack of teaching too.'[6] The cold-weather term was spent at Meerut and the summer term at Dehra Dun. The majority of the entrants to the Corps left after two years or less and did not go on to serve in the armed forces. During the thirteen years that the Corps was in existence, nearly seventy Cadets passed through the unit – 54 from the Princely States and 14 from British India. Only

---

3    See Sharma, *The Nationalisation of the Indian Army 1885-1947*, p. 16.
4    See DeWitt C Ellinwood, *Between Two Worlds: A Rajput Officer in the Indian Army 1905-21* (Lanham, Maryland: Hamilton Books, 2005), p. 155.
5    Mason, *A Matter of Honour*, p. 378.
6    Amar Singh diary, 10. 4. 1903.

eleven of these cadets were eventually, after much debate, granted commissions in the Native Indian Land Forces.

The first intake of twenty-one cadets included four maharajas and two heirs apparent, the remainder being noblemen or the sons of noblemen. Of these, only four, including Amar Singh, would graduate successfully He was somewhat different from the majority of the other cadets, being older, married and having already been to war. He had less formal education than many of his contemporaries but he was far more widely read and had a better command of English than most of them. Amar Singh was a very keen reader with a strong interest in military history, especially Napoleon's campaigns. He regularly kept a list of books which he had read which included volumes such as *The Memoirs of Baron Marbot* and *Washington and his Generals*. His attitude was resented by some of the young princes who nicknamed him 'The Rough-Rider'.

The first few days of his time in the Corps was taken up largely with drill and physical exercise. In April 1902 Amar Singh wrote a 'Note ' about his first term in the Corps. The students had set up two messes, one for Hindus (including Sikhs and Jats) and one for Muslims in order to cope with their differing dietary requirements. Amar Singh and other Rajputs, together with the British officers joined the Muslim mess which served food in the English style. Of his studies he wrote:

> These were not much. In the beginning we were taught arithmetic and algebra for a few days but these were done away with and only English was kept. We were divided into three classes. The first class (which included Amar Singh) was taught Green's *Short History of the English People* and *Treasure Island*. Besides this we were supposed to have dictation, writing summaries of what we had read, some Greek and Latin roots and English idioms. We had no lessons to prepare at home except the usual diaries. Besides polo we used to have football and lawn-tennis.[7]

Amar Singh was keeping two diaries at this time; one open to public scrutiny and his private diary from which these quotations are taken.

The first term's curriculum concentrated on a fairly basic general education with very little attempt to address military subjects. In the second term however, topography and map-reading were introduced. For their composition examination the cadets had to write a letter to a friend about life in the Corps and the day after that were examined on *A Short History of the English People*. In his Note on the second term Amar Singh wrote:

> We were not worked hard. The chief thing taught us was the correct way of speaking and writing. The Major Sahib never got angry but treated us with the greatest love. He was always in good humour and did his best to make us

---

7    Ibid., 21. 4. 1902.

understand. Among the studies may be counted the diary, which we had to write regularly, and dictation and composition. Taken all together it was quite satisfactory work. We had plenty of foot drill. I was never any good at it though I was not considered the worst. The slow marching always put me out and sometimes I used to get out of step.[8]

Amar Singh was also criticised in the riding school because he had learnt to ride as a young man in a non-military style and he now found it difficult to change. He was a keen polo player but was not good at other games and took no interest in them. In the same 'Note' he wrote about his own experience and his perceptions of the difference between the British and indian officers.

Experience clearly showed me the difference between the well-educated British officers and the native rank holders While out in China (serving with the Jodhpur Lancers) and even after our return I was under the impression that if only the natives were allowed the higher ranks they would be just as well filled. It is now that I have come to know that there is a vast difference between them. I myself know nothing at all when compared to them. Their education, their military knowledge, is far superior and I fear that it would take me twenty years or at least five to learn it all.[9]

Amar Singh also became aware of the manner in which British officers treated one another socially which he contrasted with the way in which Indians behaved.

The respect which juniors pay to seniors is simply wonderful. These people show respect but at the same time retain their independence. There is nothing like the Indian custom where if there is a big person we must all flatter him. Where respect is due they pay it and where self-respect and independence is due they maintain it.[10]

These comments are very perceptive and Amar Singh clearly recognised the potential difficulties which would face Indian officers who sought to be on a par with their British counterparts. At the end of the Note he wrote:

May God bless Lord Curzon for starting such a fine the thing (the Corps) and giving an opening to the aristocratic families of India for a good service in the British Army. May his successors follow the same policy. The Imperial Cadets

---

8    Ibid., 29. 10. 1902.
9    Ibid
10   Ibid.

Corps is a real good thing for the Indians of good family who wish to get honourable service.[11]

At the start of the third term Captain Cameron had a long chat with Amar Singh and told him that he was thought too proud and haughty and had treated some of the other cadets rather roughly as they were younger and inexperienced, to the extent that they were afraid to talk to him. He was not good at saluting, obeying orders or taking advice and had offended Captain Cameron and the Commandant on more than one occasion. Amar Singh was naturally upset at this criticism and determined to improve his behaviour. He wrote in his diary 'This term I am determined to keep all the others pleased if I can. I have asked Captain Cameron to warn me off on the slightest thing he finds wrong with me and he has promised to do so.'[12] These are the sort of issues which would affect Amar Singh throughout his military career. How much of his reaction to authority was inherent in his personality and how much due to the invidious position in which he often found himself is difficult to say.

In Amar Singh's third term there were twenty-three cadets and they were taught parts of *Forty-One Years in India* by Lord Roberts, together with reading, arithmetic and dictation. He commented ' There was not much stress laid upon studies this time.' [13] He expressed concern about the future of the Corps and what sort of commissions would be given to graduates. He was not prepared to be on an equal footing with the jemadars and risaldars who had come up through the ranks;

> If we are not to be given commissions why the devil are they teaching us military work? There is a question which everyone is anxious to know but nobody seems aware. One thing is certain we are not going to get any commissions in the British or native armies. The reason is that no British would ever like to be under a native command at present. It will require some generations before the feeling of the conqueror and the conquered, the rulers and the ruled, and of the blacks and whites, will fall away. The Imperial Cadet Corps has nothing to recommend itself in point of learning at present or of becoming useful at the end.[14]

Amar Singh discussed the role of the Corps with Captain Cameron who said that he had great trouble in convincing his colleagues that the Corps was a useful institution. British officers always told him that they would always sooner put themselves under the command of a European than an Indian. Cameron responded to that view by saying that there were exceptions and he specifically mentioned Sir Pratap Singh. Cameron told Amar Singh that he always ended any discussion with a British officer

---

11    Ibid.
12    Amar Singh diary, 22. 10. 1902.
13    Ibid., 16. 5. 1903.
14    Ibid.

by saying that God had placed India in British hands and that it was up to the British to make men of the Indians.[15]

Amar Singh's fourth term was similar to the previous three. Four of the princes who started at the same time as him had left and he felt that this lowered the prestige of the Corps and lessened the chances of the graduates being commissioned into the Indian Army as opposed to the State Forces. The fifth term was the final term for those cadets who would not qualify for commissions. Four of the most promising cadets, including Amar Singh, were selected to continue with their training for two additional terms. However, the future of those cadets who graduated was still uncertain. Curzon was unable to get senior British officers to agree to Indians being given full commissions which would entitle them to command British troops and therefore, eventually, British officers. Equally the cadets were, not unreasonably, unwilling to accept Viceroy's Commissions. There was a suggestion that a new regiment be established to be officered almost exclusively by Indians with only the commandant, second-in-command and adjutant being British. Eventually a new service known as the Indian Land Forces was set up but the Indian officers commissioned into this service were not authorised to command British troops.

Amar Singh had a conversation with Major Watson who suggested that a Viceroy appointed by a radical government in England might give Indians command over Europeans but that such a move would create a lot of discontent which he thought should be avoided. He commented in his diary:

> He said that we were the beginning of the institution which would finally end in giving posts to Indians which would enable them to command Europeans. It is this very thing that stops me from accepting a commission. Suppose that I did get a commission; I would not like to serve under any man who was my junior. My ideas are not those of a cringing man. Even here I hate it when I have to show undue respect to these officers. There are orders that we must salute every British officer that we meet on the road if he is wearing his uniform. This is all nonsense; I will not go on saluting every Englishman I come across.[16]

In the fifth term the cadets were taken out on manoeuvres. They found the practical work was more pleasant and easy than the work indoors. Amar Singh was second in the termly examination and he was delighted to be selected for the third year's course. The Commandant, Major Watson, said that only the very best had been picked and that they were sure to get some service. Amar Singh commented that now the cadets were more certain about their prospects they would work with a greater zeal. However, the Commandant returned from discussion with the Viceroy in Simla having been

---

15   Ibid.
16   Ibid., 29. 2. 1904.

told that although the cadets would get 'real' commissions, these were likely to be in the Imperial Service Troops.

By the sixth term there were only sixteen cadets in the Corps as opposed to the one-time maximum of twenty-six. The subjects covered by the Senior Class included Tactics, Topography, Fortification (making a gabion etc) and English. The cadets were taught how to lay out schemes on maps and how to make a sketch with a prismatic compass. Some years later a paper on Military Law was added to the curriculum.[17] Amar Singh was promoted to corporal within the Corps and he was second out of six in the Spring Examinations. He wrote:

> The officers were more pleased with me and the other cadets were more friendly than they had been before. Perhaps the officers were pleased because all the big swells have gone and the boys were pleased because we were so few. I have simply to say that this was the best and happiest term that I have passed. I asked Sergeant Chapman whether I would pass the final examination and he said that they would give us very easy questions as they want us all to pass, for they think that if we people don't get anything, there will be no more cadets coming.[18]

Amar Singh attended the 1903 Durbar as a member of the Corps. In 1911 he borrowed his brother's uniform and rejoined the unit. His Diaries provide a fascinating eyewitness account of these events. The British made great efforts to stimulate the devotion of the Indian troops and the ruling Chiefs to the King-Emperor and Durbars (Courts) were one way in which this was done.[19] The 1903 Durbar was organised by the then Viceroy, Lord Curzon, to celebrate the coronation of King Edward VII. The King-Emperor George V attended the 1911 event in person; 'This was, in many senses, the ultimate expression of British rule in India, never to be equalled again under the Raj.'[20]

The 1903 Durbar, a very grandiose affair, was nicknamed 'The Curzonisation.' The Imperial Cadets Corps, including Amar Singh, was near the head of the procession entering Delhi. In their distinctive uniforms and mounted on black horses the Corps was much admired and greeted with cheers from the crowds. Their team that played in the polo tournament did well. Amar Singh believed that the Viceroy was quite satisfied with them. He commented in his diary:

> As regards the show I think it was a first class one. If one looks to the expenditure it was a mere waste of money. If you look to splendour there was nothing

---

17    See Chandar S. Sundaram, 'Treated with Scant Attention', *Journal of Military History*, Vol. 77, No. 1, January 2013, pp. 41-70.
18    Diary, 25. 8. 1904.
19    See Omissi, *The Sepoy and the Raj*, p. 108.
20    Ellinwood, *Between Two Worlds: A Rajput Officer in the Indian Army*, p. 159.

wanting but it is more or less copying the Moghuls who were famous for these things though nowadays splendour is not considered a virtue and the English idea of simplicity is quite the contrary. If viewed from political points I do not know what to say. No doubt this must have impressed the foreigners who may have been thinking very lightly of India. Whether it has done the country any good I cannot say. Of course there were several meetings held of the different institutions and for these it was a very good thing indeed. Without the occasion so many men would not have come together.[21]

Amar Singh's comments from an Indian's point of view on the cost of the event as compared with its political value are significant. There is certainly an element of 'bread and circuses' about the display. One wonders how widely Amar Singh's views were shared amongst those Indians who were beginning to seek Independence.

By contrast, in 1911, the spectators were disappointed because the King-Emperor declined the traditional elephant and entered the City on horseback. Many of the Indians watching were unable to pick out the monarch among his retinue. On this occasion the Imperial Cadets Corps rode immediately behind Queen Mary's carriage with Sir Pratap Singh himself riding alongside her. Amar Singh wrote in his diary:

> It was pity that the King did not ride an elephant. A procession of elephants on this day would have been much more imposing but unfortunately the Queen did not fancy such a ride and so it was knocked on the head. This at least is the reason I have heard. Most of the people could not make out which was the King as they did not expect him to be on a horse. If I was asked my opinion I would say that the State Entry of Lord Curzon was a much more imposing show and very much more brilliant.[22]

Amar Singh seems to have taken a rather more positive view of this event than he did of the 1903 Durbar. For instance, he commented on the design of the Durbar amphitheatre which he thought very well thought out and carried out and gave a most magnificent effect. He felt that it was a great pity that all the work was so very frail that afterwards it had to be knocked down and auctioned. He wrote:

> After a few years there will be no recollection of it except in pictures and these do not show the thing really as well as one may expect. What a great thing it would have been if it had been built of marble or ordinary stone. Then it would have stood for ages and generations and been admired by posterity as the Moghul tombs and palaces are today.[23]

21   Amar Singh diary, Note on the Durbar, 1903.
22   Ibid., Note on the 1911 Durbar.
23   Ibid.

Amar Singh was quite right: all that remains today is a dusty field where boys play cricket around a memorial column to the Durbar. They are watched over by the statue of King George V which once stood under the canopy on the Rajpath together with the statues of various Viceroys which were brought here in 1947 and which are now gradually being eroded by the rain. *Sic transit gloria mundi.*

At the end of three years study, of the sixteen cadets then in the Corps, four, including Amar Singh, were granted commissions in the Indian Land Forces. These officers had a higher status than the VCOs but were not able to command European Troops. They are listed separately in the India Army List of 1906, as Second Lieutenants with commissions dating from the 4th of July 1905 as follows:-

| | |
|---|---|
| Zorawar Singh | Commandant Bhavnagar IS Lancers |
| Aga Cassim Shah (nephew to the Aga Khan) | ADC to GOC Poona Division |
| Wall-ud-dim Khan | With the Hyderabad IS Lancers |
| Kanwar Amar Singh | ADC to GOC Mhow Division |

Overall, Amar Singh did not seem to have been entirely happy during the first few terms of his three years in the Corps. Older and with a wider knowledge of the world than the other cadets, he seems to have found it difficult to fit in, especially with the young men of higher social status than himself. He found it particularly difficult to play the courtier and flatter the young princes. Although his English was good and he was well read, he did not find the academic work easy. He was clearly very disappointed by his final examination placing when he came fourth out of four. Captain Watson called Amar Singh a fighting soldier and thought that he would be better employed as a regimental officer rather than an ADC. Alternatively he might become an intelligence officer.[24]

Several years later, General Edward Barrow, GOC Southern Army, wrote to the Military Secretary to the C-in-C:

> I have reported most favourably on the Indian officers in the Indian Land forces, viz: Lt Aga Cassim Shah, ADC to GOC 65th (Poona) Division and Lt Kanwar Amar Singh, ADC to GOC 5th (Mhow) Division I consider both of them as fit to take their place among British officers of an Indian cavalry regiment whether in an educational, a professional or a social sense and I have reason to believe that they are naturally not altogether satisfied with their present position or prospects.[25]

24   See Foreign Department Proceedings, Internal Secret I, January 12905, Numbers 36/7, quoted in Sharma, *The Nationalisation of the Indian Army 1885-1947*, p. 22.
25   Appendix to the Viceroy's Note on the granting of Commissions to Indians, OIOC, L/MIL/7/19006.

Several of the graduates from the Corps, including Amar Singh, saw service in the Great War, mostly in staff roles. However, two of them did see frontline service; Lieutenant Sawai Singh with the 13th Sekhawat regiment and Lieutenant Rana Jodha Jang, Tihri Sappers and Miners, served with the 39th Garwhal Rifles in France where he was awarded a Military Cross for bravery at Givenchy.[26] He later commanded a company of riflemen, possibly the first ICC graduate to achieve this rank. A photograph reproduced in the regimental history shows him with a group of British officers and wearing the ribbon of his MC.[27]

The curriculum for the Cadets at the start of their course appears designed to bring them up to something like the general level of education of their British equivalents at Sandhurst who had had to pass an entrance exam, often with the aid of a 'crammer'. The course which Amar Singh and his fellow-cadets of the Senior Class undertook was very little different from that being offered to British cadets during this period. The curriculum at the Royal Military College, Sandhurst in 1900 covered Military Engineering, Military Topography, Military Administration and Law, French and German together with drill, gymnastics and riding.[28] Admission was by competitive examination and the course lasted one year. General Sir O'Moore Creagh, later Commander-in-Chief India, who joined Sandhurst in 1865 commented in his *Autobiography* that the entrance exam was very easy as the standard was low and there were normally more places than candidates.[29] According to him, the curriculum changed little in his years of service but the passing out test became easier. A Committee of Enquiry, set up in 1902 and chaired by the Rt Hon A Akers-Douglas MP, found that there was 'absolutely no inducement for the cadets to work' once at the Academy since a candidate's ranking, and the regiment to which he was posted, depended only on his results in the entrance examination.[30] The Committee found that too much time was spent on drill, though the young men did not learn to *take* drill. Musketry was neglected; the cadets pipe-clayed their belts but did not clean their rifles. Amar Singh, while in conversation with Colonel Pears, the resident at Jaipur, showed him the question papers of his last examination and the Colonel said that they were just what the British officers had to learn at Sandhurst or Woolwich.

The Corps failed to live up to Curzon's hopes for two main reasons. Firstly was the unsatisfactory nature of the commissions, certainly in Indian eyes, which were granted to successful graduates This was coupled with the unremitting hostility of the majority

26   See Sundaram, 'Treated with Scant Attention', p. 21.
27   D.H. Drake-Brockman, *With the Royal Garwhal Rifles in the Great War 1914-1917* (Originally published 1934 but no further details. Reprint Uckfield: Naval and Military Press, 2006), p. 73.
28   See Maj A.F. Mockler-Ferryman *Annals of Sandhurst: A Chronicle of the Royal Military College* (London, Heinemann, 1900) Appendix B, p. 284 et seq.
29   Sir O'Moore Creagh, *Autobiography* (London: Hutchinson and Co, 1925), p. 17.
30   B. Bond, *The Victorian Army and the Staff College 1854-1914* (London: Eyre & Methuen, 1972) p. 185.

of British officers to the notion that Indians could become officers on a par with them-selves. They were led by Lord Kitchener (who became Commander-in- Chief India in 1902) and who was a virulent opponent of Curzon. Kitchener commented on the perceived opulence of their uniforms; 'Had the Corps been instituted with the express object of providing the spectators with a most brilliant pageant, it could not have been more successful in that respect.'[31] Opponents of the Corps argued that a scheme devised solely for the privileged few would alienate the VCOs who were the backbone of the Army. It would also make regimental service unpopular amongst the martial races – the Sikhs, Rajputs etc – who had served the Raj for so long and so loyally.[32] These were men of limited education but long experience who would see privileged young men taking precedence over them.

There was uncertainty about the commissions right from the Corps' inception. Rule 1 of the Draft Rules had held out the possibility of graduates taking their place in the Imperial Army as British officers.[33] But this was never to be the case: gradu-ating cadets received commissions in the Indian Land Forces rather than the King's Commissions granted to their counterparts at Sandhurst. This distinction created a significant barrier between the graduates of the Corps and their English counterparts. Amar Singh himself expressed concern about the future of the Corps and the sort of commissions that would be given to the graduates. He, a Rajput nobleman, would not be prepared to be on an equal footing with the jemadars and risaldars who had risen from the ranks.

The dissatisfaction among the Indian Princes led to a decline in the number and quality of the cadets who entered the Corps. In 1907 Amar Singh attended the Viceroy's (Lord Minto) Durbar and commented on the Imperial Cadet Corps (which his brother had joined in 1905) as follows;

> I am very sorry to say that the Corps is not at all what it used to be. The boys are taught practically nothing at all except words out of the dictionary. They were all making fun of it. There is no one going on for the commission exam this year and as most of them will be leaving by the end of March and new ones will come there is no chance of anyone getting a commission for the next three years at the earliest. To make the Corps more popular two things are necessary. The first is improving the education of the Chief's Colleges and the other is finding them some sort of employment after they have had the two year course. They get nothing except permission to wear the Corps uniform. Now exactly what good is that?[34]

31   Memorandum by Lord Kitchener, 1908, para 16, OIOC, L/MIL/7/19006.
32   See Note by General Gordon in OIOC, MSS.Eur.F. 126/2.
33   See Sundaram, 'Treated with Scant Attention', p. 22.
34   Amar Singh diary, 4. 2. 1907.

Captain Cameron, who had succeeded Watson as Commandant of the Corps was asked for his views on the decline in popularity of the Corps. In his opinion some of the ruling chiefs thought it beneath their dignity to send their sons to the Corps. This was not helped by the fact that the Foreign Department had sent one or two young men to the Corps almost as a punishment in order to remove them from what were seen as pernicious influences in their home States. The Commandant believed that the Corps needed greater publicity and it should be made clear to the Princes that the invitation to join came directly from the Viceroy.[35] Because of a lack of publicity about the Corps and, above all, the uncertainty of potential cadets about their future somewhat ambiguous position should they graduate, recruitment to the Corps dwindled away. It was left to 'wither on the vine' until 1915 when the then Commandant was called to active service

General Sir O'Moore Creagh (who succeeded Kitchener as Commander-in-Chief in 1909) and under whom Amar Singh served as a Staff Officer, wrote in 1910:

> The Imperial Cadet Corps was originally started to provide for the military aspirations of Indians of noble fighting families or clans but for various reasons it has not fulfilled what was expected of it. The commissions given to the young men were not of a nature to satisfy their ambitions, or to make them feel, as they think they have the right to, that they have the same opportunities as their British confreres.[36]

Curzon may have seen the Corps as an initial step towards the Indianisation of the Army but he was opposed by the majority of the British officers. He had hoped that, in addition to its military value, the Corps would impart moral and human values to those who joined it and to which they would not have been exposed at home. The artist Mortimer Menpes who was present at the 1903 Durbar, visited the Imperial Cadet corps camp and spoke with Sir Pratap Singh. Sir Pratap was in no doubt as to the purpose of the Corps:

> His object was to make men of the Cadets and to show them that there were other things to do in this world than merely luxuriating and leading a dissolute life – for men in their position there was real and good work at hand.[37]

35   See Letter from the Commandant of the Imperial Cadet Corps to the Secretary to the Government of India in the Foreign Department, 17/9/1908., OIOC, L/MIL/7/19006.
36   Report of the Committee on the Government of India's Proposals for Commissioning Indians, July 24 1911. Appendix by HE Sir O'Moore Creagh, C-in-C, OIOC, L/MIL/7/19006.
37   Mortimer and Dorothy Menpes, *The Durbar* (London: Adam and Charles Black, 1904), p. 179.

The Corps was very much Curzons' creation; he referred to it in a speech as 'The favourite of my own heart.'[38] Unfortunately, when he left India there was nobody in government to support it. Lord Kitchener writing in 1908, stated that in his opinion only one of the eight cadets (not Amar Singh) who had successfully graduated from the Corps was making a really useful contribution to the Army. He wrote:

> I cannot escape the conclusion that the Imperial Cadet Corps as it now exists
> has failed in its two objects of opening a military career to native noblemen and
> of providing men of the standing and qualifications which would enable them to
> take advantage of such openings as have, with difficulty, been created.[39]

As we shall see in the next Chapter, Amar Singh's role as an ADC was largely confined to that of a glorified baggage master and bridge partner. Were the young men who graduated from the Corps unfitted to exercise command or were the British officers unwilling to give them the opportunity to do so?

The Imperial Cadet Corps was a small, very small, step towards increasing the professionalism of Indian officers. With only a small intake from a narrow range of potential students it was not particularly well resourced nor staffed. By contrast, when the Indian Military Academy was eventually set up in some thirty years later it was staffed by some of the best and most experienced British officers, such as Major (later Lieutenant General) Reginald Savory. These British officers were known to be sympathetic towards Indianisation.[40] Suitably qualified candidates were drawn from across the whole of the Indian Army. Alas, by then, the Imperial Cadet Corps, a promising innovation, had failed. It failed because of the inherent flaw in the initial proposal put forward by Curzon regarding the commissions to be awarded to successful cadets. Chandar Sundaram suggests that Curzon and his colleagues in the Foreign Department rejected changes which would have made the ICC more effective in order to preserve their view of a 'traditional' India.[41] However above all, it failed because of the intransigence of many senior British officers including the incumbent Commander-in-Chief India.

38   Speech at Daly College 1905 quoted in *Lord Curzon in India: Speeches 1898-1905*
     (London: Macmillan, 1906) p. 261.
39   Lord Kitchener *Memorandum on the Future of Indian Officers* para 19, OIOC,
     L/MIL/ 17/5.1746.
40   See Marston, *Phoenix from the Ashes*, p. 20.
41   See Sundaram, *Treated with Scant Attention*, p 22.

4

# An Indian Staff Officer

On graduation from the Imperial Cadet Corps, Amar Singh's commission was posted in the *London Gazette* dated 4 July 1905 and he was appointed as a special ADC to General Sir O'Moore Creagh, GOC 5th Division, Western Corps. He joined the Divisional Headquarters Mess and as a polo player was socially accept- able to his British colleagues and he seems to have been made welcome by the General who was kind to him and tried to help him to fit into his new role. The General's other ADC, Lieutenant Elliot of the Devonshire Regiment who had fought in South Africa, 'made me as comfortable as he could.'[1] Elliot taught Amar Singh the card game of bridge so that the latter could keep the General amused while on tour. During his time at Mhow Amar Singh's main responsibility seems to have been to arrange for the movement of the staff officers' horses and baggage when they were on manoeuvres or tours. He was sometimes also responsible for the messing arrangements and for planning the itinerary. He went on errands for the General seeking information or supplies as well as planning social events for the General and his wife. Ellinwood suggests that the General had a strong empathy for Rajputs such as Amar Singh.[2]

On 4 October 1907 Amar Singh was promoted to Lieutenant and in 1908 and 1910 he studied for and passed the required promotion examinations. The 1910 exam covered tactics, military engineering and topography, military organisation and administration (the easiest part according to him), military law and military history (the American Civil War). He was the only one of the original intake to have qualified for promotion to the rank of Captain before 1914 and was duly promoted that year.[3] In April/May 1908 he was allowed to practise as a Section and Company Commander and he fired on the rifle ranges. He accompanied the General on visits to Chitor and Udaipur. When visiting the latter, a difficulty arose because Amar Singh wished to be

1 Amar Singh diary, 15.9.05.
2 See Ellinwood, *Between Two Worlds, A Rajput Officer in the Indian Army*, p. 58.
3 See Sharma, *The Nationalisation of the Indian Army 1885-1947*, p. 29.

received by the Maharaja in the same manner as he would greet a British officer. He wrote: 'The Maharaja must shake hands with me. Otherwise I shall be looked down on and the Imperial Cadet Corps and the British commission will lose respect.'[4] The British Resident was unable to make an immediate reply on this sensitive issue but eventually it was agreed that if Amar Singh were in uniform, the Maharaja would receive him as an officer, but not if he were in mufti. The General and the other staff officers did not wish to go in uniform so in the end, the General went alone. This was the most delicate social difficulty which Amar Singh faced during his time at Mhow though eating and Rajput customs made occasional difficulties. It illustrated the degree of prejudice facing Indian officers, not only from the British, but also from the high class Indians.

Amar Singh was now living in two very different but overlapping worlds – the British officers' mess and his own very traditional home with all its complex family politics and intrigues. He was happy to eat European food with a knife and fork while at home he would eat Indian food with his fingers. From time to time he would meet socially with a few Indian officers, especially Rajputs whom he had known before. However he did not go out of his way to meet other Indian soldiers. DeWitt Ellinwood suggests that this was due to his concern not to interfere with men who were commanded by others.[5] He further suggests that Amar Singh had both a marginal position within the Army and a diffident, marginal attitude towards that Army.[6] He was, as the Rudolphs put it in *Reversing the Gaze,* living on the boundary between two societies and had to master the manners and outlook of both.[7] For instance, he was the only Indian guest at a British officer's wedding although at the same time his own wife was living in strict purdah.

Lord Kitchener, as Commander-in-Chief, had introduced a series of practical tests in order to improve the effectiveness and efficiency of the regiments under his command. It was expected that the whole exercise would last from 50 to 55 hours. While such a programme would be commonplace in a modern army, this move to a more realistic training schedule must have come as something of a shock to some regiments accustomed to a more leisurely approach to life. For instance, Amar Singh reported in his diary on the test of the 2nd Battalion East Surreys:

> During the advance to contact (a 15 mile march in full service order carrying 100 rounds of ammunition) a load of 28 greatcoats came off a mule. The General commented that if they could not keep loads on while on the level, God knows what would happen going up and down hills. The battalion's commanding officer, Colonel Dunsterville, was at a ford in a nullah supervising the crossing of

4    Amar Singh diary, 6. 8. 1905.
5    See Ellinwood, *Between Two Worlds: A Rajput officer in the Indian Army,* p. 207.
6    See ibid., p. 132.
7    See S.H. and L.I Rudolph, *Reversing the Gaze,* p. 21.

the baggage. This should have been done by the baggage officer or the quarter-master. The men were in quite good condition and looked fit but were drinking too freely (from their water bottles).[8]

The advance was to be followed by an attack, using live ammunition, on a position prepared by another unit. This phase was to include reconnaissance and the writing of orders. He wrote:

The attack took a long time starting – the men were allowed to have breakfast first which wasted an hour. The reconnaissance was poor. The troops didn't take much advantage of the natural conditions or ground for taking cover. The rally after the attack was quite good. The General did not approve much of the way the attack was carried out. They did not choose the right place to attack from and moved in front of the enemy's position. The men were not shooting very straight either and only a few plates (targets) were hit. The assault was not carried out properly and started before the reserves came up.[9]

The attack was to be followed by a bivouac camp with outposts which would be attacked. Amar Singh continued:

The position chosen for the camp was alright but there was not much water near. They started digging very late and little was done; the men complained the ground was too hard – but they should have seen what the 123rd did! (The 123rd, Outram's Rifles, were an Indian regiment, part of the old Bombay Army). The bivouacs were blankets supported by two rifles; the men spent the whole time putting up or knocking down their shelters. On the Frontier there would be no end of rifles stolen! The plan for the exercise expected that there would then be a night operation of some nature, probably opposed and that the troops would then prepare a defensive position to be assaulted by other troops. The final phase was to be a retirement of at least 10 miles while followed up by the enemy.[10]

The exercise revealed a number of serious failures in the battalion, failings which could have very serious consequences in battle. Amar Singh commented:

The night march was a mere farce on a metalled road in good visibility. Surrounding a village was well done. Taking up defensive positions; the trenches were not deep enough in some places – they were on the sky line and in some cases were too far back with too much dead ground. The retirement is the most

8   Amar Singh diary, 23. 1. 08.
9   Ibid.
10  Ibid., 25. 1. 1906.

difficult thing to do well; in practise few, if any, of the troops would have got back to Mhow! The men were very smart and fit and did their work well.[11]

Initially it was intended that the tests should be carried out on a competitive basis between battalions but this idea was abandoned after two years because of the difficulty of ensuring that conditions were the same for units in different parts of India.[12] Nevertheless, Lieutenant General Climo, who commanded the 24th Punjabis, commented in his foreword to the regimental history that: 'The preparedness for war of the Army in India, so far as its officers and men were concerned, was due almost entirely to the system of training inaugurated by Lord Kitchener.'[13]

Amar Singh also commented on a similar exercise undergone by the 80th Carnatic Regiment (formerly 20th Madras) in February 1906. This was a regiment recruited from the 'non-martial' races and his comments point to some of the difficulties produced by this policy though he himself appears to share the British view – or prejudice. He wrote:

> The test was the usual 15 miles march and then to entrench and attack a position. Then they had the day and night outposts and the perimeter camp and the retirement. The General thought the men and troops were not at all well trained. The officers did not seem to read their books. The position selected for defence was not good and the attack too was very badly carried out while the perimeter camp was simply awful. In fact all the British officers did not strike me of being of a very high standard. There were only two officers that were originally with the regiment. The rest were merely a collection brought in from all the other Madras regiments that have been broken up. There are seventeen of these battalions broken up and I think the officers have been rather badly treated because they had to give up their mess plate and band and such like things to the new regiments that have been raised in place of the old ones.[14]

This Regiment's war record was quite good as they were among those which fought for and conquered the Madras Presidency for the British and it had four battle honours on its colours. They were also allowed to have a third honorary colour having captured one during a battle and were allowed an extra Jemadar to carry this. This regiment was present at the taking of Mysore and as a trophy they had a big black marble cup which was supposed to have been Tippoo Sultan's. The composition of the regiment was four

11   Ibid.
12   See Anon, *History of the Fifth Royal Gurkha Rifles* (Aldershot: Gale and Polden, c 1928), p. 167.
13   Brigadier A. B. Haig, *War Records of the 24th Punjabis* (Aldershot: Gale and Polden, 1934), p. v.
14   Amar Singh diary, 23.1. 1906.

companies of Madrassi Mussulmans, one of Telegau and one of Madras Christians and Dadbers (a very low class). Amar Singh commented:

> The subedar-major is quite a nice fellow and I found out from him that nearly all the Indian officers and NCOs spoke English. This regiment has very intelligent and well-educated men and they look very smart. Their features are good but they are small and weak and most of them are as black as coal. The officers' mess has practically no war or Shikar (hunting) trophies. The mess house is quite a nice one but devoid of furniture on a large scale. I don't think much of these Madras regiments and the subedar-major told me himself that they were not such good soldiers as from northern India. They cannot stand the cold.[15]

Amar Singh took part in a Staff Ride in 1909, the first which he had attended. He commented:

> My work was very light and quite uninteresting. I had to see the carts loaded and the camp of the Director's mess struck and pitched every day. Besides this I had to obtain food from local suppliers. I preferred to ride from one place to another and not get involved in the fighting. I saw a lot of new country. I like this sort of thing when I see new places and especially when I travel with no one to bother me.[16]

Of his role in the Saugor Manoeuvres in Central India in 1910, Amar Singh commented that 'My chief job in this show was generally to look after the mess and to see that we camped in nice shady places. It was very seldom that I was taken out.'[17] Rather more usefully, in 1913 he participated in two staff rides under the direction of General Sir John Nixon GOC Southern Army of India. He wrote:

> This is the first staff ride where I have been able to pick up some knowledge. Everybody said that this was the most instructive tour that they had ever been on. General Nixon did it most splendidly. What struck me most was the manner in which he seemed to remember everything. Then all what he said he showed the people in the drill book. Not even the slightest mistake escaped his notice.[18]

Amar Singh volunteered to join the service of the Maharajah of Gwalior, who maintained large State Forces, in 1907 but was not accepted. In 1909 he hoped that he might be transferred to the staff of General O'Moore Creagh who was by now Commander-in-Chief but again was unsuccessful. Amar Singh was the first of his

15  Ibid.
16  Amar Singh diary, 5. 3. 1909.
17  Ibid.
18  Ibid., 16. 2. 1910.

colleagues to qualify for a captaincy in the summer of 1914 but by 1915 his other three colleagues who had passed out of the Corps with him were also Captains. Amar Singh had spent nine years in what was virtually a 'non-job'. It is clear that, as an ADC, he was really an errand boy for his General and that his job was to ensure that the General's life ran smoothly. While this might be the life of a typical ADC, most young officers would expect to spend only two years in such a post and would use it as an opportunity to gain experience and to make contacts which might be useful to them later on in their careers. Ellinwood suggests that his most significant contribution had been the occasional translation of official documents into Hindi.[19] At the outbreak of war in 1914, Amar Singh's role had changed very little from when he joined the staff in 1905. Though he had had the opportunity to see units in training, he remained on the outside of the real world of the Army and he had had little opportunity to perform the duties of a professional soldier.

Not only was Amar Singh's position an anomaly to the British officers but his situation vis-a-vis his own countrymen was far from clear as the episode with the Maharaja of Udaipur indicates. The graduates of the Imperial Cadet Corps were also resented, perhaps not surprisingly, by the jemadars and risaldars who had come up through the ranks and had gained their commissions through hard work and long service. General O'Moore Creagh commented to the Viceroy, Lord Hardinge, in 1910 that:

> I found that in several regiments which I inspected that the native officers objected to Amar Singh, saying that if a commission of this class was to be given, then why not give it to them who had seen service, while the Cadets had seen none, and were nothing more in the village than they were.[20]

Social status was very important in India. An Indian officer who went home on pension after years in the service would expect to be, and indeed was, treated as a person of some importance in his home village. It seems surprising that throughout his nine years as an ADC, Amar Singh seems to have made no attempt to join a cavalry regiment, even on secondment for a short period. It is difficult to believe that General could not, if requested, have arranged such an attachment – possibly to one of the State Forces if not to a regular unit. One imagines that, for instance, Sir Pratap Singh could have arranged an attachment to the Jodhpur Lancers.

When, in 1909, O'Moore Creagh became Commander-in-Chief of the Indian Army he expressed as his confidential opinion the view that the Government should give Indians full commissions of a particular sort. It would seem not unreasonable to suppose that his views on this point had been influenced by his experience with Amar

---

19    See Ellinwood, *Between Two Worlds: A Rajput officer in the Indian Army*, p. 168.
20    Letter from General Sir O'Moore Creagh to the Viceroy, 24. 7. 1911, OIOC, L/MIL/5/1750.

Singh. The General also revived the idea of a special cavalry regiment to be officered exclusively by Indians In a letter to the Viceroy, Lord Hardinge, he wrote:

> That cadets (from the ICC) should be given regular commissions in the Indian Army I consider a sine qua non. There are many native young men who are real gentleman, well educated and with a keen sense of humour.[21]

It was not to be until 1917 that Amar Singh and a few colleagues were to be granted King's commissions. However, their limited commissions still did not give them command over Europeans nor were the Indian officers paid on the same scales as British officers. The commissions were not back-dated, so that the newly commissioned officers lost seniority. What might have been a step forward for the Indian officers, though on a very limited scale, was made to seem almost a step backwards. Ellinwood put it succinctly:

> As a supernumerary ADC, Amar Singh had had few responsibilities and limited opportunities to improve his professional skills. This was part of the irony of the situation: Indian officers were not thought to have the qualities of military leadership, but at this point they were not given experiences which would test and improve such skills.[22]

Ellinwood suggests that, as far as the British were concerned, there were four key issues relating to the commissioning of Indians. Firstly, which Indians should be selected for commissioning, and how should they be educated and trained? Was a British public school education followed by attendance at the Royal Military Academy Sandhurst the only conceivable route for entry into the officer corps? Were commissions to be granted only to aristocratic members of the martial races? If so what forms of commission should they receive and for service in what types of unit? Would Indian officers serve only in selected units where the question of their commanding British officers and men would not be an issue? And, most important of all, what were the implications of commissioning Indians for the future of the Raj? In the long term, would there no longer be British officers in the Indian Army?[23] The Great War was to throw these questions into even sharper focus.

21   Ibid., and quoted in Chandar Sundaram, *A Grudging Concession.*
22   Ellinwood, *Between Two Worlds: A Rajput officer in the Indian Army*, p. 168.
23   See ibid., p. 174. and Chandar Sundaram, *A Grudging Concession*, pp. 270-272.

5

# The Great War

It is not until Great War that we find a significant amount of documentation written by Indians soldiers themselves, or to be more precise, the translations of thousands of letters written to and from home by Indian soldiers serving in France. The letters home from Indian soldiers were censored on a regimental basis in exactly the same way as those of British soldiers. In addition, however, the mail from Indian soldiers was subjected to a second level of censorship. This was imposed originally because of concerns, not altogether unfounded, about seditious material reaching the Indians. The Chief Censor, Captain Howell, originally a member of the Political Department of the Indian Civil Service, produced a monthly report for the High Command. This report was supported by translations of a sample of about sixty or seventy letters each month illustrating the points made in the report about the troops' morale etc.

The reports and translations survive in the British Library and a selection has been published by David Omissi.[1] They offer a fascinating insight into the feelings and experiences of the officers and men at the front. During the period 1914-15 the majority of letters are from infantrymen, many of them in hospital in England. This is presumably because there were more Indian infantrymen than cavalrymen in France and possibly because the authorities were more interested in the morale of the infantry who were bearing the brunt of the fighting. There are three caveats to be born in mind regarding these letters. Firstly many of them will have been actually written not by the signee but by the regimental scribe at his dictation. Secondly the soldiers were naturally fully aware that their letters were being censored; sometimes they used simple codes, e.g. 'black pepper' meant Indian troops, and in some instances attempted to obtain secret inks. Finally, although a few letters were written in English, generally one must remember that one is reading a translation into English of the original Punjabi, Gurkhali etc. Nevertheless, in spite of these caveats, the letters remain a most vital source of information.

1    See OIOC, L/MIL/5/825, 826 and 827 and David Omissi, *Indian Voices of the Great War: Soldier's Letters 1914-18* (Basingstoke: Macmillan, 1999).

The First World War marks a very significant stage in the development of the Indian Army. It was the first time that very large numbers of Indian troops had fought outside the sub-continent and had fought against a well-equipped and well-disciplined enemy. Recruitment exceeded all expectations; eventually over 1.4 million Indian soldiers and followers would serve overseas. The novelist John Buchan wrote that 'It was the performance of India which took the world by surprise and thrilled every British heart.'[2] There was an inevitable hiatus in the debate regarding Indianisation but the experiences of Indian soldiers during this war were to inform the post-war discussions. In particular, the War proved that Indian officers were capable of providing the sort of leadership which hitherto been thought to be the province of British officers only.

In 1914 the Indian Army consisted of 39 cavalry regiments and 138 infantry battalions – twenty of these being Gurkha units. The Indian artillery was limited to twelve mountain batteries.[3] When war was declared between Great Britain and Germany, the British Expeditionary Force (BEF) crossed the Channel to fight alongside their French and Belgian Allies. However, the BEF was pitifully small compared with the German Army and suffered very heavy casualties in the opening battles of the war. The Indian Army was the *only* large scale reinforcement available to aid the hard pressed BEF which was fighting desperately to stem the German tide in Belgium. The Lahore and Meerut Divisions together with the Secunderabad Cavalry Brigade received their mobilisation orders in August and the first Indian troops landed in Marseille at the end of September where they received a rapturous welcome from the French civilians. Each infantry division consisted of three brigades together with supporting troops including a cavalry regiment, signallers, engineers etc. Each Brigade contained one British battalion and three Indian battalions. The Lahore Division included two battalions of Gurkhas and the Meerut Division four. The cavalry Brigade consisted of one British regiment and three Indian cavalry regiments. One of these was the Jodhpur Lancers, an Imperial Service unit, led by the fire-eating Sir Pratap Singh together with the 16 year old Maharajah. According to the regimental history of the Poona Horse:

> Training for war, especially as regards musketry, had reached a very high standard. The Indian ranks of the Regiment were thoroughly loyal, well disciplined and imbued with esprit de corps, trained to the highest pitch and ready to follow their officers anywhere.[4]

The Indian Army of 1914 was a highly trained and professional Army but they were trained for, and experienced in, warfare on the North-West Frontier. In France they

2   Quoted in John Keay, *India: A History* (London: Harper Press, 2010) p. 471.
3   Mason, *A Matter of Honour*, p. 405.
4   Col C.B. Wylly, *The Poona Horse (17th QVO Cavalry)* (London: RUSI, 1933), Vol II, p. 75.

were to face very different conditions against an enemy armed with all the panoply of modern warfare. The sepoys were used to the cold but it was the dry cold of their native hills rather than the mist and the damp of Northern France. They had never met heavy artillery fire, machine guns and mortars or gas and flamethrowers.[5] They were ill-equipped with inadequate reserves. Casualties among the officers had a disproportional effect on the morale and effectiveness of the battalion. The British officers, known and trusted by their men, led from the front and paid the penalty for so-doing. Their loss was all the more serious because it was almost impossible to replace them with Englishmen with the requisite knowledge of the Indian languages. The Indian officers, too, were men of great experience, many of whom had served for many years in their regiments. They were looked up to by the young sepoys as father figures. Through their long service they embodied the spirit of the regiment and were equally vital to the morale and effectiveness of a battalion and their loss was equally keenly felt.

Mobilisation for war in Europe presented particular problems for a Silladar Regiment such as the Poona Horse. Originally *silladars* were land-owners who were contracted to bring in a certain number of men to the regiment, together with their horses and equipment. The silladars then received a proportion of the troopers pay. Over the years this system was modified so that uniforms and equipment, and often the horses, were bought centrally by the regiment. Mason describes a silladar regiment as 'a joint-stock company with a strong co-operative element, almost a family business.'[6] Since the style of equipment was at the choice of the commanding officer, there was a lack of uniformity among the regiments. The men had to provide a sum of money, known as an *assami*, on enlistment towards the purchase of their mount and deductions were made from their pay towards the cost of their equipment. When a man left the regiment he handed back his horse and his assami was returned to him. Such a system ensured that the men took particular care of their horses and were anxious that their mounts should not be wounded or killed in battle. Amar Singh had made enquiries in the Rajput squadron of the 27th Madras Cavalry and found that the men preferred a non-silladar regiment because they had less worries – everything was found for them.[7] For the campaign in France equipment which might have been suitable for a campaign in India had to be replaced under regimental arrangements and at regimental cost as the history of the Poona Horse explained:

> Warm clothing of the proper quality and quantity, was not only unobtainable on the open market but made a call upon regimental funds which they were quite unable to meet. All that could be done was to supply each sowar with a flannel shirt and a warm jersey.[8]

5    See Mason, *A Matter of Honour*, p. 413.
6    Ibid., p. 377.
7    Amar Singh diary, 27. 2. 06.
8    Wylly, *The Poona Horse (17th QVO Cavalry)*, Vol II, p. 77.

Accordingly, when the regiment sailed from India in the third week of September 1914, the men were wearing their tropical uniforms supplemented with those two items. However the regimental history records that by November 1914, gifts of mufflers, gloves etc from friends and well-wishers enabled the men to withstand the cold without suffering ill-health; in fact the daily average of men reporting sick was less during these winter months than the normal in India.[9] On their arrival at Marseille, the sowars were re-armed with the latest pattern rifle and at Orleans they were also issued with bayonets. The historian of the Deccan Horse wrote:

> Up till now, no one had contemplated the possibility of cavalry being utilized in any other way other than as cavalry, and it came as a shock and a surprise when an issue of infantry bayonets was made to the Brigade. What was especially unfortunate was that this particular pattern of bayonet did not fit our new rifles and fell off when the rifle was fired![10]

Thus, inadequately clad, equipped with unfamiliar weapons and lacking heavy artillery, the Indian Corps moved northwards from Marseille. In spite of these drawbacks, much was expected of them. The King-Emperor George V himself had sent them a personal message:

> You are the descendants of men who have been great rulers and great warriors. You will be the first soldiers of the King-Emperor who will have the honour of showing in Europe that the sons of India have lost none of their ancient martial instincts.[11]

Amar Singh was appointed as an ADC to General Brunker commanding the 9th (Sirhind) Infantry Brigade in the Lahore Division, and he arrived in France in October 1914. When asked by General Brunker to address the Indian officers in his Brigade, Amar Singh echoed His Majesty's words. He noted in his diary that:

> I impressed on their minds that they must make no trouble about petty caste prejudices and must combine to help the British officers. This is the first time that Indians have had the honour to fight Europeans on their own soil and that we must play up to the Government which has brought us to this level.[12]

---

9   See ibid., p. 78.
10  Col E. Tennant, *The Deccan Horse in the Great War* (Aldershot: Gale and Polden, 1939), p. 13.
11  Quoted in Ellinwood, *Between Two Worlds*, p. 363.
12  Amar Singh diary, 4. 12. 14.

The reference to caste prejudices presumably refers particularly to difficulties regarding feeding with certain foods, e.g. bully-beef, unacceptable to some soldiers.

The first Indian soldiers to reach the front line were two companies of Wilde's Rifles who went into the trenches on the 22nd October 1914. By the time that the Germans began their drive for the Channel ports at the end of that month, the regiment had been split into four separate detachments spread across a front of over five miles. The German attacks were in overwhelming strength and the Indians had no choice but to retire. The Punjabi Muslim company was almost wiped out and at Messines, where the Dogras and Afridis were posted, there was utter confusion during a German night attack. All of the British officers were killed or wounded but Subedar-Major Arsla Khan led a bayonet charge in an attempt to aid the hard pressed Dogras. When this failed he managed to retire with the remnant of his men to Messines. He was awarded the Order of British India 2nd Class. Jemadar Kapur Singh of the Dogra company fought on until all but one wounded man had been put out of action and then, rather than surrender, shot himself with his last cartridge.[13] Was it sheer desperation, a sense of *dharma* or the notion of *izzat* that made the jemadar take this fatal course?

The conditions in which the Indians fought during the winter of 1914-15 were appalling and they suffered accordingly. By the end of the First Battle of Ypres in November 1914 the Indian Corps had suffered a total of over 1600 killed and wounded. 18 British officers were killed and 28 wounded and 6 Indian officers had been killed and 22 wounded.[14] By the end of the year the Poona Horse had lost 50% of its men as casualties in action together with a high proportion suffering from sickness and exposure.[15] The weather and their living conditions affected the Indian troops very badly. The regimental history of the Poona Horse stated that the trenches which they occupied around Festubert: 'Were in a thoroughly bad state, half full of water, and many men had to stand in them up to their thighs throughout the night; the cold was intense.'[16] In spite of these conditions, morale in the regiment was high. Captain Grimshaw of the regiment wrote:

> Never a complaint that they were half frozen to death … or that they were being called upon to fight as they had never in their wildest transport of imagination pictured, armed with a weapon they had never handled before they put foot in France.[17]

13    See Gordon Corrigan, *Sepoys in the Trenches: The Indian Corps on the Western Front 1914-15* (Staplehurst; Spellmount, 1999), p. 72.
14    See Lt-Col Merewether and Lt-Col Sir F Smith, *The Indian Corps in France* (London: John Murray, 1918), p. 64.
15    See Wylly, *The Poona Horse (17th QVO Cavalry)*, Vol II, p. 100.
16    Ibid., p. 90.
17    Capt R. Grimshaw, *Indian Cavalry Officer 1914-15* (Tunbridge Wells: Costello, 1986), p. 44.

One gains some idea of the difficulties the Indian troops faced in keeping warm from the following letter from a sowar of Hodson's Horse to a friend back at the regimental depot in India:

> On my body at the present there are a warm vest, a warm shirt, a warm uniform coat, warm underpants, a pair of heavy breeches, two pairs of warm socks and boots. Even so, when I come out of my tent, I feel that I would like to have another warm shirt on.[18]

However, life was apparently not without its compensations. Lance Daffadar Ahmad Khan, 34th Poona Horse, wrote to a Daffadar in India in November 1916: 'The Indian officers are better off than they have ever been. Each one gets a bed and a French mattress and such blankets as they have never seen even in their dreams!'[19]

The trenches in which the Indians found themselves were in a poor state and in no way resembled the more elaborate fortifications of later years. Amar Singh visited the front line on several occasions. In March 1915 he wrote a long 'Note' in his diary commenting on a visit with General Brunker to the Gurkhas (either the 1st or the 4th):

> Their trenches were very bad indeed. They were ankle deep in mud and in parts seven feet deep. The constant dripping of the water had broadened them a good deal and had washed away the parapet so that it was not bullet-proof. The Gurkhas being short men had to stand on steps to reach the loopholes. In parts the trenches were quite broad at the top but narrow at the bottom. Two men had the greatest trouble to pass one another. In parts they had planks to get a firm footing but they became so slippery that one had the greatest difficulty in keeping oneself from slipping. The Germans were never more than a dozen yards from our trenches in some places.[20]

When fully equipped the Gurkhas had great difficulty in climbing out of their trenches and their rifles jammed in the mud. They were much troubled by the cold and the constant shelling and rifle fire together with the explosion of German mines. Nevertheless when they had a chance to get out of their trenches they did so 'and attacked the Germans like fury.'[21] On one occasion Amar Singh met a group of Gurkhas who had been relieved and were making their way back to their billets. 'I have never seen such miserable beings. They were dead lame and their feet were so

18  Reports of the Chief Censor, OIOC, L/MIL/5/825.
19  Ibid.
20  Amar Singh diary, Note written 31.3.15 at St Venant.
21  Ibid.

swollen that they could hardly walk. They could not even wear boots and went along supporting one another.'[22]

Amar Singh believed that the Indian troops had done well up to that point in spite of the cold:

> The average sickness has been very much below the British troops. It was not the cold that worried them so much as the dampness. The morale of the troops has been wonderfully both in the firing line and in the billets while they were resting. The great difficulty under which we have laboured is that if we fail in the slightest degree anywhere people raised a hue and cry whereas if British troops fail under the same circumstances, no one mentions it![23]

When the front line was stabilised and with the bulk of the Meerut Division now in France, the Indian corps was allotted its own section of the front line. The two divisional cavalry regiments fought dismounted while the Cavalry Brigade was kept in reserve but during the German attack around Festubert in November, the Cavalry Brigade was again thrown into the fighting as infantry. In spite of all the difficulties, drawbacks and the totally unaccustomed conditions in France, the Indian officers and men continued to display their customary courage and leadership qualities. A German attack on Festubert at the end of November was well timed, coming as it did just when the Meerut Division was being relieved in the trenches by men of the Lahore Division. German shells hit the combined Regimental Aid Post of Wilde's Rifles and the 129th Baluchis, killing both medical officers, incidentally the only Indian officers in their regiments to hold the King's Commission.[24] In this action Subedar Natha Singh of the 34th Pioneers held his position until eventually forced to retire in the face of overwhelming numbers. He was awarded the Indian Order of Merit, 2nd Class. Havildar Hawinda of the 58th Rifles was promoted to Jemadar and awarded the Military Cross for bringing in the body of a British officer while under very heavy fire.[25] Naik Darwan Singh Negi, of the 1st Garwhal Rifles, was awarded the Victoria Cross for leading the clearance of a German Trench.[26] The whole of the Indian Corps was relieved on the evening of December 22nd. When the Jodhpur Lancers withdrew from the line, five of their Indian officers were suffering from frozen feet. Captain Maxwell, who was serving with the regiment as an adviser, wrote in December:

> I wondered if they (the Germans) knew that for several hundred yards the trenches were held by Indian cavalry quite untrained to trench work and not

---

22   Ibid.
23   Ibid.
24   See Corrigan, *Sepoys in the Trenches*, p. 105.
25   See Merewether and Smith, *The Indian Corps in France*, p. 119.
26   See Corrigan, *Sepoys in the Trenches*, p. 105 et seq.

skilled in the use of the bayonet. I am sure our fellows would have done very well had they been trained, but they are very much handicapped by the circumstances and hardly have a fair chance.[27]

In December the Secunderabad Cavalry Brigade, with men from the British 7th Dragoon Guards, the 20th Deccan Horse and the Jodhpur Lancers were formed into a composite infantry regiment of 800 men. Ordered to counter-attack near Festubert, very few of the men even reached the German front line. The Deccan Horse had five out of six British officers and five out of seventeen Indian officers killed or wounded. Captain Grimshaw of the Poona Horse commented that

> The line of deployment had not in any way been marked out, no preliminary reconnaissance of the line of advance had been made, and the exact position and its extent held by the enemy was unknown. No compass bearings on which to march were available and in effect the only orders given were that the troops were to advance in two lines.[28]

These remarks, although from an officer who was notably critical of the staff, demonstrate the inexperience of the officers planning this attack.

On 10 March 1915 the Indian Corps launched an all-out attack at Neuve Chapelle, aiming to eliminate an enemy salient. The Meerut Division would be aligned along the main road to the south-west of the village while the British 8th Division was almost at right angles to the north west of the village. The two Divisions were to meet up at the northern edge of the village. The final, somewhat optimistic, objective was the Aubers Ridge. The Indian front line was held by the Bareilly Brigade and the assault would be led by the Garwhal Brigade with the Dehra Dun Brigade following up.[29] When the British bombardment ceased the Indians leapt out of their trenches. Subedar-Major Nain Singh Negi, who had already been awarded the Military Cross gained the Order of British India, 2nd Class, for leading his company of the 2/39th Garwhal Rifles forward in spite of being wounded. Jemadar Sangram Singh Negi of the same regiment was awarded the Military Cross for capturing a German officer, machine gun and crew.[30] Jemadar Pancham Singh Mahar won the Military Cross leading his men across open ground in the face of heavy enemy fire and capturing a machine gun and a number of prisoners. The highest award of a posthumous Victoria Cross went to Rifleman Gobar Singh Negi of the 2nd Gurkha Rifles who bombed and bayoneted his way along a German trench, traverse by traverse, until he was killed.[31]

---

27  Letter by Captain Maxwell, NAM, Archive No 7402-34.
28  Grimshaw, *Indian Cavalry Officer*, p. 53.
29  See Corrigan, *Sepoys in the Trenches*, p. 149.
30  See Merewether and Smith, *The Indian Corps in France*, p. 221.
31  See ibid., p. 223.

The 2/3rd Gurkhas were first into the village of Neuve Chapelle. To the cheers of the British troops, Rifleman Gane Gurung emerged grinning from one house with no less than eight prisoners, a feat for which he was awarded the Indian Order of Merit, 2nd Class. Subedar-Major Bhim Singh Thapa was also awarded the Indian Order of Merit for his gallantry, distinguishing himself by his coolness in leading his men.[32] He was later to gain the Military Cross while serving in Egypt for 'leading his platoon with great skill and gallantry through intense machine gun and rifle fire.'[33] Following the capture of the village of Neuve Chapelle there was a significant delay before the Dehra Dun Brigade could move forward thus momentum and the element of surprise was lost. The Germans put up a strong resistance to further Indian assaults and the battle eventually ground to a halt. Following the battle, Rifleman Amar Singh Rawat of the Garwhal Rifles wrote from hospital in Brighton to a friend in India on March 26th 1915:

> On 9th and 10th March we attacked the Germans. So many men were killed and wounded they could not be counted and of the Germans the number is beyond calculation. When we reached their trenches we used the bayonet and the kukri and the blood was shed so freely we could not recognise each other's faces.[34]

Amar Singh noted that only 65 Garwhalis returned alive and unwounded from the battle: 'The honour of the attack lies with the Garwhalis who fought very well indeed'[35] He wrote a long Note on the battle on April 8th 1915 and commented on the effectiveness of the initial artillery barrage which so shook the enemy that they offered little resistance to the initial attack. However, when the attack was renewed the barrage was less effective:

> The result was that the enemy remained in the trenches. Another thing was that our infantry ought to have moved out while our guns were shooting and while the Germans did not put their heads up. There was about five hundred yards of ground to be covered before we could reach the German trenches. The Germans were able to meet us and simply mowed our men down with machine-guns.[36]

He gave his views on the value of the Battle of Neuve Chapelle:

> It was worth it because a bend in our lines has been straightened out and we have got a nice commanding position. But what has been most useful to us is that

---

32   See Merewether and Smith, *The Indian Corps in France*, p. 226.
33   *London Gazette*, 13 May 1918.
34   Omissi, *Indian Voices of the Great War: Soldiers Letters 1914-18*, p. 45.
35   Amar Singh diary, 8. 4. 15.
36   Ibid.

it has proved the superiority of our guns. It has heightened the morale of our troops both European and Indian. It was about time that the Indian Corps did something after the knock they had had in December (at Festubert). Now they are all in high spirits.[37]

Neuve Chapelle was the last major offensive undertaken by the Indian Corps in France though they were to be involved in other battles in a supporting role and to suffer further casualties. At the end of 1915 the Indian infantry left France, some regiments returning to India while others were sent to East Africa, Egypt or Mesopotamia. Amar Singh too left France in December 1915 and was attached to the Headquarters of the 9th Brigade in the 9th Indian Division in Mesopotamia. The Official History gives the following figures for losses suffered by the Indian units up to 19th November 1915:[38]

|  | Killed | Wounded | Missing |
| --- | --- | --- | --- |
| British officers | 150 | 294 | 49 |
| Indian officers | 103 | 336 | 50 |
| Indian other ranks | 2,345 | 14,221 | 661 |

Individual units had suffered appalling losses. For instance, by October 1915 the 59th Rifles had no British officers and only 4 Indian officers remaining from its original strength of 13 British officers and 21 Indian officers. The 47th Sikhs were in even worse shape with no officers left at all and only 28 sepoys from the original strength.[39] It proved impossible to provide sufficient recruits of the right quality from India to replace these losses due, in part at least, to the army's adherence to the martial race theory.

Given the opportunity and in spite of the unfamiliar and difficult conditions, Indian officers were still perfectly capable of exhibiting leadership of a high order and their gallantry was undoubted. The role played by the Indian officers during the fighting in France is often over-looked in regimental histories. One exception is the Regimental History of the Central India Horse which refers to the behaviour of a number of Indian officers while the regiment was in France:

Risaldar Dilawar Khan was one of the brightest examples. He smelt the battle afar off, and where the greatest danger was, there was he. On the march neither fatigue nor cold could quell his ardour, so long as the music of the guns drew

37  Ibid.
38  See Merewether and Smith, *The Indian Corps in France*, p. 459.
39  See Merewether and Smith, *Indian Corps in France*, p. 458, quoted in A. T. Jarboe, *Soldiers of Empire, Indian Sepoys during the First World War*, Unpublished PhD thesis.

nearer; and in the trenches he was always ready to repel a German raid. Jemadar Ram Singh too, steady like all good Sikhs, would gird up his loins for a dangerous patrol and carry it through with grim determination. Imperturbable Lihaz Gul, whom no crisis could shake, would rouse himself to a fury in personal combat. Risaldar Kamaluddin Khan, an optimist like his father, was always ready for fighting. Sikhs, Ghakkars and Pathans vied with one another in facing perils and difficulties.[40]

Following the departure of the infantry, only the ten Indian cavalry regiments were left in France, now organised into two divisions. At the opening of the Somme offensive in 1916 the 1st Indian Cavalry Division was in reserve behind Gommecourt but there were few opportunities for mounted action. On July 14 1916, two regiments, the Deccan Horse and the British 7th Dragoons, took part in the attack on Delville Wood as part of the Battle of the Somme but their attack stalled with heavy losses. Meanwhile the Poona Horse had sent out two patrols, one under 2/Lt Phillips and the other under Jemadar Abdul Gafur. Of the latter's conduct, Colonel Elphinstone, commanding the regiment wrote later:

> Sent off to find and report on the road to Longueval, he, a man of very little education, went straight to the right spot and got an excellent report of the route back to HQ within an hour of his starting out. Having done the first part of his job, he then proceeded to find out the situation at Longueval and found the village partly held by the enemy and partly by our own troops and a fierce fight in progress. Many a man would have been content to send in this information but not Abdul Gafur. Leaving his patrol under cover, he worked his way into the village and eventually found a British officer who pointed out to him the position of the opposing forces, and, having sent back this information, the Jemadar kept in touch with the infantry until all chance of a breakthrough was gone, when he was recalled. It is hard to imagine a finer instance of liaison between infantry in the front line and cavalry hoping to get through.[41]

This is an excellent example of leadership and professionalism displayed by a relatively junior Indian officer.

The following year the Indian cavalry was involved in the battle of Cambrai. At the end of the November 1917 the Germans counter-attacked vigorously and the Indian cavalry took part in a number of mounted actions which helped to stem the German advance. In one of these, Hodson's Horse carried out a mounted counter-attack

---

40    Maj-Gen W. A. Watson, *King George's Own Central India Horse: The Story of a Local Corps* (Edinburgh, William Blackwood and Sons, 1930), p. 353.

41    Colonel Elphinstone, quoted in Wylly, *The Poona Horse (17th QVO Cavalry)*, p. 11.

alongside the Guards Division. Of this attack, Major Palmer of the (British) 20th Hussars wrote on 16 December 1917:

> They advanced in column, shot at from both flanks from ridges at close range. Shot at from the front much like the Valley of Death at Balaclava, they never wavered nor quickened the pace ... No troops in the world could have acted thus, had they not been bound together by that invisible knot 'esprit-de-corps.[42]

Two British squadron leaders were killed and three Indian officers were wounded in this charge. Indian officers gained a number of decorations for this action including the award of an MC to Lieutenant Dutt of the Indian Medical Services for tending the wounded under fire. A German officer who was being bandaged by Lieutenant Dutt, handed him his own Iron Cross in appreciation. In a regimental order published on 24 of December 1917, General MacAndrew, GOC 5th Cavalry Division, wrote: 'I consider the regiment the finest in France. It has all the spirit and dash of the Canadians and the extra training.'[43] A silver statuette of a charging Bengal Lancer now in the Guards Museum in London commemorates this event.

Because of the duration of the campaign in France, the Government made arrangements for some of the sowars to go home to India on leave. Indian officers had being going to London on leave for some time. Jemadar Shamsher Ali Khan of the Poona Horse commented on the arrangement:

> A few days ago, an order was issued to the effect that the British Government had, as a favour to the Indian troops in France, opened leave for them to India. Five per cent of those who have put in two year's service in France are to be granted leave for three months, and on their return another five per cent will be granted leave and so on. Thus every man granted leave will spend about a month at home.[44]

A few weeks later the Jemadar wrote to another pensioned colleague, Dafadar Taj Mahomed Khan, in the Punjab as follows:

> I went to England on leave, and have now returned to the regiment. Our generous Government made most excellent arrangements for us while on leave. One could not have secured the same results privately by the expenditure of thousands of rupees. May God speedily give victory to our gracious King, and may he blacken

---

42   A letter from Major Palmer recorded in *War Narrative of 9th Hodson's Horse*, anonymous typescript, NAM.
43   Ibid. A Regimental Order dated 24/12/17.
44   Reports of the Chief Censor, OIOC, L/MIL/5/ 826.

the face of the enemy and humiliate him, both in this world and in the world to come. Amen.[45]

On the subject of leave, Jemadar Hassan Shah of Hodson's Horse wrote in 1917:

I had ten days leave in London. Oh my friend what a thing it is to be an Indian officer! It is full of pleasure. Just think of it, what Indian millionaires can do a tour of London? Above all, to see His Majesty, and to speak to him and stand in his presence for three hours. What greater pleasure can there be than this? We got the chance of seeing places we had never dreamt of and were taken round with the greatest izzat.[46]

Indian VCOs when on leave in London were certainly very well looked after and this was clearly much appreciated as these letters show. Amar Singh was very different from the traditional VCOs who had come up through the ranks. He had much wider interests and contacts in society and he was able to visit London several times while he was serving in France. For instance, in January 1915 he went on leave to London and saw a performance of Henry V at the Shaftesbury Theatre which he enjoyed enormously. He also visited the Tower of London and Madame Tussauds and called on Lord Crewe, the Secretary of State for India. He was admitted to hospital with a fever in March and convalesced in London where he saw Sir Pratap Singh: 'He is a dear old man and most cheerful.'[47] Amar Singh was mentioned in despatches in June 1915 though the reason for this is not clear. He was the only member of the General's staff to be mentioned and this caused some resentment among his colleagues.[48]

The Indian Army Corps which landed in France in 1914, trained only to fight tribesmen on the North-West Frontier, were totally unprepared, physically or mentally for a long war of attrition with its artillery bombardments and heavy machine-gun fire.[49] The sepoys received more modern rifles when they landed in Marseille but they had little opportunity to practise their use before they were thrust piece-meal into the First Battle of Ypres. They had no Corps artillery and were under-strength compared with a British Corps. The Corps fought in conditions totally unlike anything they had experienced before and they were, initially at least, less well equipped to cope with the cold and the mud than European troops. British and Indian troops alike suffered from a shortage of artillery shells.

45    Ibid.
46    Ibid.
47    Amar Singh diary, Note on his fourth visit to England, 14.4.16
48    See Ibid: 25.6.15.
49    See Smith, 'Valour', A History of the Gurkhas, p. 44.

The British Expeditionary Force, lost nearly 15,000 men during the battle of Mons and the subsequent retreat.[50] The Indian Corps plugged the gaps during the First battle of Ypres and bought time until the relatively small British Regular Army could be reinforced by the Territorial and Kitchener Armies.[51] The Indian troops were often subjected to criticism, much of it unfair and ill-founded. Both Corrigan and Jack[52] refute claims that Indian soldiers were especially prone to self-inflicted wounds. Jack also argues that the sepoys were less dependent on their British officers than generally thought, Indian troops often being seen to re-organize and attack once again even after their British officers had fallen.[53]

As Lord Curzon wrote in his Foreword to the Official History of the Indian Corps in France:

> Neither should we forget the conditions under which these Indian soldiers served. They came to a country where the climate, the language, the people, the customs, were entirely different from any of which they had knowledge. They were presently faced with the sharp severity of a northern winter. They, who had never suffered heavy shell fire, who had no experience of high explosive, who had never seen warfare in the air, who were totally ignorant of modern trench fighting, were exposed to all the latest and most scientific developments of the art of destruction. In the face of these trials and tribulations, the cheerfulness, the loyalty, the good discipline, the intrepid courage of these denizens of another clime cannot be too highly praised.[54]

The Indian infantry involved in the ill-fated Gallipoli campaign did not take part in the initial landings and so were spared the tragedy and heroism of those events, such as 'the six VCs before breakfast' of the Lancashire Fusiliers. The 29th Indian Brigade landed five days later and consisted of the 69th and 89th Punjabis, the 14th Sikhs and the 1/6th Gurkhas.[55] After a few weeks the Punjabi regiments, which contained many Muslim sepoys, were sent to Egypt because of concerns about their reluctance to fight the Turks.[56] This was not the only example of this problem. There had already been difficulties in the 20th Punjabis. When the regiment, which recruited among

50   See Greenhut, 'The Imperial Reserve: The Indian Corps on the Western Front 1914-15',
     p. 54.
51   See R.A. McIain, 'The Indian Corps on the Western Front: A Reconsideration' in Wiest
     and Jensin (eds) *Warfare in the Age of Technology* (New York: NYU Press, 2002), p. 27.
52   See Corrigan, *Sepoys in the Trenches*, pp. 81-82 and George M. Jack, 'The Indian Army on
     the Western Front: a Portrait of Collaboration', *War in History*, 2006, Vol. 13, No. 3, p. 340.
53   Ibid., p. 352.
54   Merewether and Smith, *The Indian Corps in France*, p. xi.
55   See Anon, *History of the 5th Royal Gurkha Rifles* (Aldershot: Gale and Polden, 1928),
     p. 218.
56   Menezes, *The Indian Army*, p. 248.

the frontier tribesmen, had arrived in the Persian Gulf in 1914, the Pathan sepoys in the unit protested. They wished to fight the Germans but not their co-religionists who were Sunni Muslims. They suggested that regiments which recruited Sikhs, Dogras etc would not be affected and could be used instead. Unfortunately these feelings led to a number of desertions though, on the whole, the regiment fought well.[57] There was also a mutiny in the 15th Lancers stationed at Basra in 1916 when Muslim sowars refused to march against the Holy Places of Islam.[58] The Punjabis in Gallipoli were replaced by two more Gurkha battalions and a fourth Gurkha battalion arrived direct from France.

Overall, in the struggle to capture the Turkish positions, the four Gurkha battalions lost 25 British officers and some 730 Gurkha officers and men killed, together with 1500 Gurkhas wounded. Of the original 800 men of the 2/10th Gurkhas who embarked for the campaign, only one British officer and 79 Gurkha soldiers survived.[59] Men of one Gurkha battalion, the 1/6th, were the only Allied soldiers to reach the crest of the ridge which formed a spine down the peninsula and thus be able to look down on the Dardenelles. Unfortunately, once there, they were heavily shelled and, unsupported, they had to fall back. In one of the last battles of the campaign, the 1/6th Gurkhas together with the 2/10th Gurkhas attacked Sari Bair ridge. In a fine example of leadership, the 1/6th was commanded in the attack by Subedar-Major Gambirsing Pun because there was not a single British officer left in the battalion. He had to use the Medical Officer, Captain C.S. Phipson, as an interpreter because he did not understand English.[60]

Charles Chenevix Trench suggests that the campaign in Mesopotamia is an excellent example of Murphy's Law; 'Anything which can go wrong, will!'[61] The aim of the campaign was to protect the oil installations in Persia which were absolutely vital to the British was effort. The campaign, which eventually drew in 600,000 British and Indian troops, began extremely well. The port of Basra at the head of the Persian Gulf, which was to be familiar to British troops eighty years later, was easily captured. In order to protect the port, Allied troops moved out and captured the town of Qurna, fifty miles upstream and at the junction of the Tigris and the Euphrates. A force of some 12,000 regular Turkish troops, supported by 10,000 Arab tribesmen were defeated at the battle of Shaiba (an event known as the Miracle of Shaiba). Amara, seventy-five miles up the Tigris and Nasiriyeh, seventy-five miles up to the Euphrates were also taken and finally Kut-el-Amara, some two hundred miles north of Basra was captured.

---

57   See Anon, *Historical Records of the 20th (Duke of Cambridge's Own) Infantry 1908–1922* (London: Butler and Tanner, 1923), p. 6.
58   See Omissi, *Indian Voices of the Great War*, p. xv.
59   See Smith, *Valour*, p. 57.
60   See ibid., p. 56.
61   Chenevix Trench, *The Indian Army and the King's Enemies*, p. 75.

If only the campaign, which had by now achieved all its military objectives, had halted there all would have been well. The oil installations were now safe and the Allied casualties had been relatively light. But the cry, led by the Prime Minister, Mr Asquith, the Viceroy, Lord Hardinge, and the Commander-in-Chief India, Sir Beauchamp Duff, was 'On to Baghdad'. This suggestion totally ignored the difficulties which would face such an expedition. Mesopotamia is one of the hottest countries in the world and little was known about water supplies. The administrative and supply arrangements were sketchy to say the least. In particular, the medical support needed in order to be able to treat not only the wounded but also the men suffering from a wide variety of tropic diseases, was lamentable. Finally, the Turkish Army was now being reinforced by veterans who had returned in triumph from Gallipoli.

In spite of all these difficulties, Lieutenant General Sir John Nixon, commanding the Allied forces, was ordered to advance on Baghdad. British and Indian troops met the main Turkish defensive position at the Arch of Ctesiphon, thirty miles south of Baghdad. The Turkish line was broken but at the cost of 4,500 British and Indian casualties out of a force of 12,000. Further advance was impossible in these circumstances and the troops retreated wearily to Kut. At first sight, this seemed to a be strong position, surrounded on three sides by the River Tigris. However, there was a crucial lack of the supplies necessary to withstand a long siege and the position could be swept by Turkish artillery and machine-gun fire. The history of the 1st/2nd Punjab Regiment gives us a glimpse of conditions within the besieged town: 'It was bitterly cold. Men's hands and feet were swollen with cold and exposure, and in several cases when a man took his boots off, he was unable to put them on again for several days. Starvation stalked abroad.'[62]

Amar Singh described the country: 'The first thing I noticed was the awful condition of the country. It was ankle and in parts knee deep in mud … such a thing as a road does not exist.'[63] Any relieving force would have to fight their way past the strong Turkish positions down-river. He described one of the attempts made to relieve Kut:

> The artillery for some reason was three hours late and during this time the Turks manned their trenches and redoubts. When the advance began our troops behaved magnificently but everyone was loud in praise of the 2nd Rajputs. They had gone in about five or six hundred strong but when they returned there were only a Jemadar and about sixty men left. Our troops had been caught by machine gun fire from redoubts on both flanks.[64]

62   Cols N. Ogle and H.W.Johnston, *History of the 1st/2nd Punjab Regiment* (London: W. Straker Ltd, c 1923), p. 48.
63   Amar Singh diary, 29.1.16.
64   Ibid., 9. 4. 16.

Successive attempts to relieve Kut failed with heavy losses and the garrison surrendered on 29th April 1916. It was the greatest surrender of British and Indian troops between Yorktown and Singapore. The wretched troops were force-marched north into Anatolia in conditions which foretold those which would be suffered by captured British and Indian soldiers in Burma and Malaya in the Second World War. The Turks attempted specifically to suborn Muslim officers. They were taken before the Sultan of Turkey who tried to persuade them to transfer their allegiance. Each of the officers was offered a sword of honour as a token of the Sultan's esteem. Subedar-Major Kitab Gul of the 120th Rajputana Infantry was the first to receive his and he flung it away. His example was followed by his comrades. As punishment for their contempt, the two senior officers present suffered three weeks solitary confinement.[65] A campaign which had sought to erase the sense of failure after Gallipoli, had ended in an even greater humiliation.

Indian troops fought in Mesopotamia with their customary zeal but they were outnumbered and up against an experienced and battle-hardened enemy. In one attack Rattray's Sikh's, commanded by the son of their founder, lost sixteen out of seventeen British officers, twenty-eight out of thirty Indian officers and 988 men out of the 1,180 who were on the start line. Subedar Akbar Khan of the 2nd/1st Punjabis was wounded during the siege, returned from hospital during the siege only to be wounded for a second time. He was knocked senseless by a bomb but returned to duty for a third time, deaf in one ear.[66] There were three battalions of Marathas fighting in Mesopotamia. These were the unfashionable and 'non-martial' men whom Lord Roberts had derided but here their fighting spirit was much admired. In the attack on the enemy trenches at Kut the 117th were led forward by the Subedar-Major, all the British officers being dead. After the war the regiment was awarded the title 'Royal' in recognition of its achievements[67] Eventually Baghdad was captured but by then the emphasis had shifted to Allenby's battle against the Turks in Palestine.

In February 1918 the Indian cavalry regiments left France for Palestine to replace the British Yeomanry regiments which had been recalled to the Western Front. Once there, the Indian regiments were brigaded with the remaining British Yeomanry regiments and, together with Australian cavalry, they formed the Desert Mounted Corps. According to the regimental historian of the Scinde Horse, 'The (Indian cavalry) regiments from France had nothing whatever to learn from the mounted troops they came alongside in Palestine and could show the way to most.'[68] Jerusalem was captured in 1917 just before Christmas but in March 1918 British and Australian infantry regiments were transferred back to France in order to repel the major German offensive.

---

65    See Lt-Col F. H. James, *History of the 1st Battalion, 6th Rajputana Rifles* (London: Oxford University Press, 1936), p. 204.
66    See Mason, *A Matter of Honour*, p. 435.
67    See ibid., p. 439.
68    Col E.R. Maunsell, *The Scinde Horse 1839-1922* (Published by a Regimental Committee 1926), p. 188.

The final offensive aimed to destroy the Turkish forces in Palestine, Syria and Lebanon whilst General Allenby still had the large Mounted Corps at his disposal. The huge success of the campaign in 1918 depended on a major deception. The obvious use of his cavalry would be to send them in a big sweep around the Turkish left flank which was open desert. Allenby's plan was to do exactly the opposite. He would use his infantry to break through the Turkish defences near the coast and then send his cavalry racing northwards. They would then turn north-eastwards over the Carmel range and down into the plain of Megiddo. In order to deceive the enemy as to his intentions the cavalry were originally based in the inhospitable conditions of the Jordan Valley. On the night of September 17/18 the cavalry moved silently from right to left behind the Allied line to their concentration area at Jaffa on the coast. In order to maintain the deception, they left dummies behind them to fool any Turkish aerial reconnaissance. The attack started at 4.30 am on the morning of 19 September and almost immediately the cavalry were able to follow up the successful infantry.

As they moved forward on the morning of 19 September the leading troop of Hodson's Horse under Risaldar Nur Ahmed came under heavy fire from Turkish cavalry in a strongly entrenched position. A mounted attack by the regiment resulted in the capture of three officers, between fifty and sixty men, two guns and twelve wagons. Later, near Murkhalid, Jemadar Ali Khan's troop charged a second Turkish entrenchment. At the end of the day they halted, having advanced twenty-six miles, the last sixteen of them in action, and captured five hundred prisoners. On 21 September they entered Nazareth. On September 30th the 13th and 14th Brigades were ordered to intercept a large Turkish force (actually the retreating Fourth Army) on the Dera – Damascus Road at Kiswe. Risaldar Nur Ahmad accompanied only by his orderly penetrated Kiswe and reported that the town was full of Turks. Two troops were sent to his assistance and the Turks were taken prisoner. For their services in Palestine, Risaldar Nur Ahmed Khan IOM was awarded the Military Cross, Risaldar Dost Muhammad Khan and Jemadar Nawab Ali Khan the IOM and Risaldar-Major Muhammad Akram Khan Bahadur the IDSM.[69]

In July 1918 the Jodhpur Lancers were occupying part of the bridgehead over the Jordan which secured the British right flank when attacked by the advance guard of the 2nd Turkish Caucasian Cavalry Brigade. As a State Force regiment, they were officered entirely by Indians with only two British 'advisers'. In the fighting that followed Major Dalpat Singh led the charge. He was awarded the Military Cross for his leadership and courage on that day – one of the first Indian officers to be so honoured.

---

69    See Major F. G. Cardew, *Hodson's Horse 1857-1922* (London: William Blackwood and Sons, 1928), p. 193.

Supported only by his Trumpet-Major, he galloped on an enemy machine-gun, killed the gunners and captured the gun and followed this up by capturing the Turkish commanding officer with his own hand.[70] In addition to Major Dalpat Singh's immediate award of a Military Cross, six Indian Orders of Merit (2nd Class) and seven Indian Distinguished Service Medals were distributed amongst the Lancers. General Allenby, who visited the Brigade on the 27th, wrote that: 'The day's operations on the 14th would live as one of the great feats of the war.'[71]

As the advance continued in September, the Jodhpur Lancers, supported by the Mysore Lancers were ordered to mount a cavalry attack in order to take the port of Haifa. Major Dalpat Singh MC fell mortally wounded but the troops swept on through the town. They captured 2 German officers, 23 Turkish officers and 664 other ranks, together with two six-inch naval guns, ten field guns and ten machine guns. By any standards, the capture of Haifa on 23rd September 1918 by the Jodhpur Lancers was a magnificent feat of arms and unique in military history. The Official History of the campaign commented that 'No more remarkable cavalry action of its scale was fought in the whole course of the campaign.'[72]

Indian troops fought with great courage and determination in every theatre of operations in which they were deployed, often in very difficult conditions. Jemadar Shamsher Ali Khan of the Poona Horse wrote to pensioned Risaldar-Major Hazin Ali Khan OBI at home in India in November 1916:

> Now the rain and cold are daily on the increase. The duration of the war is being extended in an appalling manner and there is no end in sight. The hearts of the people have become depressed owing to the indefinite state of affairs. The war, coupled with the long distance from home, the separation for years, and the unsuitable climate – cold, wind and rain – have tired everyone out and crushed them.[73]

In spite of all this, the Jemadar's loyalty was undimmed:

> Who is there whom this War has not saddened and depressed; but one is bound to discharge the obligation laid on him. It was for this that our family has for generations been eating the salt of the Sirkar and receiving salary and pensions, and therefore, this is no time to be disturbed in mind and for turning one's face away from duty. Rather it is the time for showing valour; and, please God, but a few days remain for the end to come.[74]

---

70    See R.B. Van Wart, *Sir Pratap Singh* (London: Oxford University Press, 1926), p. 219.
71    *War Diary of the Jodhpur IS Lancers*, August 1914- December 1918., TNA, WO/95/587.
72    Capt. C. Falls and Major A.F. Becke, *Military Operations in Egypt and Palestine from June 1917 to the end of the War* (London: HMSO, 1930), Vol II, p. 538.
73    Reports of the Chief Censor, OIOC, L/MIL/5/ 826.
74    Ibid.

The paragraph indicated the very strong feelings of loyalty and obligation which many Indian soldiers expressed in their letters home in spite of their hardships and casualties. The sense of *dharma* and *izzat* remained strong, possibly being linked to their religious beliefs

Their devotion throughout the war was suitably recognised with awards and decorations. Distinguished Indian officers were not infrequently granted an audience with the King, who presented them personally with their decorations. This was much appreciated, reinforced their loyalty and had a significant effect on morale. Risaldar Muhammad Akrim Khan wrote to a friend in Peshawar in April 1916:

> You have no doubt heard of my good service from other people. I am not given to self-praise and you know the proverb; 'It is not the perfumer who gives the perfume to his wares.' On March 26th I went to London to have an interview with His Majesty The King. The King spoke to me in his own auspicious tongue. I am profoundly grateful to His Majesty for his kind treatment and am always praying to that God in justice will grant him the victory.[75]

Indian officers leaving their regiments were treated with great honour and respect by their British comrades. For instance, when two senior officers from Hodson's Horse went home to India in 1916. Antar Singh of the regiment wrote:

> Indur Ram Singh and Jai Ram left for India today, one on pension and one on leave. The officers treated them with great 'izzat'. The General sent his motor car to take them to the railway station and the Colonel and Major Rowcroft with an escort of seven sowars went to the station to see them off.[76]

Loyalty to the regiment and to the King-Emperor was a key factor in the Indian soldier's concept of service and of *izzat*. A Subedar of a Garwhali battalion wrote home in February 1915: 'If I am to die for the sake of the great Emperor, then what could be more glorious?'[77] Mir Jafar, who became Risaldar-Major of Hodson's Horse in 1915 wrote a charming letter to a friend in Peshawar in May 1916:

> My service extends to 33 years, but I tell you truly that, if in this war I were to lose my life for my King, I would count it as gain. I have been in Hodson's Horse for the whole 33 years. During a railway journey when two people sit side by side for a couple of hours, one of them feels the absence of the other when he alights, how great then must be the anguish I feel at the thought of having to sever myself from Hodson's Horse. I have heard it rumoured that the CO

75  Ibid.
76  Ibid.
77  Ibid

Sahib Bahadur contemplates sending me back to India. Although, no doubt, I should be pleased to see again my country and my people, that pleasure would be as nothing compared with the sorrow I should feel at having to part with the regiment.[78]

Ressaidar Badhu Singh of the Scinde Horse (attached 29th Deccan Horse) was the only Indian cavalry officer to win the VC during the Great War. In the Jordan Valley in September 1918 during a charge by his squadron, he noticed that heavy casualties were being caused by fire from a Turkish position on a small hill. Without hesitation he collected six sowars and with an entire disregard of danger he charged and captured the position. He was mortally wounded but not before the Turkish troops had surrendered to him. In a very different situation, Jemadar Abdul Gafur's leadership of his patrol of Hodson's Horse to which reference has already been made displayed leadership skills of a very high order. Ressaidar Badan Singh of the Poona Horse offers another example of leadership in difficult conditions. He was in command of a squadron of the Poona Horse at Festubert in December 1914. Their attack began in the early hours of the morning of the 21st and in the evening he sent a message back to the British lines asking whether or not he and the remnant of his men should retire. They had been lying out in no-man's-land all day, a short distance in front of the German trenches, having taken cover when the enemy's fire made it impossible to advance further. There they had been subject to British artillery fire as well as German bullets. However, mindful of an earlier instruction by Major Molloy that no retirement was to take place without his express order, the Ressaidar had held his ground. The Ressaidar was also in charge of bombing. Major Molloy wrote:

He proved a tower of strength; whenever an unpleasant situation called for my attention I was sure to find him already in the thick of it, his dour face stretched into a huge grin.[79]

In addition to their personal bravery, Indian officers did their best to encourage their troops and to keep up morale. Naik Buland Khan of the 69th Punjabis wrote to the son of Subedar Muhammad Khan in October 1915 to inform him of his father's death:

He showed himself the pattern of valour and he was a pattern of loyalty to the Government. He was ever on the look-out for the faint-hearted, and if he heard anywhere of a young man who was troubled in mind he went to him and talked to him in such a way that all his discomfort, exile and homesickness faded away.[80]

78    Ibid.
79    Major Molloy diary, quoted in Wylly *The Poona Horse*, p. 91.
80    Reports of the Chief Censor, OIOC, L/MIL/5/ 826.

In spite of all the difficulties facing them, the Indian troops in all theatres had rendered invaluable service. They had suffered heavy casualties, especially among their British and Indian officers, and this, together with the difficulties of providing suitable reinforcements, led to the withdrawal of the Indian infantry from France in 1915. Previously Indian officers had had little experience of independent command and were not educated or trained to the level of their British counterparts. Because of this, the Indian troops relied at times too much upon their British officers. This meant that they were very adversely affected by casualties among the British officers. However, the loss of Indian officers who were known and trusted by their men had equally as great an effect on the fighting ability of units as did the death of the British officers. In spite of it all, as R. A. Mclain points out, Indian officers often showed considerable bravery, resource and initiative when opportunity offered.[81]

After the war the Indian veterans returned home less innocent but with a wealth of new experiences.[82] In recognition of the contribution made by India, both in manpower and material, a number of promises were made after the war by the British to the Indians.[83] However, as the size of the Indian army was reduced to its pre-war level and as time passed, many of these promises, especially with regard to Indianisation, came to lack urgency in their fulfilment. The Great War changed forever the relationship between ruler and ruled in India.[84] This, together with the increasing demands for Independence in India, led to a growing realisation that Indian officers would have to play a much greater role in the Indian Army than hitherto.

81  See McIain 'The Indian Corps on the Western Front: A Reconsideration', pp. 1–31
82  Ibid., p. 28
83  See Cohen, *The Indian Army*, p. 73.
84  See McIain, 'The Indian Corps on the Western Front: A Reconsideration', pp. 1–31.

# 6

## Squadron Commander

When the Indian infantry left France at the end of 1915, Amar Singh went too, leaving Toulon on 21 December for the Middle East. On arrival, he was attached to the Headquarters of the 9th Brigade of the 9th Division in Mesopotamia. He was given little to do; as he had been in France; he was responsible merely for seeing to the movement of horses, tents and other supplies and he had difficulties when British soldiers refused to obey his orders. He was sent back from the front because he couldn't eat beef for religious reasons and presumably there was no other meat available. In June 1916 he left Basra and returned to India. In September 1916 he was appointed ADC to General Knight, commanding the Bombay Brigade. In this role he was given a more meaningful responsibility than any he had held previously. In particular he visited Convalescent Camps and Transit Camps where Indian soldiers were staying in order to ensure that their conditions were as good as possible. He was treated kindly by the General and spent two years in Bombay until July 1918 when he was commissioned into the 2nd (Gardner's) Horse. As this regiment was still abroad at the time he was almost immediately transferred to the 16th Cavalry in Delhi.

In 1917, as a small recognition of India's contribution to the War, nine Indian officers, including Amar Singh, all of them former graduates from the Imperial Cadet Corps, were given full King's Commissions. Pradeep Barua argues that this was only a limited step and not connected to the mainstream effort to create an Indian officer Corps. It was a political move rather than a step towards Indianisation.[1] The regiments into which these officers were commissioned appear to have been selected in order of seniority, taking the first five cavalry regiments and the first four infantry regiments. There appears to have been no attempt to take into account any experience, family links, class ties or indeed preferences which the officers might have had. Amar Singh was granted a King's Commission in the rank of Captain with promotion to Major expected in 1927. He would have expected promotion to that rank in 1920

---

1    See Barua, *The Army Officer Corps and Military Modernisation in later Colonial India*, p. 62.

under the terms of his previous commission. In other words, after service through the Great War, he 'lost' seven years seniority; after twelve years of service he was placed on the same level as British captains with only four years service. After protests from the officers concerned it was agreed that their pensions were to count from 1905 but there was no change in their seniority. This decision was grossly unfair and was the cause of considerable anger among the Indian officers concerned.

Amar Singh noted in his diary for April 1919:

> I have been agitating (about my commission) through my commanding officer and found that we will be allowed to count our service from the date of our commissions in the Indian Land forces but as regards seniority we have to take the date of our captaincy from 25.8.17. The C-in-C has duly considered the matter and was not going to discuss the point any more.[2]

In fact the Commander-in Chief had wanted to commission all of the Indian officers as Second Lieutenants.[3] Amar Singh discussed the issue with other Indian officers who were in the same position:

> I told them simply and plainly that I was fed up with the whole thing and would go as soon as I had done my eighteen years and was eligible for my first pension. I told them that my Maharaja (of Jaipur) was not on good terms with my family and that the minute he found I was losing the support of the British officers he would pounce on me.[4]

Amar Singh joined his new regiment on July 15th 1918 and the following diary entry offers a description of a typical day in his life during his service with the regiment:

> In the morning I woke at about half past five and after washing, dressed myself and had tea. Then I went on parade and had riding school practice with the lance at the dummies and jumping until eight when I came to the mess and had break-fast. After that I saw the paper and then went to stables and attended the stables and offices of both B and C squadrons. Then I went to the regimental office and after that came to the mess and read *The Pioneer*. Just then a veterinary officer came from Meerut and I took him to the horse hospital. When he had gone I came to my house and read a little of *Vanity Fair* by W M Thackeray. After that I read a little of a Sanskrit drama translated into Hindi.[5]

2   Amar Singh diary, 14. 4. 19.
3   See Ellinwood, *Between Two Worlds*, p. 461.
4   Amar Singh diary, 14. 4. 19.
5   Ibid., 3. 11. 19.

He seems to have got on well with his fellow officers with whom he hunted, played polo, tennis and billiards. However, he did not enjoy the more rowdy side of life in the officers' mess. His commanding officer, Colonel Mears, seems to have tried his best to give Amar Singh a clearer insight into the duties of a squadron commander, sending him out on activities such as road reconnaissance and field exercises. Amar Singh commented:

> Colonel Mears explained to us the general idea of the field operation that we were going to have. The hill near the water towers was to be defended by the 72nd Punjabis who were supposed to be one battalion. The Bedfordshire Regiment were to attack and take it while one squadron of the 16th Cavalry was to dismount and deliver a flank attack as a surprise on the left of the Bedfords. We moved off to the east and then came to Basantnagar where we dismounted and I took my squadron and attacked the hill. The 72nd did not see me until I was within 150 yards. I rushed the position and the umpire told me I had taken the hill. I now began firing on the backs of the remainder of the 72nd. The Bedfords were very late in coming up. Our Divisional commander got fed up and rode away. The second phase of the operation was that our other squadrons were to take up the pursuit and then throw out a line of outposts. This was done but General Nugent had had enough and so the 'Dismiss' was sounded. All the officers were collected and the General criticised the whole of the operations.[6]

Amar Singh was involved in the usual regimental round of training activities such as riding, musketry etc. This included 'coming into dismounted action with great promptitude, outposting (or picqueting) and night drill.'[7] Experience of a different kind came when his knowledge of Indian languages was used in the examination of British officers who were required to pass test in at least one language in addition to Urdu, the lingua franca of the Army. He wrote:

> At about half past one I had to go over to the mess and examine six officers in colloquial Hindustani. Major Hill and I were on the Board; we passed four and failed two – Lieutenants Warren and Cantwell both of the 16th.[8]

This meant that the two officers who failed were from his own regiment.

The retirement of a senior Indian VCO from the regiment was an occasion for special festivities. Agya Ram Bahadur OBI had joined the service in 1886 reaching the rank of Risaldar Major in 1914. Amar Singh recorded:

6    Ibid., 13. 2. 19.
7    Ibid., 8. 10. 19.
8    Ibid., 5.4.19.

We went to our lines where the Indian officers had given a tea party in honour of Risaldar-Major Agya Ram who is going away on pension. When the Colonel arrived Risaldar Hoshya Singh read out a speech extolling the virtues and services of the retiring officer. After that Agya Ram read out his speech in a very fine and becoming manner.

The next day the British officers also gave a farewell tea-party for the Risaldar Major. Of this event, Amar Singh noted:

> The Colonel read out a very fine and complimentary speech in Urdu full of praise of the good work of the retiring Risaldar-Major who then replied. This over we had our tea while the Indian officers sat at their table and we gave them tea as well.[9]

It would appear that the Indian officers were not sitting at the same table as the British officers – including, one assumes, Amar Singh.

Amar Singh had no previous experience of serving in a regular cavalry regiment; he had passed nearly twenty years as an ADC doing little and learning less. When he first joined the regiment he was put in C squadron under Major Digges La Touche. Amar Singh commented:

> The Commandant and the Adjutant were the only two officers senior to me in length of service in the regiment. I knew nothing at all of regimental work so I did not mind. It was the hot weather and most of C squadron were on leave so there was practically no work to be done. I learned some work in the office and La Touche was awfully good to me and taught me a lot of things.[10]

After various changes in squadron commanders Amar Singh went to the Colonel to ask which squadron he wished him to go to. Amar Singh recorded their conversation:

> He asked me whether I thought I could command a squadron. I told him it was not for me to say do, it was for him to judge. He said that he did not think I was able to and asked if I would mind working under Major Wing in D squadron. I said that I did not mind in the least.[11]

However, Major Wing left and the squadron was taken over by a less experienced British officer. Dissatisfaction with this situation led to Amar Singh asking for

---

9    Ibid., 26. 2. 19.
10   Ibid., Notes about how I got command of a squadron, 25. 6.19.
11   Ibid.

command of a squadron. The Colonel told him that he could have had it at any time he asked for it – he was only waiting for Amar Singh to ask:

> I said that this was most kind of him. To this he said that there was no kindness about it. It was my right and he had not given it me before because I had not been ready to command a squadron.[12]

However, some of the British officers thought that Amar Singh was only with the regiment for instruction and did not count as a regular officer and he commented that 'the Indian officers specifically had this idea.'[13] These remarks highlight the uncertainty of Amar Singh's position and status within the regiment, both vis-à-vis the British officers and also the Indian VCOs. The latter may well have resented someone whom they saw as a relatively inexperienced officer who was on a higher and more privileged footing than they were.

Amar Singh took over command of B squadron in March 1919:

> This morning I went to B squadron which I have taken over. I went all round and saw the horses. When that was over I went to the squadron office and worked for over half an hour ... I hear that the Indian officers are very sorry that Lieutenant Crittall is going. I do not wonder at this because Critall allowed them to run the squadron exactly as they liked. He himself knew nothing about India. I am an Indian and the officers know that they will have to be more careful.[14]

Perhaps Lieutenant Crittall was young and inexperienced and the Indian officers recognised that Amar Singh was older and less likely to have the wool pulled over his eyes. The 16th Cavalry was sent to Delhi in March to help to control the riots which followed the passing of the Rowlatt Acts which abolished normal legal processes for all political offences. However, Colonel Mears kept Amar Singh out of involvement in internal security issues:

> The Colonel said that he did not wish to put me in a position that was not to my liking. The Colonel does not think me fit to command a small mixed force and there was also the difficulty of an Indian officer commanding British troops. He told me that I had started learning rather late in life.
>
> I did not tell the Colonel anything but thought that a man who does not talk about himself gets left behind. I have passed more examinations and have

12   Ibid.
13   Ibid.
14   Ibid., 12. 3. 19.

14 years of service and still I am not considered to know as much as Wordswill or Brown (two young British officers).[15]

These events also point to the difficulty facing an Indian officer such as Amar Singh. There is doubt as to his ability to adopt an impartial position towards the rioters and the old issue of an Indian in command of British troops raises its thorny head once again. In spite of his age and experience, Amar Singh has once again to play the part of a junior officer.

On 9 October 1919 the regiment was ordered to mobilise for operations in Waziristan. Amar Singh wrote:

> I saw Colonel Mears yesterday (the 16th) and he told me that he did not think that I knew enough to command a squadron in the field and asked whether I thought that I could command it. I told him that it was no use asking me as I would probably say that I could command the whole Waziristan Field Force. It was for him to judge whether I was capable or not. He told me that while he had a capable officer like Scott with war experience he did not find himself justified in risking the lives of a whole squadron as I was quite inexperienced – I could not have learnt much as an ADC. I said that I never even had a proper ADC's work either and if he thought that I could not command I would not grouse at him taking the squadron from me.[16]

In the event Amar Singh served under Major Hill who was senior to him but who might be posted away in which case Amar Singh would be in command of the squadron.

Eventually Amar Singh took over command of B squadron and even, for a short time in the Colonel's absence, he was actually in command of the whole regiment as it entered Waziristan. This has some historical significance as it appears to be the first occasion on which an Indian officer commanded a regiment of the Indian Army, even though it was only for a short period. The regiment was involved in guarding lines of communication and was frequently split up with the squadrons acting independently. At the beginning of November the regiment 'got news of a seventy strong band of Waziris in a pass not far from us. It was their intention to make a raid. The telegraph wires were cut and one troop of C squadron was sent out to get the damage repaired.'[17] However, despite news of the raiders, contact with them was infrequent. Much of the time was spent in training. Amar Singh wrote: 'My squadron practised crossing a

15   Ibid., 28. 6. 19.
16   Ibid., 17. 10. 19.
17   Ibid., 5. 11. 19.

nullah as an advanced guard would. The Commandant and C squadron officers were watching and I was very pleased that my men did not make a single mistake.'[18]

Amar Singh's position within the regiment was not an easy one and some of the junior British officers were prepared to challenge his authority. One of these was 2nd Lieutenant Wilks who had been a clerk at Simla and had been commissioned from the ranks. Possibly because he was unsure of his own position, he attempted to make himself independent of Amar Singh, who was his squadron commander, for instance by appearing late on parade and behaving in such a manner that he would not have attempted with a British officer. The other British officers noted this behaviour and Lieutenant Scott told Amar Singh that Wilks was getting too bumptious and that he must show him his proper place. Wilks then went to the Colonel and said that he would not take orders from Amar Singh. The Colonel said to Amar Singh that he had told Wilks off and ordered him to go back on parade and not be a bloody fool. According to Amar Singh, the Colonel had said that 'I was his squadron commander and he was to take orders from me.'[19]

Wilks was replaced by another young British officer. Amar Singh commented: 'The Colonel told me to tell off anyone who did not obey but as soon as the parade was over to forget it all.'[20] The tricky position in which Amar Singh could find himself among the British officers is further exemplified by another diary entry:

> Last night after dinner I smoked a cigar and talked in the mess until about eleven. I get into a rather delicate position these days when these young and hot-headed boys start talking about the late riots at Amritsar and defend General Dyer. They extol him as a hero while I look on him as nothing more than a murderer. I try not to speak at all but when it comes to an acute point I cannot contain myself.[21]

It was General Dyer who had ordered his troops to fire on unarmed protesters trapped in a courtyard in Amritsar with consequent heavy loss of life.[22]

For some unexplained reason, there was a major difference of opinion in the following year between Amar Singh and Major Hill together with his Colonel. Amar Singh wrote that 'Major Hill has given me a thoroughly bad confidential report though the General has added some excellent remarks.'[23] There is, unfortunately, no explanation in the diary as to the nature of Major Hill's report. Now totally dissatisfied, Amar Singh planned to take six months leave and then retire under the new pension rules. Unfortunately, he then found that he could not retire until he had completed 18 years

18   Ibid.
19   Ibid., 17. 11. 19.
20   Ibid.
21   Ibid., 27. 9. 20.
22   See Mason, *A Matter of Honour*, p 448.
23   Amar Singh diary, 7. 7. 20.

service. He commented that 'There are three more weary years to get through though I hope the greater part of them will be on leave.'[24] He noted in his diary for the 5th of July 1920 that he began his sixteenth year of service that morning. In spite of these difficulties, when Sir Charles Cleveland from Jaipur asked him how he got on with his brother officers and how they liked his being with them, Amar Singh replied that:

> From the CO to the latest joined subaltern they are all very good to me and I have no complaint. They respect me and I respect them. I do not try to mix too much amongst them and still I do not try to hold off too. Of course I am in rather a difficult position as I am too junior for my age and too old for my rank.[25]

At last Amar Singh had his chance – the opportunity to command a squadron in a regular cavalry regiment of the Indian Army – yet he seemed to be reluctant to seize the opportunities when they presented themselves. Although he lacked experience of regimental duty, one might have thought that he would have been less diffident and more confident than he appeared to have been. He might well have had command of a squadron in the regiment earlier but, in spite of his age and experience, he did not immediately push for command of a squadron. While his experience as an ADC had undoubtedly been limited, this may have been, in part at least, his own fault. If he had asked he could almost certainly obtained a secondment, if not to a regular regiment, then to one of the State Forces units. His only active service had been as a squadron commander with the Jodhpur Lancers thirty years earlier.

Colonel Mears seems to have treated Amar Singh well though he appears to have thought him inexperienced and possibly lacking in confidence; he may have been being tactful when he referred to his late start. Nevertheless, Amar Singh was perfectly correct to draw attention to the anomaly that his experience was much greater than that of younger British officers who were somehow supposed to know more than he did. The attitude of Wilks in publicly flouting Amar Singh's authority and in refusing to take orders from him illustrates the other side of the double bind in which Amar Singh found himself. It is difficult to reconcile Amar Singh's comments to General Cleveland with his argument with Lieutenant Wilks and his disagreement with Major Hill and the Colonel. Was he giving Cleveland a tactful answer or just what he thought that the General wanted to hear? Perhaps a mixture of both.

In April 1921 Amar Singh asked General Holman for two years leave pending retirement and he left the 16th Lancers at Kohat in June of that year. However, in October 1922 he received a telegram from the 2nd Lancers (to which regiment he had been originally gazetted) to join them at Poona. On arrival he was told by the Commandant that the regiment was very short of officers and that he must serve with them for a few weeks at least until some other officers arrived. This was a totally

---

24   Ibid., 28. 7. 20
25   Ibid., 5. 7. 20.

unexpected turn of events and he is again listed in the Army List among the officers of the 2nd Lancers but as on leave and then very briefly as with the 6th Lancers and still on leave. In his diary he does not mention this second change of regiment and he finally left British service in January 1923.

The comments in his Diary during his service with the 16th Lancers shows very clearly some of the ambiguities of his position and highlights some of the issues faced by Indian officers holding the King's Commission. The VCOs, the risaldars and jemadars who have risen through the ranks, were uncertain of his status and role. An Indian, he is however to be treated as a British officer. On the other hand, when the regiment is sent on internal security duties to Delhi, Amar Singh is left behind, in order that he may not be put into an invidious position vis-à-vis the rioters. Such consideration would not be extended to the VCOs who would be expected, if required, to lead their troops against their fellow countrymen. To what extent did very experienced Indian officers such as the Risaldar-Major, who had come up through the ranks, resent what they might see as Amar Singh's privileged status? There is resent-ment, too, by at least one British officer in the regiment who declines to accept Amar Singh's authority. Amar Singh is one of a new breed of Indian officers though, their position within the hierarchy was still uncertain. Would they eventually replace the British officers? Would they eventually remove the need to have VCOs? These were major questions to be addressed in the period between the two World Wars.

Figure 1 The late Mohan Singhji in the library at Kanota with Amar Singh's diary.
(© Author)

Figure 2 Amar Singh in the uniform of the Imperial Cadet Corps. He is wearing his medals for the China Campaign and the 1903 Durbar. (© Kanota)

Figure 3  Sir Pratap Singh and officers of the Jodhpur Lancers, winter, China 1901.
(© Kanota)

Figure 4  The first intake of cadets in the Imperial Cadet Corps. Amar Singh is fifth from the
left in the back row. (© Kanota)

Figure 5  General Sir O'Moore Creagh with his staff, including Amar Singh. (© Kanota)

Figure 6  Graves of Indian soldiers, Lillers Communal Cemetery, Northern France.
(© Author)

Figure 7  The Indian War Memorial, Neuve Chapelle. (© Author)

Figure 8  Teen Murti, the Memorial to the 15th (IS) Cavalry Brigade, New Delhi. (© Author)

Figure 9 An Indian cavalry patrol. Amar Singh was a keen amateur photographer and this photograph is almost certainly by him. (© Kanota)

Figure 10 A postcard of Amar Singh in France. (© Kanota)

# 7

## The Progress of Indianisation Between the Two World Wars

'The most significant by-product of India's great material and manpower contribution to the Allies in World War I was the pledges and promises offered by the British to the Indians.'[1] Unfortunately, as Stephen Cohen points out, as the Indian Army reverted to its peace-time establishment, there were second thoughts about the promises made regarding Indianisation.[2]

The period between the two World Wars saw a rising tide of nationalism in India. Inevitably, the future role and composition of the Indian Army within an independent India formed part of the discussions. Indian nationalists were beginning to speak of the Indian Army as a mercenary force, officered by men of the occupying power and they looked down on the army as an instrument of colonial oppression.[3] There was no doubt that the army, in addition to its defensive role on the NW frontier, also had a police role and was called upon from time to time to come to the aid of the civil authorities. Indian officers might therefore be seen as collaborators by the more extreme Indians who were agitating for their freedom.[4] However, the wiser nationalists, men such as Senathi Raja from Madras and Sirdar Gurmukh Singh from the Punjab, realised that a free and independent India would need a professional and dependable army which would be officered entirely by Indians.[5] Unfortunately the British government of the time was reluctant to consider the possibility of such a situation ever arising. Nevertheless, discussion on the key issue of Indianisation (the introduction of Indians to the higher ranks of command) continued. Not only was it an important military matter but it was also of major political significance.

In 1911 the Committee of the London All-India Moslem League wrote a letter to the Secretary of State for India on the subject of Indianisation. They quoted an

---

1    Cohen, *The Indian Army*, p 73.
2    See ibid., p. 76.
3    See Omissi, *The Sepoy and the Raj*, p. 154.
4    See ibid., p. 154.
5    See Sundaram, *A Grudging Concession*, pp. 284-285.

article in a service paper entitled *Broad Arrow* as follows: 'Do not Indian records from the early days of Indian rule down to those of the consolidation of the British raj teem with instances of great results achieved under native leadership?'[6] They also drew attention to the anomaly whereby Indians in the civil services could reach high rank compared to those in the military service who could not.

The debate regarding Indianisation had begun in the nineteenth century with the writing of men like Briggs, Lawrence and Chesney. It was to be a long, drawn-out and at time painful, debate. This Chapter might be sub-titled 'A Series of Committees' because the period between the wars is characterised by the setting up of one rather tentative committee after another, each of which seemed to take two steps forward followed by one step back. Viscount Morley, who for a brief period in 1911 became once again Secretary of State for India, set up a special committee to advise on the whole issue of Indianisation and to look specifically at the promotion of Indian officers to the higher ranks. The report declared that:

> In our view the time has come when the loyalty and devotion to the Crown of the Princes and nobles of India must be recognised by the admission of members of their families to the military service of the Empire and we hold that the only condition on which such an offer can be made with honour, can be received with dignity, and can result in contentment, is that of absolute equality of rank, power and employment with British officers of that service.[7]

However, the committee was constrained by Morley's use of the word 'advise' and in Chandar Sundaram's view 'the committee's recommendations were very conservative and subtly obstructionist.'[8]

The Secretary of State for India, Sir Edwin Montagu, announced in 1917 that the aim of the British Government was 'the progressive realisation of responsible government in India as an integral part of the Empire.'[9] The Montagu-Morley proposals which were enacted in 1919 saw the formation of a two-tier system of government for India. Eight provincial assemblies were to be responsible for education, health, agriculture and the state budget. However, the role of the central Viceregal Legislative Assembly was to be a largely advisory body, with power retained in the hands of the British. In recognition of their status within the community, officers and NCOs of the Indian Army were among those who made up the all-male electorate for the

---

6   Article in *Broad Arrow* 27.11.09, Letter from the London Committee of the All-India Moslem League to the Under-Secretary of State for India, 27. 1 1911, quoted in Chandar Sundaram, *A Grudging Concession*, p. 284.
7   Report of a Special Committee appointed by the Secretary of State for India, OIOC, L/MIL/7/19006, quoted in Chandar Sundaram, *A Grudging Concession*, pp. 291-292.
8   Sundaram, *A Grudging Concession*, p. 208.
9   Quoted in Mason, *A Matter of Honour*, p. 447.

Assembly.[10] In 1919 the Esher Committee was established in order to report on the organisation and administration of the Indian Army but recommended few changes and made no recommendation for any increase in the number of King's Commissions awarded to Indians.[11] However following publication of the Committee's report, a resolution was moved in March 1921 in the Indian Legislative Assembly as follows:

> The King-Emperor's subjects should be freely admitted to all arms of His Majesty's military, naval and air forces in India, and every encouragement should be given Indians – including the educated middle classes – to enter the commissioned ranks of the Army.[12]

The comment regarding the middle classes is significant. These were not generally men from the martial classes and had therefore been excluded from recruitment into the Army as a matter of policy. The Assembly wanted one quarter of all new commissions in the Indian Army to be reserved for Indians, pending the creation of an 'Indian Sandhurst'. Moderate Indian politicians, members of the National Liberal Federation, who were looking towards Independence, were agitating for an Indian army officered by Indians. As General Rajendra Nath points out: 'Without an efficient Indian Army, officered by our own nationals, self-government for India must be a very unreal and shadowy thing.'[13] A politician in the Legislative Assembly commented that 'The question whether a Military College shall or shall not be established in India is a question of life or death to the people of this country.'[14]

Morley's Committee made it clear that all Indians seeking the King's commission would be expected to attend the Royal Military Academy at Sandhurst and that the Imperial Cadet Corps might provide some sort of preparation for the Academy. This proposal was accepted at an informal conference concerning issues relating to the Princely States held in Agra in 1907.[15] The status of those VCOs presently serving would be raised in order to prevent disaffection among those unqualified for entry into Sandhurst who might otherwise see themselves being downgraded. However, there was considerable variation among the views of the Committee members as to how to tackle the perceived thorny issue of British officers and men serving under Indian command. Different ideas were put forward by different members of the Committee, none of which were entirely practicable. The suggestions included giving Indian KCOs

---

10   See Lawrence James, *Raj: The Making and Unmaking of British India* (London: Little, Brown and Co, 1997), p. 459.
11   See Menezes, *The Indian Army*, p. 313.
12   Quoted in Omissi, *The Sepoy and the Raj*, p. 166.
13   Maj-Gen Rajendra Nath, *Military Leadership in India: The Vedic Period to the Indo-Pak Wars* (New Delhi: Lancer Books, 1990), p. 252.
14   Pandit Madan Mohan Malvivsa in the Legislative assembly 1928, quoted in Nath, *Miiltary Leadership in India*, p 252.
15   See Sundaram, *A Grudging Concession*, pp. 251/2.

an initial posting to prestigious units within the British Army Alternatively Indian KCOs would have an initial period serving with a British regiment.[16] In spite of their opening fine words, the Committee's final recommendation was that the whole question of Indianisation be referred back to India for further consideration. The urgency of the First World War overtook the debate but it was to return with renewed significance afterwards.

When the Indian Corps had fought on the Western Front, there had been very heavy casualties among the British officers. Indian officers had sometimes been unable to take over in these circumstances due to their lack of adequate training before the war. Lord Kitchener had been aware of the problem well before the outbreak of war:

> The heavy casualties which may occur in a few minutes fighting shows that Indian officers commanding platoons must be trained to take the place of their British officers in command of companies. The failure of Indian officers on various occasions in the present war (on the North-West Frontier) has been largely due to them not having been trained in peace for the duties and responsibilities appertaining to higher rank. The Indian officers lack the initiative to carry on because they have never been in a position to command, and consequently have never been taught initiative.[17]

There were sixteen Indian officers in an infantry battalion in 1914 and this number was increased to twenty in 1920, presumably in recognition of the effect of casualties on a unit's effectiveness.[18] Captain Bonham-Carter writing after the War of the need to train Indian officers made the same point: 'The failure of Indian officers on various occasions in the present war has been largely due to them not having been trained in peace for the duties and responsibilities appertaining to higher rank.'[19] As a short-term measure, a school to train Indian KCIOs was formed at Indore in October 1918 with forty-three students. Thirty-nine of these passed the course and thirty-two eventually received full King's Commissions in 1920. The school was closed down in 1919 after the war had ended.[20] Two of the graduates of this course, K.M. Cariappa and A.A. Rudra, were to become generals in the Indian Army post 1947.[21] Cariappa was also the first Indian officer to graduate from the Indian staff college at Quetta, the first Indian

---

16   See Sundaram, *A Grudging Concession*, pp. 296-297.
17   Lord Kitchener, Memo on the future of Native officers, 1908 OIOC, L/MIL17/5/1746.
18   See *The Army in India and its Evolution* (Calcutta: Superindent of Government Printing, India, 1924), pp. 102-103.
19   Capt. B.H. Bonham-Carter, 'The Training of Infantry Platoon Commanders' in *JUSII*, Vol LII, No 229, Oct 1922, p. 370.
20   OIOC, L/MIL/7/19018 and see Chandaram, *A Grudging Concession*, p. 399.
21   See Ellinwood, *Between Two Worlds*, p. 609.

to command an infantry battalion and became the first Indian Commander-in-Chief in 1949.[22]

Indian officers returned from the Great War with a wealth of experience. Ian Grant records how, as newly joined officer in the Bengal Sappers and Miners, he gave a lecture to his men on anti-gas drills. He thought it had gone well but was reminded of his men's prior experience of the subject when the elderly Sikh subedar remarked 'What you said was absolutely right Sahib. I remember in the first gas attack at Ypres.'[23] Indian troops had passed through a baptism of fire during the War and had they seen their British officers swept away, leaving them without their accustomed leaders. They were aware that in the French and Russian armies men of African and Asiatic origin were given full commissioned rank and they had seen Turkish officers bravely leading their men in the Middle East. According to Lt-Gen Menezes: 'They must ask themselves why to Indians alone this privilege was denied.'[24]

British prejudice against the notion of Indian officers remained strong, even in men such as Lord Roberts (Commander-in-Chief in India, 1893–1893), who was devoted to the Indian Army and revered by the sepoys:

> I have known natives, whose gallantry and devotion could not be surpassed, but I have never known one who would not look to the youngest British officer for support in times of difficulty and danger.[25]

He must have been aware of the courage shown by the Guides who fought to the death when surrounded at Kabul but perhaps he had overlooked the actions of men such as Subedar Sundar Singh of the 1st Punjabis. Fighting against rebel tribesmen in the Tochi Valley in 1897, all of the British officers from a small party from the 1st Sikhs and 1st Punjabis were killed or wounded. However, a steady and disciplined retreat was carried out under the command of the Indian officers, the Subedar being killed. Later in the same year, Subedar Sayead Ahmed Shah of the 31st Punjab Infantry was awarded the Indian Order of Merit for gallantry when, in command of a small outpost, he had continued to direct the defence although wounded.[26] In spite of these and other examples of the leadership shown by Indian officers, Roberts remained of the opinion that an infantry battalion needed at least thirteen British officers in order to exercise effective command in modern warfare.[27] One point which contributed to the British view was a concern that Indian officers would be unable to

---

22    See Barua, *The Army Officer Corps and Military Modernisation in later Colonial India*, p. 65.
23    George Cooper and David Alexander (eds) *The Bengal Sappers 1803-2003: An Anthology* (Chatham: Institution of Royal Engineers, 2003), p. 95.
24    Menezes, *The Indian Army*, p. 311.
25    Quoted in ibid., p. 308.
26    See Michael Barthorp, *Indian Infantry Regiments 1860-1914* (London: Osprey Publishing, 1992), p 14.
27    See Omissi, *The Sepoy and the Raj*, p. 160.

stand aside from the religious and/or caste issues of their men and to adopt a disinterested view in the way in which British officers were able to.[28] There were also concerns expressed as to whether men of one race would follow an officer from another.

As Mason quite rightly points out, Robert's criticism was very unfair as the Indian officers were often simply reacting as they had been trained to do.[29] A different view was taken by General Sir George Macmunn who, in spite of being a strong proponent of the martial races theory was 'one of a small clique in Simla who urged that Indians be granted commissions when the Government was searching for boons to be granted at the time of King George's visit to India in 1912.'[30] General Sir O'Moore Creagh, who succeeded Kitchener as Commander-in-Chief India, proposed that Curzon's idea of the Imperial Cadet Corps should be followed up by the creation of irregular regiments, three of foot and one of horse, which would be officered entirely by Indians.[31] His view may have been coloured by the fact that he had had Amar Singh, one of the first graduates of the Imperial Cadet Corps, on his staff before the outbreak of war.

The first Indians to obtain the King's Commission were doctors who, in 1912, were permitted to hold regular commissions in the Indian Medical Service of the Indian Army; nearly 700 were commissioned during the War.[32] However, although more than one million Indians served abroad in the Great War and some 60,000 died, none of the 9,000 officers granted temporary King's commissions in the Indian army during the war were Indian, though four Indian officers had been commissioned in to the Royal Flying Corps.[33] Of these four, two were killed and one was awarded the DFC. A speaker at the Thirtieth Session of the Indian National Congress in 1915 drew attention to the anomaly: 'Indians are allowed to have commissions to go into dangerous positions to heal people; are they to be refused commissions to kill the enemies of the country?'[34] After the war Indian soldiers were given pensions, grants of land and 200 selected VCOs were awarded honorary commissions with pay and pension benefits. Due to their age, these officers would not be expected to be on the active list for long, if at all. In addition, the Viceroy proposed that, in recognition of the contribution of the Indian army to the war effort Indians would in future be able to obtain the King's Commission and that ten places a year would henceforward be reserved for suitable candidates at RMA Sandhurst. These would be for 'selected representatives of families of fighting classes.'[35] However, at this rate it would have

28   See Marston, *Phoenix from the Ashes*, p. 15.
29   See Mason, *A Matter of Honour*, p. 348.
30   MacMunn, *The Martial Races of India*, p. 344.
31   See Menezes, *The Indian Army*, p. 309.
32   See Chenevix Trench, *The Indian Army and the King's Enemies 1900-1947*, p. 116.
33   See Menezes, *The Indian Army*, p. 313.
34   Shri R. C. Banerjee, Report of the 30th Session of the INC quoted in Sharma, *The Nationalisation of the Indian Army 1885-1947*, p 42.
35   Quoted in Omissi, *The Sepoy and the Raj*, p. 162.

taken over a hundred years to produce a substantial proportion of Indian officers in the Indian Army.

The Secretary of State for India, Edwin Montagu, wrote in a secret memorandum to the Cabinet in July 1917:

> The granting of King's commissions to Indians had been under consideration for many years, both in India and at home but no progress has been made with it owing to the unwillingness of the War Office to concede the principle of giving Indians command over Europeans.[36]

He proposed that places at Sandhurst were to 'be allotted to Indian youths who by birth, character and education are fitted to aspire to high military rank.'[37] On leaving Sandhurst, successful cadets would spend a year with British unit before being posted to an Indian regiment. In addition, commissions would be awarded to exceptional Indian officers for services in the field and to distinguished Indian officers whose age and defective education meant that they were unfit for the higher commissioned ranks. The granting of commissions in this way was intended to reward representatives of the martial classes who had fought so well beside the British during the war. It was argued that men of the martial races could only be handled by officers of the same race and that the martial races were entitled to the lion's share of the commissions as they had made the greatest sacrifices during the War.

However, it was not easy for young Indians to enter Sandhurst. The entrance examination had to be taken in England and many of the cadets lacked the education or the physical and mental robustness to cope with a demanding course designed for the products of the English public schools. Of the first 25 Indian boys admitted to Sandhurst, only ten passed out successfully. In the period 1918–1926, only 243 Indians competed for the 83 places available to them at Sandhurst. The failure rate among Indian cadets at Sandhurst was 30%, compared with 3% for British cadets. By 1925, only 25 Indians had been commissioned into the Indian Army. During the same period, 672 British officers had been commissioned into the Indian Army.[38]

The Army found itself caught in a trap of its own making with its insistence on recruitment from the so-called martial races. Lt-Gen Cobbe wrote:

> It is an unfortunate fact that the fighting races of India, from which the Indian Army is recruited, are the very classes who are most backward as regard

---

36    Secret Memo from the Secretary of State for India to the Cabinet, 20 July 1917, OIOC, L/MIL/7/19006, and quoted in Sundaram, *A Grudging Concession.*
37    Ibid.
38    See Sundaram, *A Grudging Concession*, p 404.

education, and on the other hand those classes whose intellectual qualifications are the highest are generally regarded as lacking in martial qualities.[39]

The lack of suitable candidates was ascribed, on the one hand, to the reluctance of those who could afford a good education to go into the army, and on the other, to the unsoundness of the education of most of the boys who wished to enter the army. The education of the average Indian appeared to be quite unsuitable for the army's require-ments, either scholastically, physically or socially. Many candidates were rejected on medical grounds and there was an apparent ignorance among the Indian public gener-ally regarding exactly what King's Commissioned service in the Army involved.[40] The Report of the Indian Sandhurst Committee concluded that: 'It is not too much to say that until quite recently the educated middle classes have been definitely debarred from a career as military officers'.[41] This may well have been due to the lack of publicity regarding the entry requirements and application process.

In his evidence to the Indian Sandhurst Committee, Lt Col McCleverty, the Commanding Officer of the 1/7th Rajput regiment, referred to the Indian cadets as having a dislike of responsibility and being too easily content with the second best where the best was never good enough. They were unable to give orders properly and they had a general education which was not up to that of the British Sandhurst cadet.[42] A Minute by 'E.G.B.' written in 1917 stated:

> The bulk of the officers we require for the ranks of jemadar and subedar have not the education necessary to absorb the teachings of a school on the lines of Sandhurst. Few of them know English and any attempt to insist on such knowledge as a qualification would be most unpopular. It is not necessary to give (Indian) officers the high standard of training which Sandhurst implies. The Sandhurst boy can aspire to the highest ranks in the army and to appoint-ments requiring the highest attainments. The class from which we get our native officers is quite unfitted for any such positions.[43]

The War Office remained very reluctant to grant full commissions to Indians. In spite of the difficulties noted above which might have been overcome, this reluctance was due almost entirely to racial prejudice, a refusal to countenance the idea that Indians might then be in a situation where they would be in command of European troops. General Sir Beauchamp Duff, Commander-in-Chief, India, wrote: 'There is

39  Lt-Gen Cobbe, Secretary to the Military Department in the India Office, quoted in Byron Farwell *Armies of the Raj*,(London: Viking, 1989), p. 296.
40  Report of the Indian Sandhurst Committee, OIOC, L/MIL/17/5/1785.
41  Ibid.
42  Report of the Indian Sandhurst Committee, evidence of Lt-Col McCleverty, OC 1/7th Rajput Rifles, OIOC, L/MIL/17/5/1785.
43  'E.G.B.', Minute signed and dated 20 March 1917,OIOC, L/MIL/7/19006.

no lack of physical courage among Indians, but I think there is a distinct lack of that moral courage which is involved in unhesitating acceptance of heavy personal responsibility.[44] A letter from the War Office to the India Office written in July 1917 stated:

> The Army Council after careful consideration have come to the conclusion that to grant commissions to natives of India would entail a great risk from the military point of view, in that it involves placing Indian officers in a position where they would be entitled to command European troops.[45]

However, as the Viceroy, Lord Hardinge, suggested, 'It is not, I believe, as the C-in – C's note indicates, the British soldier who will be unwilling to accept the Indian officer's orders but the British officer.'[46] The lack of prejudice by British soldiers was referred to by the Chairman of the Indian Sandhurst Committee in the Committee's Report:

> The curious thing as regards the attachment of young Indian officers to British units is that no prejudice is shown by the British soldier at all. The attached Indian officer always says that he gets on very well with his men.[47]

Colonel Walshe, Commandant Royal Artillery, Eastern and Western Command responded to this comment by saying 'If the individual is good and plays games with his men, and they feel that he is a sportsman and a gentleman, he gets on all right.'[48] Nor were the Commander-in-Chief's sentiments on the inadvisability of giving King's Commissions to Indians shared by all British officers. General Dyer, the Governor General, North-West Frontier wrote:

> My twenty-five years of service across India have been spent in intimate contact with warlike races amongst whom I have known men who by character and hereditary instinct had every qualification to become with proper training thoroughly efficient officers, the equal at least of the average officers of any army.[49]

The Military Requirements Committee was established in 1921 under the chairmanship of Lord Rawlinson in order to frame a progressive policy. They proposed the

44   Appendix by C in C India to a Note by the Viceroy on the granting of commissions to Indians, October 1915, OIOC, L/MIL/7/19006.
45   Letter from the War Office to the India Office, 5 July 1917, OIOC, L/MIL/7/19006.
46   Note by the Viceroy, October 1915, OIOC, L/MIL/7/19006.
47   Report of the Indian Sandhurst Committee, OIOC, L/MIL/17/5/1783.
48   Ibid: Evidence of Col Walshe, commanding RA, Eastern and Western Command, OIOC, L/MIL/17/5/1785.
49   Appendix the Governor General North-West Frontier, OIOC, L/MIL/7/19006.

eventual replacement of British officers by Indians so that eventually the Army would be fully Indianised. The basis of recruitment would also be broadened.[50] However, these proposals were not acceptable in Whitehall. The Government of India proposed that the number of commissions granted to a particular community should be in proportion to the number of men of that community serving in the army.[51] This would go at least some way to ensuring the maintenance of the 'martial-race' theory and practice. Unfortunately it was not generally those men who were the best educated. A further concern of the Committee was the issue of the future prospects for British officers who might resent their places being taken by less well-educated and experienced Indians.

Yet another Committee was set up in 1922 under Lt-Gen Shea to consider the issue of the introduction of Indian officers into the Army. Their report proposed that total 'Indianisation' (excluding Gurkha units) should be completed in three phases. If the first phase taking fourteen years was successful, the second phase would be completed in nine years and the third phase in seven. From the beginning of the second phase, British officers would cease to be commissioned into the Indian army and eventually the VCOs would disappear. At this rate, the Indian army would be completely 'Indianised' by 1955. Eventually Whitehall reluctantly agreed to six battalions and two cavalry regiments being Indianised to begin the process. These units were chosen so as to include as many different classes of Indian troops as possible.[52] No more British officers would be posted to the eight units being Indianised and eventually all of the officers in them would be Indians, holding the King's Commission. The old VCOs would eventually disappear although it might be possible for some of the youngest and most promising to obtain a King's Commission – the majority were too old and lacking in education to be considered. It was suggested that setting up segregated units in this way would give the Indian officers a chance to succeed on their own merits and would also provide a test of the efficiency of such a unit.[53] Of course, at the same time the scheme ensured that British officers would not be deterred from joining the Indian Army as they could continue to serve in all of the other units without fear of competition for promotion from Indian officers. However, when he was Commander-in-Chief India, Lord Rawlinson expressed the concerns of some British officers, stating that 'Old officers say that they won't send their sons out to serve under natives.'[54]

In order to accommodate the new Indian KCOs in the eight units the old VCOs would be eliminated and Indian officers were placed in command of platoons – a system known as 'platoonisation'. This idea was unpopular with the newly commissioned Indian officers who felt that, although newly commissioned British officers

50   See Menezes, *The Indian Army*, p. 323.
51   See Omissi, *The Sepoy and the Raj*, p. 167.
52   See ibid., p. 174.
53   See Andrew Sharpe, 'The Indianisation of the Indian Army', *History Today*, Vol 36, March 1986, p. 48.
54   Quoted in Mason, *A Matter of Honour*, p. 454.

commanded platoons in the British army, their British counterparts in the Indian Army commanded companies. Their chances of reaching command of their regiments would therefore be reduced from 3:1 to 8:1.[55] At the same time, the sepoys saw their chances of reaching commissioned rank virtually disappearing although there were to be exceptions. For example, Naik Ghalam Mohd, son of Subedar Karam Khan, of the 16th Punjabis, entered the Indian Military Academy in 1934 and eventually rose to command his father's regiment. One difficulty in the Indianisation process was the setting up of criteria for selection for prospective officers – a problem not solved until the Second World War.[56] Nor was the Indianisation scheme popular among the British officers. Philip Mason wrote:

> No one could disguise the fact that most Englishmen believed that hardly any Indians were really good enough to lead Indian troops. Almost every British officer believed that only the British public-school system could produce the right sort of officer and only the right kind of officer could give Indian troops the leadership they needed.[57]

The Progress of Indianization Committee which met in 1923 expressed the view that those Indians who held the King's Commission should resemble British officers, i.e. men who had been to British public schools, as closely as possible. Officers, and potential officers, were judged not only on their professional qualities but on their social behaviour as well – the sort of behaviour which was taught in the public schools. In his evidence to the Committee, Colonel Maynard, commanding the 4th/6th Rajputs, stated that: 'By the right type of man, I mean a boy like the one I have under me. He has been to an English public school as he belongs to a Rajah's family.'[58] The year which the newly-commissioned Indian officers spent with a British regiment before joining their Indian units was also seen as an important part of this education. Colonel Maynard wrote again:

> The mess of a British regiment creates a social environment which is of high educational value, especially in the case of officers now entering the army as they are drawn from a much wider field than was the case before the war.[59]

The setting up of The Indian Sandhurst Committee chaired by Lt-Gen Andrew Skeen in 1926 was a turning point.[60] The Report, published in 1927, recommended

---

55    See Farwell, *Armies of the Raj*, p. 299.
56    See Cohen, *The Indian Army*, p. 64.
57    Mason, *A Matter of Honour*, p. 456.
58    Report of the Indian Sandhurst Committee: evidence of Lt Col Maynard, 4/6th Rajputana Rifles OIOC, L/MIL/17/5/1785.
59    Ibid.
60    See Mason, *A Matter of Honour*, p. 463.

an increase in the annual number of vacancies at Sandhurst to 20, increasing in successive years by four until the Indian Sandhurst was established in 1933. In fact it was opened as the Indian Military Academy at Dehra Dun in 1932 with sixty places for candidates from the regular army and forty from the States Forces. Vacancies for Indian cadets at Sandhurst were to continue after the opening of the IMA and Indians were to be eligible for commissions in the Artillery and Engineers. It was planned that half of the total number of officers in the Indian Army would be Indian by 1952.[61]

Entry to the IMA at Dehra Dun was by open competition for 15 places, with the remainder being made up by nomination, care being taken to ensure representation from the minority communities. There were cadets from all castes and creeds – Hindus, Muslims, Sikhs, Parsis and Anglo-Indians – and they came from all strata of society.[62] The course lasted two and a half years as opposed to the Sandhurst two year course to allow for more academic preparation. Three cadets from the first intake were to become Commanders-in-Chief of their respective Armies – Field Marshal S.H.F.J. Manekshaw in India, General Mohammed Musa in Pakistan and General Dun Smith in Burma.[63] The course was on the Sandhurst model with a strong emphasis on drill and 'spit-and-polish' in the early stages. The syllabus aimed to develop the qualities of leadership, discipline and fitness in the cadets as well as a high sense of duty and honour.[64] However, the salary, allowances and conditions of service of the Indian Commissioned Officers (ICOs) passing out of the IMA were less favourable than those of the KCIOs from Sandhurst and the fact that Indian officers could only command Indian troops further lowered their status.

The establishment of the Prince of Wales Royal Indian Military College was an attempt to give selected Indian boys 'a public-school education' and a social training so that they might compete on equal terms with their British counterparts for the rigorous demands of the course at Sandhurst later Dehra Dun. Those who were selected for places at the College came from families whose loyalty to the Government was unquestioned.

General Thimmaya was one of the first Indians to pass out of the Prince of Wales College. He then went to Simla to sit the Army Entrance Exam – a daunting process which involved interviews with the Commander-in-Chief and the Viceroy. It would appear that his prowess at games was a significant factor in his obtaining entry.[65]

61  See Report of the Indian Sandhurst Committee, OIOC, L/MIL/17/5/1785.
62  See Lt-Gen T. Thomas and Jasrit Mansingh *Lt-Gen P.S. Bhagat PVSM VC* (New Delhi, Lancer International, 1990).
63  See Menezes, *The Indian Army*, p. 329.
64  See Brig L. P. Collins, 'The Indian Military Academy', *JUSII Journal*, Vol. LXIV, 1934, p. 320, quoted in Sharma, *The Nationalisation of the Indian Army 1885-1947*, p. 137.
65  See Barua, *The Indian Army Officer Corps and Military Modernisation*, p. 67.

Viscount Chelmsford was now Viceroy and in his view:

> The best guarantee for the elimination of racial prejudice and the reception of young Indian officers by their British counterparts in a spirit of camaraderie is to give them such an education as will ensure them starting on their careers with the manners, ideas and speech of an English gentleman.[66]

Speaking to the Legislative Assembly in February 1923, Lord Rawlinson, the C-in-C India, said:

> The responsibility which lies before these young (Indian) men who will officer the Indianised regiments is no light one. They will have in their hands not only the lives of their men but also the task of maintaining untarnished the high and ancient traditions of the regiments to which they are appointed. Their success or their failure will mean much to India.[67]

Major (later Field Marshal) Cariappa giving evidence to the Indianisation Committee in 1939 commented that;

> The boys who passed out of the Indian Military Academy as officers were of good quality and very much more practical and useful than those from Sandhurst.[68]

Initially there were uncertainties about the status of the ICOs and their relationships with the older VCOs. In one regiment the ICOs were made to live and eat with the VCOs and were not allowed into the British officers' mess. Nor was prejudice confined to the British. Brigadier Yadav recounts how, as a young officer, his Subedar Major had suggested to him that he, an Indian, did not understand the men in his regiment as well as the British officers who took pains to study their habits and way of life. This VCO had served for 31 years and had fought in the First World War and on the North-West Frontier where he had been decorated. Although he was an extremely experienced and competent regimental soldier, he lacked education and was actually proud of the fact that he could not sign his name.[69] Risaldar Sardar Khan, the Indian Adjutant at Dehra Dun, reporting to the Indian Sandhurst Committee, also foresaw difficulties regarding the relative social standing of Indians holding the King's and Viceroy's commissions: 'It might happen that a KCO had not much wealth or landed property in comparison to a VCO serving in the same unit in which case the former

66    Letter from the Viceroy to the India Office, 17 April 1917, OIOC, L/MIL/7/19006.
67    Quoted in John Gaylor *Sons of John Company: The Indian and Pakistan Armies 1903–1991* (Tunbridge Wells: Spellmount Ltd, 1992) p. 23.
68    Cariappa Papers, quoted in Sharma, *The Nationalisation of the Indian Army 1885–194 7*.
69    See Brig H.S. Yadav 'Tips from the Subedar-Major', *JUSII*, Oct/Dec 1965, p. 249.

will be looked upon with some lack of respect not only by the latter but also by the rank and file who come from the same part of the country.'[70]

In order to accommodate the additional Indian officers who would emerge from the IMA, it was decided that three cavalry regiments and twelve infantry battalions were to be eventually officered entirely by Indians but these plans were overtaken by the outbreak of the Second World War. The VCOs returned and 'platoonisation' ended. Courses at Dehra Dun were shortened and Emergency Commissioned Officers (ECOs) appeared – both British and Indian. Whereas regular officers passing out of the IMA had undergone two years of training, these ECOs received only a few months training. Such were the numbers of Indian officers produced under these arrangements that where formerly there had been ten British officers to each Indian officer, by 1945 there were only four British officers to each Indian. In 1927, in order to judge the success of the scheme, the Commanding Officers of the eight Indianised units were asked to answer questions regarding the efficiency of and recruitment to, their units post Indianisation, and the performance of their Indian officers within their units post-Indianisation.[71] The comments on the Indian officers were not entirely encouraging. The CO of the 7th Light Cavalry reported that when given command of a squadron or given a staff job, 'the best of them can do it as well as British officer' The Colonel of the 2nd/1st Punjab was less positive; 'I find that the Indians lack team spirit, power of command, initiative and drive.'[72]

Lieutenant General Shea, the Adjutant General in India, stated that:

> When the British officers have been eliminated, it will be out of the question from the point of view of organisation to contemplate having in one unit Indians holding two types of commission. The VCO who is at present responsible to a great degree for the working of the interior economy of the unit has acquired during his service considerable power in and knowledge of it. All this is placed at the disposal of the British officer who controls it. I question whether the same relationship could possible exist between Indian officers holding the King's and Viceroy's commissions, especially where a difference of caste exists. We will be faced with the elimination of a class of soldier which is an invaluable asset to the army, and it remains to be seen whether his successor will adequately replace him.[73]

The VCO was therefore still seen by the British as important link between the British officers and the men, living, as they did, in such close contact with the latter.

---

70   Report of the Indian Sandhurst Committee, evidence of Risaldar Sardar Khan, Indian Adjutant and QM, RIMC, Dehra Dun, OIOC, /MIL/17/5/1785.
71   See Reports of Officers Commanding Indianised units, OIOC, L/MIL/7/19088.
72   Quoted in Marston, *Phoenix from the Ashes*, p. 19.
73   Report of the Indian Sandhurst Committee, evidence of Lieutenant General Shea, Adjutant General in India, OIOC, L/MIL/17/5/1785.

Indian officers living alongside their British counterparts in their officers' mess would not have that close contact with the sepoys. Risaldar Sardar Khan pointed out in his evidence to the Indian Sandhurst Committee that:

> The VCO lives in the lines and can very well look after his men in the way of discipline and interior economy; he has thus got a better influence upon the men than the officer who lives outside the lines.[74]

Many sepoys enlisted with the hope that they might eventually become VCOs but could never aspire to the King's commission. VCOs were held in great respect in their own communities. The committee report stated that:

> The VCO is treated with extreme cordiality and great consideration wherever he goes. The senior NCOs of the British army when they enter social life are given no consideration by their people. A retired Indian officer is in a very different position.[75]

The outbreak of the Second World War found the Indianisation programme far from complete. John Gaylor illustrates the effect of Indianisation by reproducing two pages from the Army List of 1939. In the 1st battalion of the 7th Rajput regiment – an Indianised unit – there are only three British officers – the Commanding officer and two out of the four company commanders (there is no second-in command shown). Two out of the 25 Indian Officers have passed the Staff College course. There were only 8 VCOs, even the VCO Head Clerk has been replaced by an Indian Warrant Officer. By contrast, in the second battalion of the same regiment, a non-Indianised unit, there are still 18 British officers. There is one honorary Indian officer listed, together with 25 VCOs, including the Head Clerk.[76]

David Omissi shows the extent of Indianisation in the eight units in 1932 in the table below.[77]

---

74 Report of the Indian Sandhurst Committee, evidence of Risaldar Sardar Khan, OIOC, L/MIL/17/5/1785.
75 Ibid.
76 See Gaylor *Sons of John Company*, pp. 26-27.
77 See Omissi, *The Sepoy and the Raj*, p. 185.

| | King's Commissioned officers | | | |
| | 1923 | | 1932 | |
| | British | Indian | British | Indian |
|---|---|---|---|---|
| 2/1 Punjab | 20 | 0 | 8 | 8 |
| 5/5 Mahratta | 16 | 2 | 9 | 8 |
| 1/7 Rajput | 19 | 2 | 9 | 10 |
| 1/14 Punjab | 20 | 0 | 10 | 8 |
| 4/19 Hyderabad | 16 | 0 | 10 | 10 |
| 2 Madras Pioneer | 20 | 0 | 10 | 8 |
| 7 Light Cavalry | 18 | 0 | 7 | 10 |
| 16 Light Cavalry | 20 | 0 | 8 | 10 |
| Totals | 149 | 4 | 71 | 72 |

The Regimental History of the 1st/14th Punjab recorded that:

> Difficulties were many. Disappointments were not a few. Weaknesses were evident. But there was a will to work with the new order and on the whole it worked well. By the outbreak of war in 1939, of the British officers only the Commandant and four company commanders remained. All other officer appointments were filled by KCIOs and ICOs. The last VCO, the Subedar-Major, had been replaced.[78]

Many of the VCOs retired in order to make room for the new ICOs. In October 1938 Subedar-Major Kehr Singh, a Dogra, generously took early retirement so that one more VCO might have the honour of holding that position. That in itself is a comment on the status accorded to the Subedar-Major within a regiment. Their role in future would be undertaken by a Regimental Warrant Officer. There must have been disappointment among some of the older VCOs that they would no longer have the opportunity of rising to that position and the NCOs would no longer have the incentive of promotion to VCO. On 3rd September 1939 'a new band of keen young officers had assumed responsibility, found their feet and acquired the regimental spirit.'[79] The reference to 'regimental spirit' is interesting; it is certainly a factor on which much emphasis was, and still is, placed. This spirit and loyalty to the regiment was deliberately fostered and closely linked to *izzat*.

---

78   G. Pigot, *History of the 1st Battalion, 14th Punjab Regiment* (New Delhi: The Roxy Printing Press, 1946), p. 166.
79   Ibid., p. 180.

The Indianisation programme did not entirely remove racial prejudice. Indian officers overheard, and at times were meant to hear, racial slurs. Indian wives, some of whom were still in purdah, sometimes had difficulties in attending social functions and not all British wives were understanding or helpful. A few British commanding officers had to forbid their British officers from joining the British Clubs in those garrison towns which barred Indian officers from membership.[80] S.P.P. Thorat, later a Lieutenant General, when posted to his battalion (1st/14th Punjab) found that the attitude of some of the British officers was not what it should have been, and stated that 'This was particularly noticeable in their social behaviour which bordered on hostile. They made no secret of the fact that Indians were not wanted as officers. We were treated as outcasts.'[81]

General Auchinleck, the much respected and last British commander of the Indian Army was firmly in favour of Indianisation and did much to smooth the path for Indian officers. He was only too aware of the difficulties which had been placed in their way and of the resentment which some of them felt. After the war he wrote:

> The policy of segregation of Indian officers into separate units, the differential treatment in respect of pay and terms of service as compared with British officers and the lack of manners by some, by no means all, British officers and their wives, all went to produce a deep and very bitter feeling of racial discrimination in the minds of the most intelligent and progressive of the Indian officers.[82]

Indian officers were well aware of Auchinleck's efforts on their behalf. The Indian Commanding Officer of the 1st Bihar Regiment wrote to him;

> The ICOs thank you for all the kindness you have shown them during your command. It seems that the welfare of the ICOs is constantly in your mind. I thank you for all this and all that you have done for us.[83]

Auchinleck, perhaps the best C-in-C that the Indian Army ever had, wrote after the war to Leo Amery MP who had been Secretary of State for India:

> In my opinion, we have been playing a losing hand from the start in this matter of Indianisation. The Indian has always thought, rightly or wrongly, that we never intended the scheme to succeed and expected it to fail. Colour was lent to this view by the fact that the way in which each new step had to be wrested from

---

80   See Farwell, *Armies of the Raj*, p. 295.
81   Quoted in Barua, *The Indian Army Officer Corps and Military Modernisation*, p. 92.
82   Quoted in Farwell, *Armies of the Raj*, p. 300.
83   Quoted in Marston, *Phoenix from the Ashes*, p. 223.

us, instead of being freely given. Now that we have given a lot we get no credit because there was little grace in our giving.[84]

The number of VCOs had been progressively decreased in the Indianised battalions as shown above, but upon the outbreak of war, their numbers were brought up to the same complement as in the non-Indianised units. During the War, very many more Indian officers were to receive the King's Commission and to fight as equals alongside their British counterparts. It is regrettable but, given the entrenched attitudes of many British officers, almost inevitable, that Indianisation should have proceeded so slowly between the two World Wars. More Indian officers in senior posts and with experience of higher command could have helped the Indian Army significantly not only during the Second World War, but after it. As Andrew Sharpe has pointed out:

> Indianisation in the inter-war years provides a history of wasted opportunity. Had the intention existed, Britain could have bequeathed a firm, impressive legacy to India in the existence of a highly professional Army very much earlier. That this eventually happened was due to the massive expansion caused by the war, and also to the exceptional qualities of the Indian officers, and to some senior British officers and the younger British officers who lacked the prejudices of their elders. That the transfer of power in 1947 was completed with relative ease was more by luck than judgment.[85]

84    Letter from Auchinleck to Leo Amery MP, 1940, quoted in Farwell, *Armies of the Raj*, p. 300.
85    See Sharpe, 'The Indianisation of the Indian Army', p. 143.

## 8

## Commandant of the Jaipur Lancers

Until the end of the Great War, Jaipur's only contribution to the Imperial Service (IS) scheme had been a Transport Corps which had gained a high reputation for itself. The Annual Report on State Forces in 1924-25 states it was: 'A very efficient Corps which does much work for the State and has a fine record of service.'[1] In 1923 a cavalry regiment and an infantry battalion were to be established which would come into the Imperial Service scheme. The quarrel between Amar Singh's family and the Maharaja was resolved and he was appointed as the first Commandant of the Lancers with the rank of Major. The regiment was to consist of a Headquarters, Headquarters Wing and three squadrons with a total of 530 men. The Annual Report on Indian State Forces for 1924-25 commented that:

> One squadron of cavalry has been completed. The commanding officer is very keen and in time a good regiment should be raised. New lines (barracks) of a very good pattern have been commenced for the cavalry and infantry.[2]

The barracks which Amar Singh had built still stand in Jaipur and are now the Headquarters of the 61st Cavalry, the only mounted regiment remaining in the Indian Army. This regiment incorporates the traditions of the Gwalior, Jodhpur, Mysore and Patiala Lancers.

Amar Singh's diary records his initial impressions of his command which were not good. The men were old and their equipment and barracks were in a poor state.[3] The majority of the horses were unfit for service. With his experience commanding a squadron in a regular Indian cavalry regiment, he would have had a very clear idea of the standards expected but this situation was not unusual in the State Forces. General Sir O'Moore Creagh, who took command of the Alwar State Forces in 1886, found

---

1    The Annual Report on Indian State Forces for 1924/25, OIOC, L/MIL//17/6/56.
2    Ibid.
3    See Amar Singh diary, 30. 8. 23.

that many of his men were so old that they could hardly walk and that they were totally ignorant of all but the most basic military knowledge.[4]

It was decided to raise one squadron at a time rather than a whole new regiment and Amar Singh arranged to obtain instructors and Indian officers from the Nagra Muslim squadron of the 30th Lancers which was being disbanded. New colours were presented in October 1923 but Amar Singh was still having difficulties in finding a sufficient number of fit horses for the first squadron. Gradually, however, things began to improve. After Major Reynolds, the British Adviser, had inspected the squadron in January 1924, he congratulated Amar Singh on his success in getting the squadron up to standard in such a short time.[5] As an experienced officer, Amar Singh had very clear ideas on the standard of discipline that he expected within the unit. He wrote some years later:

> Discipline is not maintained by harsh treatment and strictness only. The secret of success is that all ranks must not only be afraid of you but they must also love you. Fear and love ought to be combined in equal proportions.[6]

Amar Singh was keen to recruit young men wherever possible as he believed that he could train them more easily than he could older men. As well as expecting a very high standard of smartness and equitation, Amar Singh was very clear about the importance of education and military training to a first class unit. He went to some lengths in order to ensure that his men were trained in the sort of situations which they might expect if on active service. The Annual Report on State Forces for 1931/32 commented on the Lancers that:

> Educational training is carried out as laid down for the Indian Army. The whole regiment was in camp for six weeks. One squadron attached for manoeuvres with the Nasirabad Brigade. One cadre class has been held (on field work and tactics). Tactical training has improved as a result of the six weeks in camp and it is hoped that better and more systematic progress will be made in training this year.[7]

Amar Singh was obviously passing on his previous experience and training to his officers although he had a clear perception of the difference between a regular cavalry regiment, such as the 18th with whom he had served, and a State Force regiment such as his own or the Jodhpur Lancers. There was a good-natured rivalry between the Jodhpur and Jaipur regiments. In 1930, he had a discussion with Mrs King, the wife of the Military Adviser in Jaipur. She told him that he should aim at the Jaipur

4     O'Moore Creagh, *Autobiography,* p 173.
5     Amar Singh diary, 31. 1. 24.
6     Ibid., 20. 12. 31.
7     The Annual Report on State Forces for 1931/32, OIOC, L/MIL/17/6/56.

Lancers being as good as the Royal Deccan Horse (her husband's regiment) or any other regular Indian cavalry regiment. He replied that the Jaipur Lancers were on a par with the Jodhpur Lancers in most areas but were behind on field work and collective training. In two years time they would be their equal but they could never be on a par with regular Indian cavalry. This was because the State officers could never be of same standard as British officers because they did not have the same education. If the Jaipur Lancers were to be mobilised Amar Singh would ask for four British officers on the basis of one per squadron not to command but to see that they did not make a mess of things.[8]

Having served with British officers, Amar Singh was under no illusions regarding the capabilities of the men under his command:

> I told Major Burdett (the Inspecting Officer in 1927) that it was very silly of the State officers trying to ape the British officers. They have not the education nor have the means of living up to that standard. The officers of the State Forces are not fit to command a service. They may be quite good enough as a fighting unit as far as the actual fighting is concerned but when it comes to understanding the actual orders and scheme they would fail.[9]

In 1927 the Jaipur infantry and cavalry were used to assist the police in quelling rioting which took place as a result of attempts to stop gambling. The Resident, Mr Coventry, wrote that ' The Jaipur Lancers showed extra-ordinary self restraint and confidence under most trying circumstances and the coolest and most confident was Colonel Amar Singh who never lost his temper.'[10] This is significant in that the regiment was obviously sufficiently trusted to behave in a proper and steady manner when confronted by rioters.

When the Maharajah suggested that the officers should pay for their own uniforms, Amar Singh replied that they could not afford to because the pay was very low, much less than that of the Jodhpur Lancers. The Maharaja pointed that it was an older regiment and the Jaipur Lancers must first reach the standard and then ask for a rise in pay. Amar Singh replied: 'In no way are we behind them. Our men were finer riders, our horses were of a better stamp and our field work and the training of the officers was better.'[11] In 1930 Colonel Macnabb, the Resident at Jodhpur, suggested to Amar Singh that he should visit the Jodhpur Lancers. Amar Singh wrote:

> I told him that I knew the regiment very well as I had served with it myself. It is a very good regiment. He told me that hearing the way in which I go for it

8    See Amar Singh diary, 10. 9. 30.
9    Ibid., 15. 2. 27.
10   Ibid., 4. 9. 27.
11   Ibid., 14. 2. 30.

one would think that I have a very poor opinion of it. I told him that this was all between Dalpat Singh (the commander of the Jodhpur regiment) and myself when we pull one another's legs. We really had great respect for each other.[12]

The Annual Report on Indian State Forces for 1926/27 commented on the Jaipur Lancers that:

> This new unit is getting on satisfactorily. Lt Colonel Thakur Amar Singh is keen on his work. Some of the State's officers, who are mostly pensioned officers of the Indian Army, and have been useful in raising and training the unit, are getting a little bit old and might be discharged when the regiment is complete.[13]

The following year when the Military Adviser in Chief visited personally, the Report read as follows:

> He (Amar Singh) is well served by his officers who are up to the standard of the Indian army. There has been a great improvement in this unit since it moved into new lines. I foresee that in a couple of years this unit is going to be first-class. There is now an atmosphere of keenness throughout and a keen spirit. All that is required is an organised system of training and plenty of work in the field. Not yet fit (for service).[14]

Throughout his career Amar Singh was always ready to defend the status of VCOs although he was well aware of their limitations, especially in terms of their education. Whilst in London in April 1915 he had met the son of Kutub Chandar Sen who was working with Indian students in London and who argued that the government should give more commissions to Indians. Amar Singh commented in his diary:

> When I did not agree with him he said the VCOs should be eligible to rise to the rank of Captain. I said that this cannot be done because these fellows have not got the education and they are quite idiots when compared with British officers. It is quite another thing to run a battalion and to be able to live up to the standard of a British officer.[15]

At the same time as admitting their limitations, he believed that VCOs were not being accorded the respect and status that they deserved. He wrote:

12  Ibid., 27. 6. 30.
13  The Annual Report on Indian State Forces for 1926/27, OIOC, L/MIL/17/6/56.
14  The Annual Report on Indian State Forces for 1927/28, OIOC, L/MIL/17/6/56.
15  Amar Singh diary, 14. 4. 15.

However, in my opinion the VCO status ought to be raised and the British Tommies and sergeants must be made to salute them. That is the only way in which these fellows will be respected. I hear that in Egypt, Tommies have to salute Egyptian officers – why not Indians?[16]

On the other hand, Amar Singh was very much against Indianisation and his diaries give us a rare and significant glimpse of the perception of one experienced Indian officer at this period. Amar Singh was always very conscious of differences between different classes and religions within the Army and the conflicts which could arise. Talking with Major Oswald in 1930:

I said that the feelings between the different classes and the different religions were still so bitter that I did not think that there was any chance of it succeeding. I was afraid that it would be the ruination of the Indian Army.[17]

Amar Singh was also very concerned about the type of men being commissioned and drew attention to the potential difficulties. In discussion with Lieutenant General Sir Cyril Deverell, he commented that:

However fair an Indian might be he could not overcome the hatred and jealousy prevalent among the various classes. They will never trust one another. Human nature will not allow it. I asked where they were going to get the right sort of officers from. The people to whom the British are giving commissions to at present are not the right sort. Commissions are being given these days to people whose relations are serving as sepoys in those very regiments. How can they command the necessary respect? Probably a number of those in the ranks hold higher social standards than these officers and the thing would not work. Where our Indian officers fail is that they are not as highly educated as the British. The majority of Indians who go to the Academy are highly educated but they are not the right class. Lots of people tell me that I have a King's Commission and would make this regiment as good as any in the Indian Army. To this I always tell them they expect the impossible from me. There are 13 British officers in a regular Indian cavalry regiment. How can I do the work of them all?[18]

He recorded in his diary for 1930 a discussion with Captain King, the British Military Adviser to the Jaipur State Forces:

16  Ibid., 27. 1. 16.
17  Ibid., 2. 2. 31.
18  Ibid., 2. 2. 32.

I told him that Indianisation could never be a success at present, the reason being that there is great enmity amongst the various classes and they will never be able to pull amicably together. I told him that I was as level-headed and as little prejudiced as anyone you could find but even I always have a leaning towards the Rajputs.[19]

Class or social standing was very important to Amar Singh. He himself was a high-class Rajput, a Thakur and therefore a man of property, and he was always very conscious of the fact. He felt that some of the Indians being commissioned are socially inferior – possibly even to the men whom they will command. Some of his difficulties in the past had been because of his determination not to take orders from those whom he believed to be socially inferior to him or the failure of junior officers, such as Lieutenant Wilkes of the 16th Lancers, to accord him the proper respect due to him and his rank. Social standards were all-important to him. He noted in his diary for October 1931:

Social standards should always be kept in view. It is only owing to the observance of this that the maharaja sahib asks the cavalry officers to dinner and not from the other units. The other day I could not invite Sardar Khan to dinner because of his social standing; he is only of the social standing of an Indian officer and a very poor one at that.[20]

In the following year he recorded a discussion with Colonel Craster who had come to Jaipur as Chief of Staff. The Colonel wished to get Ressaidar-Major Bharat Singh of the 16th Lancers to command the Jaipur Lancers. Amar Singh told him it would not do: 'You cannot bring a man of his rank to command officers who are Captains. As regards social position he is not in the same street nor as professionally well qualified.'[21]

Visiting the Officers' Mess of the 2nd Lancers (in which regiment he had briefly served) in the thirties, he was very impressed by what he saw:

In the mess all officers mix freely from 2 i/c to newly joined subaltern. There is hospitality for visitors, tradition, pictures and photos of all the old commandants. The officers who have retired still keep up their connections with the regiment and send presents.

He noted the photographs of past regimental commandants in the mess and wrote that: 'The Commandant is a mere stone in the life of the regiment. If the present man

19   Ibid., 17.9.30.
20   Ibid., 7. 10. 31.
21   Ibid., 12. 10. 31.

does not take any interest in his predecessors he may be sure that his successors will not in him.'[22] He met Captain Rajendra, who was serving with the 2nd Lancers, and commented:

> He is the only Indian officer with a King's Commission in the regiment. The officers were a happy family. The British officers did not like it at first but that they know that this has to come and they do not mind it. There is really more trouble with the VCOs when King's Commissions are given to people of their own social standing.[23]

Amar Singh discussed Indianisation with the officers of the regiment, remarking:

> In my view it was bound to be a failure if they hurried things. India must first form into a nation before they could dream of such things or they would know it to their cost at the first outbreak of a fairly big war. India is not a nation. People have nothing in common with one another and they are awfully jealous of one another. The men will have nothing to look forward to except to rise to non-commissioned officer. The pay of Indian officers if the same as British officers will be less than in the Indian Army. Officers in the British army and certainly in the cavalry served for the honour and glory of it and not to make money. Their pay does not even cover their mess bills.[24]

Amar Singh was not enthusiastic about men from the State Forces attending the Indian version of Sandhurst. In 1932 Colonel Craster asked him if he had any cadets from his regiment that would like to go there:

> I said that I had not and then explained to him that this scheme would not work. If a man is educated well enough and had four thousand rupees to pay for his expenses he would take a King's Commission in the Indian Army where pay and conditions were far better than in the States. Even if the States paid their expenses they would be inclined to go to the Indian Army and would be awfully discontented if there were forced to come back to the States.[25]

Colonel Craster said that the States did not propose paying their expenses. 'I said that in that case there was no hope of anyone going.'[26]

---

22    Ibid., 26. 2. 35.
23    Ibid., 16. 2. 31.
24    Ibid., 20. 4. 31.
25    Ibid., 2. 4. 32.
26    Ibid.

Amar Singh's comments are particularly significant at a time of rising unrest and politicisation. He does not accept the concept of 'India' as a single nation, but rather sees the country as a collection of separate groups and states. During a visit to Kashmir in April 1932 Amar Singh met up with an old friend, Captain Brown, and they too discussed Indianisation:

> I said that it was rather premature. The racial and religious feelings were so bitter that the thing will prove a failure. However much a man may try to be impartial he could not really be so. There would be too much pressure on him from all around. Then, making the examination open was a mistake. This would mean that all the clever mischief-mongers would get in the army. I said that before Indianisation was tried on a large scale they ought to try out some of the Indianised regiments on active service to give the scheme a thorough trial to make sure that it would succeed.[27]

Nor was Amar Singh alone among Indians in his objection to Indianisation. He records that when one Indian officer, Pratap Singh from Jamnagar, was ordered to join an Indianised regiment, he sent in his papers (i.e. resigned) as 'He did not want to join that crowd of undesirables.' Amar Singh commented that:

> 'If this was the case with an Indian officer how could one expect the British to mix with them? When giving commissions to Indians they (the British) ought to be careful and give them only to people of the highest class and education.'[28]

In 1931 Amar Singh was appointed as a special ADC to the Viceroy to attend on him when he was in Rajasthan. He accepted the post on condition that he would be treated in exactly the same way as a British ADC. In that same year he was also appointed Corps Commander of the Jaipur State Forces, cavalry, infantry and transport corps, with the rank of Colonel. However, this was not to be a happy move. Amar Singh commented:

> It is merely an empty shell. All the powers are with Colonel Craster (the Chief of Staff). It has never been my principle to quarrel with British officers but when things got beyond a limit one had to take a stand. I am treated merely as a post office between Colonel Craster and the unit commanders. I have practically no powers and no authority. If he wants to run the whole show then he might as well appoint himself Corps Commander and I am perfectly willing to revert to

27   Ibid., 15. 4. 32.
28   Ibid., 11. 11. 31.

commandant of the Jaipur Lancers. I do not want an empty title. Colonel Craster as a staff officer should have no powers.[29]

He wrote later: 'I know that by the enmity with Colonel Craster I will gain nothing and would eventually lose a great deal but my fate carries me the wrong way.'[30]

In March 1936 Amar Singh was compulsorily retired with the rank of Major General. Amar Singh was awarded a special pension for his services and in September his name was put forward for an OBE but as he was retired the honour could not be awarded. In any case Amar Singh saw this as palliative. He felt that he had been pushed out because he had successfully opposed the views of the British officials. He wrote in his diary:

> I was feeling very depressed and occasionally stopped writing (the diary) when my thoughts wandered to very soon breaking off all connection with the army and especially with my pet child the Jaipur Lancers. I had raised the regiment from the beginning and was very deeply associated with it. It has been like a family to me.[31]

Major King (who had been Military Adviser in Jaipur) wrote to Amar Singh:

> We were awfully sorry to hear about (your retirement) and it must be rotten for you having to give up the Jaipur Lancers in which you took so much interest. However in a way you have been lucky. It is not given to many of us to have a constructive job of building up a new regiment and you can always look back on the fact that you made a first class job of it.[32]

In March 1930 Amar Singh noted in his diary:

> The Ressaidar-Major said that the regiment would be very sorry when I leave them; they will never get another commandant like me. He told me that he had seen eight commanding-officers in his old regiment but not one of them was up to my standard in tactfulness or in managing inspections or dealing with superior officers.[33]

29    Ibid., 29. 9. 31.
30    Ibid., 4. 2. 34.
31    Ibid., 31. 5. 34.
32    Ibid., 19. 4. 36.
33    Ibid., 22. 3. 30.

Amar Singh himself when talking to Captain Patterson said:

> As a rule the Indian has a narrow mind. He does not want his subordinates to shine or come to the foreground. I worked on different lines and was more open-minded. I pushed my officers and encouraged them to come to the Club and mix with bigger and better people than themselves. I made them play polo and other games. I treated them as my own sons. The majority of my officers were not educated and came straight from the villages.[34]

Amar Singh's view that his fellow officers needed to broaden their outlook and to widen their range of social contacts was a very far-sighted and liberal notion. He was well aware of the poor education of many potential and serving Indian officers and was anxious to give them opportunities for self-development. He used his previous experience of serving in the Indian Army to ensure that at least some of his comrades did not face the discrimination which he himself had met. All of the difficulties and ambiguities of Amar Singh's role seem to come together at the end of his military career. He was not unaware of his faults. As he wrote: 'I have spent the last twelve years in quarrelling and fighting with my senior officers.'[35]

Amar Singh's Diary provides a most valuable ethnographic study, giving, as it does, a detailed picture of life in an upper class Indian family in the first half of the nineteenth century. His diary, contained in 82 bound volumes, provides us with a unique account from the Indian perspective of part of the painful process of the transformation of the Indian Army. In 1931 he showed his diary to two British friends: 'They wondered how I found time to write so much and how very constant and persevering I must be. They told me that in one hundred years time my diary would be very valuable.'[36] He was undoubtedly a shrewd observer of the scene around him and although the entries devoted to military matters form only a small part of the whole, they are nonetheless most interesting. His diary provides a thread running through the great changes which took place in the Indian Army during the first half of the twentieth century and throws an informed light upon them. He took part in the failed experiment of the Imperial Cadet Corps and comments shrewdly on its reasons for failure. He spends ten unsatisfactory years as an ADC because the British are uncertain as to what to do with this new breed of officers who held commissions in the Indian Land Forces. His comments on the contribution made by the Indian Corps in France and the difficulties which the troops faced are also a most important commentary on these events as seen from the Indian standpoint. He was one of the very first Indians to command a squadron in a regular cavalry regiment and he raised, and commanded, a very efficient regiment in the State Forces. His views regarding

34   Ibid., 23. 9. 36.
35   Ibid., 9. 3. 36.
36   Ibid., 18. 3. 31.

Indianisation are also highly significant, coming as they do from an Indian officer of considerable experience. As a high class Rajput, Amar Singh held very strong views on the matter of social class. Indeed it might be said that he is, in his own way, just as prejudiced as many of the British officers with whom he comes into contact.

As an Indian officer he had to live in two very different communities with very different social mores and he could never be entirely at ease with either group. A high caste Rajput, he was very conscious of his social standing within Indian society while at the same time he was painfully aware that many British officers looked down on him as socially inferior. He respected many British officers as individuals and yet he found it almost impossible to show them the respect as a group which convention demanded. Neither could he be at ease with the vast majority of the Indian officers who had risen through the ranks and who were uncertain of his standing within the hierarchy. His experiences illustrate very clearly the difficulties facing Indian officers as they tried to make their way into what had previously been an all-British society.

## 9

## The Second World War and Independence

---

*The Indian army was comparatively less ready in fact for a jungle war with Japan than it had been in 1914 for a trench war with Germany.*[1]

In the Second World War Indian troops were to fight in a number of totally different theatres of operations. Men fought with the Eighth Army in the deserts of North Africa, the Middle East and the mountains of Italy. Indian soldiers also fought with the Fourteenth Army defeating the Japanese in the jungle and open plains of Burma. At the outbreak of the Second World War the Indian army comprised some 160,000 soldiers plus a further 35,000 enrolled non-combatants organised into ninety-six infantry battalions and eighteen cavalry regiments.[2] In addition there were four Class A Indian State Forces cavalry regiments and seven infantry battalions fit and ready for active service. Of the cavalry regiments, only two were partially mechanised; it was not until the end of 1940 that the last regiment, the 19th Cavalry, relinquished their horses.

As in 1914 the Indian Army was a well-trained and effective force fighting on the North-West Frontier and engaged in internal security duties. It was not, however, equipped and or prepared for conventional warfare. There was an acute shortage of modern equipment. Just before the war a restructuring in order to mechanise the infantry and to provide them with more modern weapons was planned. Battalions were each to consist of four companies together with a headquarters company. They were expected to have 44 light machine guns, 4 mortars and 6 anti-tank rifles and there should be 12 King's Commissioned Officers and 17 Viceroy's Commissioned Officers.[3] Unfortunately when war came almost none of the battalions were fully equipped or at full strength. The number of VCOs had been progressively run down

---

1    Menezes, *Fidelity and Honour*, p. 347.
2    See Farwell, *Armies of the Raj*, p. 304.
3    Mason, *A Matter of Honour*, p. 468.

but their number was now increased as all units were to be equally 'Indianised'.[4] By 1942-43 the companies in Indian battalions were commanded by British officers and the platoons were commanded by Jemadars with Subedars acting as the Company second-in-command. Modern warfare brought with it a need for much more sophisticated skills in order to handle the more complex weaponry. One man who broke the axle of a 15cwt truck by driving it over a large boulder grumbled that 'a bullock cart would have got over it!'[5]

A massive expansion of the Indian Army was put in hand. In 1940, for instance, the Sikh Regiment was immediately ordered to raise two new battalions. The regiment had started the war with five battalions, together with a training battalion. It ended the war with eight battalions, plus a specialist Machine-Gun battalion and a garrison battalion. In order to raise these new units, the existing battalions were mercilessly 'milked' of experienced officers and men. In order to create the two new battalions of the Sikh Regiment, each of the pre-war battalions was to provide a nucleus of some ninety Indian ranks. In addition, each battalion received a further 250 recruits from the Training Battalion.[6] Just six days before the 1st Battalion left the North-West Frontier for Burma, one British officer, two VCOs and 100 men were drafted to the 5th Battalion in Malaya.[7] The remnants of this battalion surrendered at Singapore. In another example, the 1st Battalion 14th Punjab Regiment which had built up a strong cadre of officers, had to lose every British officer except two, every KCIO and numerous VCOs in order to officer other newly raised units.[8] There were few replacements available, other than reservists who were, in many cases, unfit for service overseas, The departure of experienced men from the battalions which they knew and in which they were known was bound to have an unsettling effect on both the men and the units from which they were taken.

From January 1940, all British and Indian officers joining the army were given Emergency Commissions. By January 1945 the ratio of British to Indian officers in the Army was 4.2:1.[9] Arguments about the Indian officers powers of punishment over British troops were not finally resolved until 1943.[10] By August 1943 there were 97 Indian Lieutenant Colonels, but only six of them commanded fighting units.[11] The vast majority of the Colonels were in the Medical Services. The Staff College

4    Menezes, *Fidelity and Honour*, p. 344.
5    Mason, *A Matter of Honour*, p. 469.
6    See Col Birdwood, *The Sikh Regiment in the Second World War* (Norwich: Jarrold and Sons, nd), p. 18.
7    See ibid., p. 85.
8    See G.Pigot, *History of the 1st Battalion, 14th Punjab Regiment* (New Delhi: The Roxy Printing Press, 1946), p.182.
9    See Marston, *Phoenix from the Ashes*, p. 222.
10   See ibid., p. 224.
11   See ibid., p. 225.

at Quetta in 1940 included only four Indian officers and there were no Indian instructors. In 1942 there were 21 Indian students out of a class of 140 and by 1944 there were four Indian instructors.[12] By January 1944 the 2nd/1st Punjab Regiment was commanded by an Indian Colonel with an Indian second-in-command and as well as an Indian company commander there were three other Indian officers, all Captains.[13] General Auchinleck, Commander-in-Chief in India at this time, strongly encouraged Indian officers at all levels and was at pains to make his ideas clear throughout his command. His views carried great weight and did much to encourage the success of Indianisation throughout the Army and to ease the path of individual Indian officers.

Three mule transport companies went to France in 1939, where they did sterling work before they were evacuated from Dunkirk. The first major Indian formation to see action was the 4th Indian Division early in December 1940. Italy entered the war alongside Germany on 10 June 1940. Some 400,000 Italian soldiers were spread across Abyssinia, Eritrea, Italian Somaliland and Tripolitania. Opposing them General Wavell had only 80,000 men including two brigades of the 4th Indian Division.[14] The Allied troops defeated the Italians at Sidi Barani and then continued to attack the Italians in Libya with immediate success, destroying the greater part of five enemy divisions. In the fighting in North Africa, the Indian Divisions utterly destroyed the Italian armies in Abyssinia and Libya taking 130,000 prisoners before sweeping on to Benghazi. Jemadar Dhers Singh of the 2nd Punjab Regiment won the Indian Order of Merit for 'continuous good work and the exhibition of sterling qualities of leadership'.[15] The 4th Indian Division then joined the 5th Indian Division in Eritrea There was severe fighting at the strong position at Keren where a main road led through a defile, thus forming a formidable defensive position. Subedar Richpal Singh of the 4/6th Rajputana Rifles was awarded a posthumous Victoria Cross for his gallantry in leading an attack against the enemy position here.

However, the situation changed dramatically with the arrival of General Rommel and the German Afrika Korps in North Africa. The first German attack came in March 1941 and the British and Indian troops were compelled to fall back towards Tobruk. The battle swung back and forth across the desert, each side advancing in turn and then being forced to halt at the end of its supply lines and/or because their vehicles needed overhaul. The port of Tobruk was besieged twice by the Germans; on the first occasion the Allies were able to hold out until relieved but the port fell after the second siege. The fighting was extremely fluid in the open and featureless desert; there were no fixed battle lines so that vehicles coming towards one through the dust

---

12   See ibid., p. 226.
13   See ibid., p. 229.
14   See Birdwood, *The Sikh Regiment in the Second World War*, p. 16.
15   Narinder Singh Desri, *Sikh Soldier, Vol III, Policing the Empire* (Uckfield: Naval and Military Press, undated), p. 381.

might turn out to be friend or foe. In these circumstances, the initiative and determination of often quite junior officers was of vital importance. As Mason has pointed out: 'It was a war for young men and professional soldiers, and in the opening stages, the Indian army was highly professional.'[16] Surrounded at Meikili in March 1941, the 3rd Indian Motor Brigade was able eventually to break out. Major Rajendrasinhji of the 2nd Lancers captured 300 prisoners on the way back to the British front line and was the first Indian officer to be awarded the Distinguished Service Order (DSO).[17] Major (later General) P. P. Kumaramangalam commanding the 7th Indian Field Battery also received the DSO for his defensive action at Bir Hakeim.[18] During the attack on the Fatnassa Heights in Tunisia, Subedar Lalbahadur Thapa was second in command of D company of the 1st /2nd Gurkhas. Fighting his way up the feature with a handful of men he reached the crest with only two riflemen. They killed several Germans before the rest fled. His gallantry led to the capture of this vital feature and he was awarded the Victoria Cross, the first to be awarded to a Gurkha during the Second World War[19] The landing of the mainly American forces together with the British First Army in Tunisia under the overall command of General Eisenhower led to the final defeat of the German forces in North Africa as they were caught between two pincers. During the final days of fighting in Tunisia, Jemadar Dewan Singh of D Company of the 1st Battalion, 9th Gurkhas was awarded the Indian Order of Merit for his courage in continuing to fight although having a dozen wounds on his head alone which had been inflicted by the Germans with his own kukri.[20] The 4th Indian Division was one of two divisions transferred from the Eighth Army to the First Army. General (as he then was) Montgomery commented 'I sent First Army my best – 7th Armoured and 4th Indian.'[21]

An officer of the Jodhpur State Infantry, Major Ram Singh, was the first Indian to set foot in Europe since 1940 when he landed at Salerno as part of the 'beach-block' tasked with organising and controlling the invasion beach. He was awarded the DSO for his work in the bridgehead. The fight up Italy was a long, slow and bitter struggle with a particularly difficult hard-fought battle at Monte Cassino. The terrain favoured the defence as the Allies fought their way past a succession of mountain ranges It was in Italy that Indian sappers built the so-called 'Impossible' Bridge. The retreating Germans had destroyed the bridge across the river Moro which ran along the bottom of a thickly wooded ravine. British, Canadian, Polish and New Zealand engineers had all declared that it was impossible to build a new bridge on that site. The Sikh Subedar of 69 Company, the Bengal Sappers and Miners, agreed to take on the task. The parts

16    Mason, *A Matter of Honour*, p. 480.
17    See ibid., p. 483.
18    See Pradeep, *The Army Officer Corps and Military Modernisation*, p. 146.
19    See Smith *'Valour' A History of the Gurkhas*, p. 80.
20    See Lt-Col G.R. Stevens OBE *Fourth Indian Division* (Toronto: McLaren and Son Ltd., nd) p. 238.
21    Quoted in Chenevix Trench *The Indian Army and the King's Enemies 1900-1947*, p. 229.

of the Bailey bridge were carried by hand across the river at night, the bridge was built on the far side and launched back across the gap from the enemy side.[22] On the slopes of Monte Cassino Subedar Subramanyan of Queen Victoria's Own Madras Sappers and Miners threw himself on a German shrapnel mine which was about to explode in order to save the lives of his comrades. He was awarded a posthumous George Cross – the first to a member of the 4th Indian Division.[23] A second George Cross was awarded to Jemadar Balbahadar Gurung of the 6th Gurkha Rifles for an incident which occurred in a cantonment in India. He was a passenger in a lorry loaded with mortar bombs which swerved off the road, hit a tree and caught fire in front of the married quarters. Having helped the driver and other passengers out of the vehicle he tackled the blaze fully aware that the cargo could have exploded at any minute. According to the Regimental Newsletter: 'The fine courage of the Gurkha Officer and his coolness in a situation of extreme danger to himself saved further injuries and loss of life which would have undoubtedly occurred had the fire in the lorry not been checked immediately.'[24]

Whilst their comrades were fighting in North Africa and Italy, British and Indian troops were fighting a very different war in the jungles of Burma and Malaya. On the 7th December 1941 Japanese aircraft attacked the American base at Pearl Harbour, sinking five battleships. The Japanese then attacked Hong Kong which was only lightly held by under-equipped Allied forces. Kai Pak airfield was bombed and its obsolete aircraft destroyed on the ground. The mainland was evacuated and the island forced to surrender on Christmas Day. Japanese operations against Malaya began with an attack on Siam to the north. Bangkok was occupied on December 8th and the Siamese government was forced to sign a treaty of alliance with the Japanese.

Meanwhile, British airfields in the north of Malaya and ports, including Singapore, were bombed by the Japanese who enjoyed almost total air superiority. British troops weighed down by heavy equipment, dependent on motor transport and untrained for jungle warfare were at a severe disadvantage. The Japanese soldier was lightly clad and equipped and prepared to live on a ration scale which would have been quite unacceptable to British and Indian troops.[25] When Allied troops took up a blocking position astride a road, the Japanese put in a frontal holding attack while their main force melted into the jungle and encircled the British and Indian soldiers who hurriedly retreated lest they be cut off. By January 7th, the British had been pushed back almost halfway to Singapore. The city surrendered on February 15th, a massive blow to British prestige in the Far East. Over 70,000 British, Australian and Indian troops were taken

---

22   See George Cooper and David Alexander, *The Bengal Sappers 1803-2003. An Anthology* (Chatham: Institution of Royal Engineers, 2003), p. 200.
23   See Stevens OBE *Fourth Indian Division* pp. 295-296.
24   Regimental Newsletter, 6th Gurkhas, June 1941. Gurkha Museum, Winchester, The Gibbs Papers.
25   See Birdwood, *The Sikh Regiment in the Second World War*, p. 80.

prisoner, many of whom died in captivity.[26] There were individual examples of bravery even in defeat. For example, Jemadar Mohammad Hassan of the 5th/2nd Punjabis was commanding a platoon when his battalion was ordered to retire. The order did not reach him and, ignoring a summons to surrender, he fought his way out and rejoined his unit. He was awarded the Military Cross.[27] Jemadar (Acting Subedar) Ajit Singh of the 5th/1st Sikhs was given an immediate award of the Indian Order of Merit for his defence of a ferry which was a vital line of retreat for a Gurkha battalion.[28]

The Japanese success in Malaya opened the way for an advance on Rangoon and the Burma Road along which supplies went to the Nationalist troops fighting in China. To defend Burma, the British had only two weak divisions. Rangoon was abandoned on March 7th as the Allied troops fell back northwards towards the Chindwin river. During the retreat from Burma the 7th/10th Baluchis, a young, wartime battalion, were holding the line of the Bilin River. During the night of the 11/12 February 1942 they fought a Thermopylae-style battle against much stronger Japanese forces. An immediate DSO was won by Captain Siri Kanth Korla who, commanding the Dogra company, led several counter-attacks, was captured by the Japanese and escaped.[29] Eventually, the defeated and exhausted British and Indian soldiers struggled back into India.

As Daniel Marston has pointed out: 'Defeat in the Malaya and Burma campaigns convinced the Indian Army that new tactics and training were required.'[30] The lessons learnt in battle were disseminated in *Army in India Training Memoranda* and *Military Training Pamphlets*. Veterans from the campaigns were sent out to other units to share their experiences. It was recognised that the soldiers, both British and Indian, must be taught to see the jungle as their friend and not to be afraid of encirclement by enemy forces. Their training would include a strong emphasis upon patrolling, both for reconnaissance and for taking the fight to the enemy. Even if apparently cut off, the allies would be supplied by air. The basic recruit training of Indian soldiers was increased to nine months followed by two months of jungle warfare training.[31] In 1943 two training divisions were set up specifically to train recruits who spent a month at a base camp in the jungle learning individual battle skills before spending a second month on longer exercises out in the jungle.[32] General Bill Slim, who was eventually to command the 14th Army in Burma, also realised that only a completely fresh mental approach and a strong sense of moral values would enable his men to defeat the Japanese. He firmly believed that his soldiers needed an object worth fighting for as well as a strong belief that they were all contributing to the achievement of that

26    See Mason, *A Matter of Honour*, p. 488.
27    See ibid., p. 487.
28    See Birdwood, *The Sikh Regiment in the Second World War*, p. 115.
29    See Chenevix Trench, *The Indian Army and the King's Enemies*, p. 200.
30    Marston, *Phoenix from the Ashes*, p. 79.
31    See Menezes, *The Indian Army*, p. 364.
32    See Marston, *Phoenix from the Ashes*, pp. 97-98.

object.[33] He set out, though a series of talks to his troops, to ensure that they all shared his belief and values.

In January 1944 British and Indian troops were attacked in the Arakan, the western coastal strip of Burma. They were held by a strong Japanese offensive, known as 'Ha-Go'.[34] The Japanese plan was that, while the bulk of the Allied troops were engaged in the Arakan, the main Japanese thrust, known as 'U-Go', would be in the north, taking the Tamu-Imphal-Kohima route into Assam and so through into India and on to Delhi.[35] The British had established an 'Admin-Box' in the Arakan and the Japanese troops, lightly equipped and with the bare minimum of food, relied upon its capture to re-supply them. But the 'Box', defended by a scratch force of non-infantrymen supplied by air, held out, often mounting determined counter-attacks, against wave after wave of Japanese attacks which were put in with their usual unswerving ferocity, Meanwhile, to the north, the tiny garrison at Kohima, with only one British battalion alongside the Indian troops, held out in a fight which raged across the District Commissioner's tennis court. Such was the intensity of the fighting in these battles that two posthumous Victoria Crosses were awarded. One went to L/Cpl P.J. Harman of The Royal West Kents at Kohima and the second to Jemadar Abdul Hafiz of the 9th Jats for gallantry in clearing the road to Imphal.[36] The twin defeats of the Japanese at Kohima and Imphal in March 1944 mark the turning point of the war in the Far East. At the end of their over-stretched supply-lines, the Japanese were forced to retreat. Thereafter, in spite of the monsoon, appalling terrain and the suicidal tactics of the Japanese, the enemy was remorselessly pushed back across the Chindwin and Rangoon was eventually recaptured in May 1945.

Indian soldiers fought throughout the war with their customary valour. The first Victoria Cross to be awarded to an Indian officer went to Second Lieutenant (later Lieutenant General) Premindra Singh Bhagat of the Indian Engineers. In February 1941 the Italians were retreating through Eritrea. The minefields that they had laid had to be cleared swiftly in order to allow the British pursuit. Bhagat carried out the task non-stop for forty-eight hours in spite of having his Bren Carrier blown up twice beneath him and having both his eardrums damaged.[37] During the advance on Mandalay a company of a British regiment, the Buffs, was caught on the enemy side of the Shweli River with all its officers dead. A newly arrived Indian sapper subaltern, M. R. Rajwade, was awarded the Military Cross for organising the company's defence and preparing for the evacuation of the wounded.[38] In Burma, Lt Karamjeet Singh

33  See Mason, *A Matter of Honour*, p. 255.
34  See Birdwood, *The Sikh Regiment in the Second World War*, p. 297.
35  See Mason, *A Matter of Honour*, p. 501.
36  Ibid., p. 297.
37  See ibid., p. 314.
38  See Chenevix Trench *The Indian Army and the King's Enemies*, p. 279.

Judge of the 4th/15th Punjabis was awarded a posthumous Victoria Cross for leading charges against ten Japanese positions before he was mortally wounded.[39]

In February 1945 Japanese forces were attacking the isolated positions of C Company of the 14th Battalion, 13th Frontier Force Rifles. Jemadar Prakash Singh, a Dogra, was hit in both ankles but he dragged himself about on his hands and knees encouraging his men and firing a Bren gun. Wounded twice more he shouted the Dogra war-cry so loudly that his men took it up and drove the Japanese from their position. Jemadar Singh was finally killed when a Japanese hand-grenade hit him in the chest.[40] He was awarded a posthumous VC for 'his inspired leadership and outstanding devotion to duty.'[41]

In total, the officers and men of the Indian Army earned thirty-one Victoria Crosses during the War, twenty of them in Burma. Three of these went to a single battalion, the 2nd/5th Royal Gurkha Rifles.[42] In all, 4,028 awards were made to Indian soldiers for gallantry in action.[43] In the vicious close-quarter fighting against the Japanese in Burma, four Victoria Crosses were won by Sikh soldiers. Naik (later Jemadar) Nand Singh won his for 'his determination, outstanding spirit and magnificent courage'. Uniquely, he was to be awarded India's second highest decoration for valour, the Mahavir Chakra in 1947, fighting in Kashmir. Sadly, this award was posthumous as he was mortally wounded leading a bayonet charge.[44]

Gallantry in very different circumstances was shown by a number of Indian officers who were captured by the Japanese. Captain Mahmood Khan Durrani of the Bahawalpur State Forces resisted all Japanese attempts to suborn him over a long period. In spite of being tortured most cruelly he refused to join the Indian National Army which the Japanese were attempting to form to fight against the British. He was awarded the George Cross.[45] The same award went posthumously to Captain Ansari of the 5th Battalion 7th Rajput Regiment for his defiance of Japanese propaganda and their attempts to undermine his men's loyalty.[46] Subedar-Major Harising Borha of the 2nd Battalion of the 2nd Gurkhas, captured at Singapore, was savagely beaten to death by the Japanese for protesting about the treatment of his men. He was awarded a posthumous Indian Order of Merit.[47]

---

39    See Ian Summer, *The Indian Army 1914-47* (Oxford: Osprey, 2001), p .27.
40    See Mason, *A Matter of Honour*, p. 502-503.
41    *London Gazette*, 1st May 1945 quoted in Brig W.E.H.Condon *The Frontier Force Rifles* (Aldershot: Gale and Polden, 1933), p. 461.
42    See Mason, *A Matter of Honour*, p. 507.
43    See Farwell, *Armies of the Raj*, p. 314.
44    Narindar Singh Dhesi, *Sikh Soldier, Vol III, Policing the Empire* (Uckfield: Naval and Military Press, undated), pp. 109 et seq.
45    See Chenevix Trench *The Indian Army and the King's Enemies*, p. 194
46    See Gaylor *Sons of John Company: The Indian and Pakistan Armies 1903-1991*, p. 155.
47    See Smith, *'Valour' – A History of the Gurkhas*, p. 95.

A million troops fought in South East Asia, nearly two-thirds of them Indian or Gurkha. During the war the Indian Army expanded to 180,000 men, everyone a volunteer.[48] At the beginning of the war, fewer than one thousand Indians held the King's Commission; by the end of the war there were 16,000 Indian officers with the most senior of them commanding battalions or brigades. The Fourteenth Army, led by General Bill Slim, was the largest wholly volunteer army in the world and had a 700 mile battle front.[49] The casualties suffered by the Indian Army was as follows:

| | |
|---|---|
| Killed | 24,338 |
| Wounded | 64,354 |
| Missing | 11, 754 |
| Prisoners | 79,489 |
| Total | 179,935[50] |

At the end of the War, General Slim said, 'My Indian Divisions were the best among the best in the world. They would go anywhere, do anything, go on doing it and do it on very little.'[51] He told General Savory that he regarded the 1st/11th Sikh Regiment and the 1st/4th Gurkha Rifles as the best two battalions within his command.[52]

The regimental history of the 1st/17th Dogras refers to Major Ghulam Qadir who was killed near Imphal.

A most gallant leader. A Pathan (Muslim) in a Hindu Battalion, the Dogras would have followed him anywhere; an amiable and attractive personality with a natural sense of humour, he was essentially a soldier, and an absolutely first-class one at that.[53]

In the Second World War Indianisation was of enormous value to the Indian Army providing as it did the necessary impetus to make the process a reality.[54] The only way of meeting the needs of a vastly expanded army for more officers was by granting many more commissions to Indians and these new arrivals were to acquit themselves well. By the end of the war there were some 32,750 British officers and nearly 16,000 Indian officers in the Indian army.[55] 25% of the officers in the combat arms were

---

48    See Chenevix Trench, *The Indian Army and the King's Enemies*, p. 255.
49    See ibid., p. 316.
50    See Pradeep, *The Army Officer Corps and Military Modernisation*, p. 137.
51    Quoted in Mason, *A Matter of Honour*, p. 509.
52    See Birdwood, *The Sikh Regiment in the Second World War*, p. 325.
53    Quoted in Mason, *A Matter of Honour*, p. 512.
54    See Chenevix Trench *The Indian Army and the King's Enemies*, p. 117.
55    See Mason, *A Matter of Honour*, p. 511.

Indian.[56] Professor Stephen Cohen has pointed out that 'When queried about the special merits and demerits of Indian officers, British commanders agreed almost unanimously on the superior ability of the Indian officer to handle his troops.'[57]

It was in the crucible of the Second World War that the future leaders of the Indian and Pakistani Armies were to learn their trade, though it was unfortunate that none of them reached the more senior ranks during the war. Captain S.H.F.J. Manekshaw led one of the few British counter-attacks in the early part of the war on Burma. His energy and drive led to the award of a Military Cross in 1942. After Independence he became a Field Marshal and commanded the Indian army in its successful campaign in East Pakistan in 1971.[58] By 1943, in addition to the 2nd/1st Punjab battalion, three other battalions were being commanded in action by Indian officers; Lt-Colonels K.S. Thimmaya, L.P. Sen and S.P.P. Thorat. Thimmaya became the first Indian to command a Brigade.[59] The most senior Indian cavalry officer was Colonel J.N. Chaudhari who commanded an armoured car unit, the 16th Cavalry, in Burma.[60] After Independence Thimmaya and Thorat both became Army Chiefs and Sen a senior General in 1947. Brigadiers K.M. Cariappa and J.N.Chaudhari completed the first post-war course at the Imperial Defence College and were the first Indians to pass out of this establishment.[61] Cariappa was to become the first Indian Commander-in-Chief and a Field-Marshal.

As Roger Beaumont has stated, 'Partition came with a whimper for Britain but with a bang for India.'[62] The British were almost totally unprepared for the separation between India and Pakistan and almost to the end hoped that it might somehow be possible to keep a united Army serving the two countries. As late as March 1946 there was not a single contingency plan to prepare the Indian Army for partition.[63] The most favourable pre-war estimates of the progress of Indianisation suggested that it would not be before the mid-1950s that Indian officers would be attaining high rank. At first Auchinleck resisted calls to bring the process forward arguing that long experience was required to be a good senior officer in order to allow them to acquire the necessary judgment, wisdom, patience and understanding of human nature.[64] He was over-ruled by the politicians and Indian officers were given accelerated promotion over the heads of their more experienced British colleagues.[65]

---

56   See Marston, *Phoenix from the Ashes*, p. 227.
57   Cohen, *The Indian Army*, p.145.
58   See Pradeep, *The Army Officer Corps and Military Modernisation*, p. 149.
59   See Pradeep, *The Army Officer Corps and Military Modernisation*, p. 96.
60   See ibid., p. 151.
61   See ibid., p. 165.
62   Beaumont, *Sword of the Raj*, p. 186.
63   See Farwell, *Armies of the Raj*, p. 348.
64   See Gautam Sharma, *Nationalisation of the Indian Army*, pp. 187/8.
65   See Barua, *The Indian Army Officer Corps and Military Modernisation*, p. 162.

The Indian Army was divided with roughly two-thirds/one third with the smaller portion, the Muslims, going to Pakistan. Of the ten existing Gurkha regiments, six were allotted to the Indian Army and four joined the British Army. Generally speaking, the army's cantonments and training areas were in Pakistan whilst the armament factories were in India. Pakistan inherited the main recruitment areas of the Indian Army.

Traditions of loyal service were deeply embedded as were military expectations of preferential treatment from the organs of state. Recruits had been drawn from the same clans and hereditary networks for generations.[66]

It was particularly unfortunate that there was a significant lack of experienced battle-hardened Muslim officers to fill the upper levels of command in the new Pakistan. So severe was the lack of trained senior officers in Pakistan that in the process of raising four new divisions the number of regular officers in a battalion had to be significantly reduced. The situation was even worse in the Pakistan Air Force.[67] There had been no all-Muslim units in the Indian Army. In the Armoured Corps, for instance, there were only eight Muslim squadrons in the six regiments allocated to Pakistan although there were nineteen Muslim squadrons in the Corps.[68] In the majority of cases, regiments and battalions had to be divided as the Sikh and Hindu soldiers were separated from their former Muslim colleagues. There were poignant farewell scenes and, not infrequently, men of one faith returning home were escorted by their former comrades through the murder and mayhem which was taking place immediately before and after partition. For instance, the Sikh squadron of the 19th Lancers was escorted through Peshawar by the Punjabi Muslim Squadron of the regiment.[69]

Individual regiments did all that they could to control the chaos into which India was descending. For example, according to Colonel Eustace:

The 2nd battalion of the 6th Gurkha Rifles was largely instrumental in preventing the communal violence in Delhi from becoming worse than it was. The conduct of the battalion at all times enhanced its high reputation.[70]

The now famous 4th Indian Division was to form a key part of the new post-Independence Indian Army. It's final duty under the Raj was to be the nucleus of the hastily formed Punjab Boundary Force consisting of 50,000 troops under General T. W. 'Pete' Rees. From the outset the Force faced an almost impossible task, with

---

66    Keay, *A History of India*, p. 523.
67    See ibid. p. 171.
68    See Gaylor, *Sons of John Company*, p. 298.
69    See Chenevix Trench, *The Indian Army and the King's Enemies*, p. 294.
70    Last Years in India. Note by Col N. Eustace DSO, Commandant 5/6 Gurkhas, in The Gibbs Papers.

the collapse of law and order over a vast area. Murderous gangs roamed the Punjab, burning, raping and pillaging. At a meeting of regimental Commanding Officers and Subedar-Majors General Rees told them that they, representatives of the old Indian Army, constituted the last bulwark against chaos and that the future of India depended upon their steadfastness and fidelity.[71] The eventual break-up of the Punjab Boundary Force marked the final stage in the dispersal of an Army in which Hindus, Sikhs, Muslims and all the other races of the sub-continent had served together in harmony for a common cause. As the historian of the Fourth Indian Division has commented, 'In many ways the Indian Army had been the only truly Indian entity in the Indian Empire. In its last service its great actuating tradition remained.'[72]

With the coming of Independence and full Indianisation, the position of the VCO within the Army might be seen as no longer required. However, no less a person than the future Field Marshal and Commander-in-Chief, Brigadier K. M. Cariappa, argued strongly for the retention of an intermediate rank as 'economical sub-unit commanders.' The VCO had originally been the link between the British officer and the sepoys and with an all-Indian Army such a position might be thought unnecessary. Cariappa pointed out that India is a huge country and that the Indian officer coming from part of the country might be unfamiliar with the language and customs of his men who came from a different area. Nevertheless, Cariappa saw this co-ordinating role as second to the VCO's primary concern which was to command a platoon or other sub-unit. He wrote in a report to Field-Marshal Auchinleck:

> I am of the firm conviction that the VCO rank must remain in the Indian Army in the interests of India. It is an economical and yet an efficient rank which provided an incentive to a very large number of young Indian other ranks with limited educational qualifications.[73]

The spirit and traditions of the British Army of the Raj lives on in the Indian Army of today. VCOs may have been replaced by Junior Commissioned Officers but their importance in the regiment is unchanged, 'The JCOs were a powerful breed who practically ran the squadrons.'[74] According to Corrigan, class regiments and class companies are not officered by men of their own race and this is the reason why the JCO continues to exist. Thus, for example, a Sikh regiment will have Sikh NCOs and JCOs but will be officered by, for instance, Rajputs or Mahrattas.[75] Lieutenant General Ajai Singh recounts the influence which Risaldar-Major and Honorary Captain Prag

---

71    See Stevens, *Fourth Indian Division*, p. 410.
72    Ibid., p. 413.
73    Letter from Brigadier Cariappa to General Auchinleck, 5 Nov 1945, National Archives of India, Private Papers of FM Cariappa, Part 1 Group 1.
74    Brigadier Amrik Singh Virk in '*Fakhr-E-Hind*' *The Story of the Poona Horse* (Dehra Dun: Agrim Publishers, 1993), p. 181.
75    See Corrigan, *Sepoys in the Trenches*, p. 13 footnote.

Singh MC had on him: 'It was as if the whole Regimental personality was reflected in this one man.' His parting words to the General on the day of the Risaldar-Major's retirement were: ' Ajai Sahib, I have worked hard on you. I hope you rise high and thereby prove that the effort expended by this old man was not in vain.'[76]

Field-Marshal Auchinleck, the last British Commander-in-Chief of the Indian Army, broadcast in March 1946: 'The magnificent divisions of the Indian Army are world-renowned. The Indian soldiers will go down in posterity as among the finest fighting soldiers of the world. Let the Indian Army guard its good name. The Indian army may well be the instrument which will ensure that this great period in history will pass peacefully and in a spirit of goodwill on both sides.'[77]

---

76   Lieutenant General Ajai Singh in 'Fakhr-E-Hind' The Story of the Poona Horse, p. 151.
77   Quoted in Menezes, The Indian Army, p. 407.

# 10

## The Education, Training and Selection of Indian Officers

---

In 1875 Lord Napier wrote that:

> There is nothing in the military history of any of the Native armies of India to justify a belief that with fair opportunities the Native soldier is not capable of becoming an efficient troop or company commander, under the careful selection, education and training of his troop officer.[1]

Prior to the Mutiny, promotion to and within the officer ranks in the Bengal Army was solely on the basis of seniority within the regiment. This inevitably meant that they were old men by the time that they reached the senior rank. Sita Ram was promoted to Jemadar after 35 years hard service and to Subedar thirteen years later at the age of sixty-five. He commented:

> I would have been much better fitted for this position thirty years earlier. What could I do now at the head of my company? Could I double-march or perform Light Infantry drill? But I was expected to be as active as ever and no allowance was made for my 48 years service.[2]

An even more extreme example was the Subedar-Major of the 8th Bengal Light Cavalry who was killed charging at the battle of Ramnuggar. He was 78-years-old with 60 years' service.[3] The situation only changed after the Mutiny and then rather slowly, so that for a number of years afterwards, there were still elderly and unfit senior Indian officers serving with their regiments.

---

1     Response by Lord Napier to a letter from the Military Department, 1875. OIOC, L/MIL/7/7240.
2     Lunt, *From Sepoy to Subedar*, p. 172.
3     Ibid., p. 148.

According to Mason, 'There was a time when a recruit was looked on with disfavour if he could read and write.'[4] At the beginning of the nineteenth century, when promotion went by seniority, the Indian officer's education – or more usually complete lack of it – was of little significance. All that was required of him was that he knew the words of command and stood bravely in front of his troops. Indeed there was at times a positive reluctance to recruit educated men. Chandar Sundaram recounts the experience of Gurmukh Singh who had been a schoolteacher before he enlisted. However, he was repeatedly passed over for promotion and was told by his commanding officer that the Indian Army actually discouraged the promotion of educated men.[5]

However, as tactics and weaponry became more complex, their lack of even a basic education became an increasingly significant handicap for many Indian officers. This was a problem which was to last until at least the Second World War and may be the one of the reasons why the Indian army has retained a role for Junior Commissioned Officers who have not attended the Indian Military Academy. Regimental schools went some way to mitigating this difficulty but one suspects that they received greater encouragement in some units than in others. The 1st Battalion 14th Punjab regiment appointed an Education Jemadar in 1920 in view of the fact that passing educational tests had become an essential step to promotion.[6] Captain Morton of the 24th Punjabis wrote in 1907:

> 90% of recruits enlisted are entirely illiterate, and the ambition to rise in their profession will, at best, only come after several years service in the ranks, combined with a good deal of unpalatable instruction in the Regimental School. Only a comparatively small percentage of men enlist with any idea of completing the full term of twenty-one years service.[7]

The level of training once the NCO became an officer was also variable and there seems to have been an almost total lack of any formal leadership training for the Indian officers. They were expected to have developed their leadership skills through their many years of experience as an NCO. In the 1920s schools known as King George's Schools were founded in order to give a basic education to boys who might be potential VCOs. Kitchener College provided a preparatory course for Indian young men seeking commissions.[8] This situation, lasted into the Second World War, except for those relatively few Indians who received Indian Commissions having attended

---

4    Mason, *A Matter of Honour*, p. 466.
5    See Sundaram, *A Grudging Concession*, p. 286.
6    See G.Pigot, *History of the 1st Battalion, 14th Punjab Regiment* (New Delhi: The Roxy Printing Press, 1946), p. 162.
7    Captain S.Morton, 24th Punjabis, 'Recruits and Recruiting in the Indian Army', *JUSII*, Vol. XXXVI, No 91, January 1900, p. 53.
8    See Menezes, *The Indian Army*, p. 327.

the Military College at Dehra Dun and were known as King's Commissioned Indian Officers (KCIOs).

The pre-Mutiny system of promotion by seniority meant that young men of greater ability could be passed over in favour of their older, less able and more senior colleagues. A sepoy who entered the service at 16 could not expect to become a naik before he was 36, havildar at 45, jemadar at 54 and subedar at 60. Their duties were generally monotonous and irksome unless on active service. The system produced 'a great feebleness of character and physical incapacity arising from age and infirmity in the higher native officers of the service.'[9] The problem persisted after the Mutiny. In 1872, Inspection Reports show that in 26 out of the 49 regiments of infantry in the Bengal Army, one or more Indian officers were unfit for service. By 1874, this figure had risen to 34 regiments, ie nearly 70% of the whole. Typical comments were: 'old and worn-out, too old for active service, six officers unfit on account of age and infirmities'.[10] There were implied reservations in the reports of the inspecting officers as to the capacity of the existing Indian officers for the more extended duties imposed by the new regimental organisation, though there was no doubting their smartness and willingness.

Immediately after the Mutiny the degree of trust which had existed between the Indian sepoy and his British officers was shattered and would take many years to rebuild. The loyalty of the Indian troops and especially that of their officers who might, perhaps, lead the men in any future uprising, was a major concern. Some British officers still had serious doubts regarding the abilities of the Indian officers and there was 'very vehement and persistent opposition from men representing the old school.'[11] The objections were based on the perceived inefficiency of the Native Officers, especially in Madras, and the consequent necessity of having more British officers. The lack of trust which followed the Mutiny meant that it was felt that there were dangers in giving the Indian officers too much responsibility and authority. However, some British officers still believed in the importance and value of the Indian officer. Sir Henry Norman wrote:

> I do not conceive it possible to have a satisfactory Native army without thoroughly good Native officers. We should have thoroughly efficient and, if possible, thoroughly loyal and contented Native officers; and I think we do our best to secure them under a system under which we give our Native officers responsible and honourable positions, with a suitable and adequate training.[12]

9    Captain Macan, Parliamentary Papers 1831-32 XIII (735-v) House of Commons, p. 150.
10   Abstract of Confidential Reports on Native Regiments as to the efficiency of Native Officers, OIOC, L/MIL/7/7240.
11   Departmental Minute No 438 of 1876, p 4, OIOC, L/MIL/7/7240.
12   Sir H Norman, Note on the organisation of the Indian Army, 11.10/1875, Chap 1, para 15. OIOC, L/MIL/7/7240.

The system of promotion based purely on seniority changed and VCOs were now compulsorily retired after 32 years of service.

The Mutiny brought a number of officers who had received immediate postings as officers into the Army. These were usually men of influence within their communities and such a privilege was usually dependent upon the number of recruits which the potential officer brought with him. For instance, when the 2nd Punjab Regiment was raised in 1849, Tota Ram and Nasrullah Khan who had each brought in a complete troop from Hindustan, were given command of their respective troops. The practice of giving direct commissions to men who brought in a sufficient number of recruits appears to have continued at least until 1865 when Mamara Kan, the son of the late Risaldar-Major Lahras Khan, was appointed as a Jemadar in the 2nd Punjab for bringing in 14 men with 250 rupees each.[13] The practice of linking rank to the number of man and horses which a recruit brought with him harked back to the Moghuls and was employed by James Skinner when he was raising his irregular regiment (later known as Skinner's Horse). This arrangement had brought a number of advantages. Lord Napier wrote:

> In recent years some men have become Jemadars and Subedars more quickly and many of them were immediately promoted if they brought young men for enlistment during the Mutiny. This is a much better system. These officers were young and full of spirit, men of influence and were much more highly regarded by the sepoys, being looked upon as fathers of the company.

Supporting the system of promotion on merit, he wrote that there were some British officers 'who have never believed in the ability of the Native Officer and have never thought of selecting the best men, and cultivating and bringing them out' and that 'The opinion of those officers who have tried and proved the capacity of Native Officers should carry more weight.'[14]

However, not everyone was pleased by the new arrangements and the sepoys were concerned at the possibility of unfairness and favouritism: 'They now have examinations and promotion goes by supposed merit, which means in effect at the pleasure of the commanding officer, which is very precarious thing to depend on for promotion.'[15] Nor did the changes have immediate effect. In 1872 the Duke of Argyll inspected the system adopted in 1857 for the selection and training of Indian Officers and reported little change or marked improvement overall although there had been some advance in the Bengal Army.[16] The sons of the Indian Rajahs and Maharajahs were seen as

13   Anon, *History of the Second Panjab Cavalry from 1849 to 1866* (London: Kegan, Paul, Trench and Co, 1888), p. 19.
14   Lord Napier, Memorandum, OIOC, L/MIL/17/5/1674.
15   Lunt, *From Sepoy to Subedar*, pp. 172-173.
16   See Lord Napier, Memorandum, OIOC, L/MIL/17/5/1674.

an alternative source of Indian officers and it was hoped that such 'Native gentlemen' might be encouraged to accept direct appointment. The Secretary of State wrote in 1876:

> The selection and appointment of a few Native gentlemen of good family, of approved loyalty, and of good education to hold the position of Native commissioned officers … could not fail, especially if they had the further claim of being sons of distinguished Native officers, to promote a feeling of professional pride and self-respect among other members of the same class and enhance the dignity and importance of their position.[17]

Unfortunately these hopes were not generally realised; Indian young men of good family had little taste for the boring routines of regimental life. Major Elsmic of the 56th Punjab Rifles commented that:

> It is highly desirable that, in conjunction with other improvements, the standard of education of native officers should be gradually raised. Perhaps in the distant future we can picture an Indian Sandhurst, peopled by the sons of well-educated Indian gentlemen and sending forth a race of native officers, loyal to the State, high in principle, active in body, intelligent in mind and devoted to duty.[18]

During the nineteenth century the recruits were mainly illiterate peasants; they could not read or write their own language and did not speak any English. In an effort to remedy these difficulties, regimental schools were established. For instance, in Madras in 1830 two schoolmasters were authorised per unit while it was in garrison. There was, however, a fear among British officers that if the Indian officers became too highly educated they would be tempted by higher paid jobs in the civilian life. Lord Napier had reservations:

> If we educate too highly we shall be unable to satisfy either the social wants or the ambition of the Native officer. The amount of education contemplated in the regimental schools is sufficient for our purposes.[19]

In spite of the opposition, schools were established and were effective. The Record Book of the 28th regiment Bombay Infantry shows that in 1869: 'the number of men who can read and write is large and creditable to the educational efforts of the past

---

17   The Secretary of State for India to the Governor General, 10.8.1876, para 11, OIOC, L/MIL/7/7240.
18   Major A.M.S.Elsmic, 56th Punjab Rifles FF. 'Native officers of the Indian Army' in *JUSII*, Vol XXXVI, No 16, April 1907, p. 45.
19   Lord Napier, 1875, OIOC, L/MIL/7/7240.

year' and that in 1870 the Commander-in-Chief remarked 'with pleasure on the number attending school in the regiment.'[20] Some British officers went further in their suggestions. Captain Hennell, writing in *the Journal of the Indian United Services Institution* suggested that Soldiers' Institutes be established:

> My proposal for the establishment of Soldiers' Institutes in the Native Army must be divided into three parts:- First – as a preliminary measure – I would advocate the extension of our present regimental school system. Second, I would advocate the formation of small regimental libraries and recreation rooms. Thirdly, I would suggest the establishment of a service printing press at every large station.

He refers to a great improvement in regimental schools and to the fact that in recent years girls' schools had been formed in every regiment in the Bombay army at the instigation of Lord Napier:

> There are now 3 or 4 classes where English is eagerly studied by sepoys seeking promotion. Native officers now read English newspapers and take an interest in the world around them of which they knew little or nothing before. Company orderlies now keep their pay accounts and rolls in English. English copies of the 'Field Exercise' and 'Rifle Instruction' now may be seen in a good number of regiments.[21]

However, the continuing lack of English among many of the sepoys at the end of the nineteenth century is indicated by an enquiry recorded in the letter book of the 2nd Gurkhas as to whether it was necessary for candidates for the signalling class to have a knowledge of English.[22]

As early as 1888, the idea of a Military College for Indian officers was being put forward by enlightened officers such as Sir George Chesney, Military Member of the Supreme Council. He recognised the lack of education among the Indian officers as a major handicap: 'Good officers as they are according to their lights, brave, faithful and intelligent, their education is defective and they cannot come into line with our own officers until it is improved.' The ability of the Indian officer to speak English was seen as crucial; as he wrote:

---

20  Record Book, 28th Regiment Bombay Infantry National Archives of India.
21  Captain R. Hennill, 'Soldiers' Institutes for the Native Army of India' in *JUSII*, Vol 5, 1876, p. 71.
22  Letter dated 16.6.83 from Dehra Dun in the Regimental Letter Book, 2nd Gurkhas. Gurkha Museum Winchester.

A man can have all the military instruction, but until he can transact regimental business in the English language and study his profession in it, he cannot take his place in the Army alongside the English officer.[23]

Chesney proposed the addition of a senior department for military training to the schools which already existed for the education of Indian princes and nobility. If student numbers were small, a single military school might give the best results. However, their lack of a basic general education remained for many years as a further handicap for the potential Indian officers. Major Laing of the 12th Pioneers wrote in 1909 that: 'It is manifest that the educational qualifications of both native officers and NCOs are generally of the poorest quality due to want of early schooling.'[24]

Before promotion to lance-havildar, soldiers were expected to be in possession of the 3rd class educational certificate (the 3 Rs, a little geography etc), havildars to have the 2nd class certificate and VCOs the 1st Class.[25] In order to further improve the situation, it was proposed that military schools would be established to provide training for NCOs and that, in future, no Indian NCO would be promoted to jemadar unless he had attended one of these schools. However, this training was not to be the equivalent of the training offered at Sandhurst; a minute by 'E.G.B.' suggested that:

The bulk of the officers we require for the ranks of jemadar and subedar have not the education necessary to absorb the teachings of a school on the lines of Sandhurst. Few of them know English and any attempt to insist on such knowledge as a qualification would be most unpopular. It is not necessary to give (Indian) officers the high standard of training which Sandhurst implies. The Sandhurst boy can aspire to the highest ranks in the army and to appointments requiring the highest attainments. The class from which we get our native officers is quite unfitted for any such positions.[26]

Indians soldiers in France during the First World War noted the value and importance of education. The Chief Censor commented that:

The Indians have not been slow to draw a moral from the close connection between wealth and knowledge which they have seen in the West, and there is no doubt the cause of education had received a large impetus.

---

23    Sir G. Chesney, Military Education for the Natives of India, 23.1.1888, p. 6, OIOC, L/MIL/5/2202.
24    Major F.C. Laing, 12th Pioneers, 'Education in the Native Army' in *JUSII*, Vol XXXVIII, 1909, p. 193.
25    Report of the Indian Sandhurst Committee, evidence of Col Walshe RA, OIOC, L/MIL/17/5/1785.
26    Minute by 'E.G.B.' signed and dated 20.3.1917, OIOC, L/MIL/7/19006.

and that:

> Under the stress of necessity many Indian soldiers during their stay in Europe
> have learned to read and write their own languages, and primers and spelling
> books have come in large quantities from India to the Army.[27]

For instance Fateh Yar Khan of the 19th Lancers wrote home: 'Get the children
(boys and girls) taught to read and write well. Here teaching is obligatory.'[28] However,
literacy was to remain a problem for some sepoys until 1947. Brigadier Bristow who at
one time commanded of the Dogras' Regimental Centre in the 1940s reported that.
'Some recruits arrived illiterate, probably because the nearest school was too far from
home; the rest would have been to primary school, and a fair number to secondary
school.'[29] This problem affected the technical arms especially. At the same time at the
Jodhpur Lancers' Training Centre: 'Education was another problem as comparatively
few educated boys were prepared to enlist as recruits.' This affected the armoured car
regiment especially 'because of the technical nature of their role and so basic education
had to be included alongside the technical training.'[30] At the end of the Second World
War the Dogra Regimental Centre had accumulated a significant amount of money
in its private funds. The Indian officers, both ICOs and VCOs, urged that as much
of the money as possible should be set aside to provide a scholarship fund for the sons
of soldiers of the regiment. They recognised that only through an improved education
could they hope to regain their traditional influence within the community.[31]

In addition to the need to improve the general level of education among the Indians,
there was also a need to implement more specific military training. The first steps to
improve the standard of horsemanship and training in the Madras cavalry were taken
in 1787 when a riding master was appointed. A cavalry riding school was established at
Arcot in 1807 for the instruction of joining officers and recruits and a recruit training
depot was set up at the same place in 1816 for the Madras Cavalry regiments.[32] This
depot was to train 200 recruits at a time. Unfortunately, the depot was closed in 1820
and the training of recruits became, once again, a regimental responsibility. When
Ensign O'Moore Creagh joined his British regiment (the 95th) in the 1870s:

---

27   Chief Censor's Report, 18.12.15, OIOC, L/MIL/5/825.
28   Ibid.
29   Brig R.C.B. Bristow, *Memories of the British Raj* (London: Michael Joseph, 1974), p. 101.
30   Maj-Gen R.C. Duncan., *History of the Jodhpur State Forces in the War 1939–45* (Jodhpur:
     Jodhpur Government Press, 1946) p. 170.
31   See Bristow, *Memories of the British Raj*, p. 141.
32   See Maj-Gen Singh Sandhu, *The Indian Cavalry* (New Delhi: Vision Books, 1981), p. 57.

Military training was practically confined to barrack-square parades and
musketry; exercises were never carried out outside of the cantonments; parades
only took place twice a week on average.[33]

Later during the nineteenth century Schools of Instruction were set up and appro-
priate qualifications awarded. The Cavalry School at Saugor opened in 1910. The
course was six months long and most officers and a large proportion of NCOs attended.
The curriculum included equitation, skill at arms, remount training, cavalry training
and its tactical handling. Two other schools which cavalry officers attended were the
Small-Arms School at Pachmarhi and the Machine-Gun School at Ahmednagar.
Each regiment had a least one officer and a few NCOs trained in the handling of the
Vickers machine gun.

The Permanent Order Book of the 2nd Punjab Cavalry offers some valuable insights
into the training of Officers and NCOs in that regiment. An entry for 8th December
1884 sets out the proposed regime of training:

> The training in detail of the work of Native Officers and NCOs is of the greatest
> importance and up to the present time there has been no organised system of
> instructing them. Indian officers and NCOs were to be trained to parade in all
> positions. In addition, the duties of reconnoitring parties, scouts, advanced and
> rear guards, and outposts should be considered. Musketry instruction and theory
> will require to kept up. To these principal points might be added questions on
> the conduct of Native Officers and NCOs in detached command of small parties,
> either on duty at the outposts or on service, in any contingency that might arise.[34]

In 1898 the practice of examining NCOs every Wednesday in drill, riding school
drill and detached duties was introduced:

> In the next Squadron training native officers should be placed in charge of patrols.
> They should be instructed how to prepare a rough sketch of the enemy position,
> together with a report on the strength of the enemy, nature of the surroundings
> and the most suitable line of attack. Native officers will be expected to acquaint
> themselves with the use of the compass.[35]

This training, though welcome, seemed to deal very much with specifics and not to
address wider issues such as leadership and morale.

---

33  O'Moore Creagh, *Autobiography*, p. 67.
34  Permanent Order Book, Sam Browne's Cavalry, entry for 8.12.84, National Archives of
    India.
35  Ibid.

By the end of the nineteenth century there was growing support for the idea that a college should be set up specifically to train Indian officers. The syllabus for such a college might include elementary topography, map-reading, tactics, fortification, law, company accounts with the students being taught in Urdu.[36] H W Norman, writing in 1878, argued that the experience of the Franco-Prussian and Turkish Wars showed that more officers would be needed per unit. There were now higher officer casualties due to more accurate weapons and the tactic used by snipers of picking off the officers first. His view was that for the Indian Army in such a situation, the onus would fall upon the Indian officers who would therefore need to be trained to take over in such an eventuality. He wrote:

> It seems to me that if heavy casualties occur among the European officers, we must expect companies and troops often to fall under Native officers, and naturally the command will devolve upon the latter after much loss and at critical times. They should therefore be habituated to command, which cannot be the case in any system by which there is a large number of European officers.[37]

'J McD B' made the same point even more forcefully a few years later:

> Does the system of training in vogue tend to prepare the native officers for this contingency (British officers becoming casualties)? Most decidedly not. Every shred of individuality is denied him. Until self-dependence is recognised, inculcated and encouraged, we most assuredly court disaster. British officers assume command – even if inexperienced – to the detriment of native officers. Many instances might be cited from the records of our own small campaigns in which the native officer has borne himself intelligently and with credit to his regiment. We must devote more time than now to practical battle training.[38]

The anonymous writer asserted that, properly selected and trained and given the right experience, the average native officer was quite capable of leading his men on as European battlefield. He also wished to see opportunities for Indian officers to rise to ranks higher than subedar-major and risaldar-major.

When Lord Napier became Commander-in-Chief India in 1850 he instigated changes in methods of training. Earlier, training had been mostly confined to the parade ground and the endless repetition of drill movements. Napier made field training, which had previously been restricted to sham fights lasting a few hours, more realistic by introducing exercise camps. The *Cavalry Training* manual which was distributed in

---

36   See Captain A.L.Barrett, 'The appointment of Native Officers in the Indian Army', *JUSII*, Vol XXXVI, No 167, April 1907, p. 177.
37   H. W. Norman, 'Note on officering the Indian Army', 5.7.1878,OIOC, L/MIL/17/5/1686.
38   J.McD B, 'The Higher Training of infantry officers', *JUSII*, Indian ol. XIV, 1892, p. 251.

the 1880s preached 'shock tactics' and laid great stress on the drilling of the troops, and in succession, the squadrons, the regiment, the brigade and finally the division.[39] When he was a staff officer, Amar Singh observed infantry battalions going through the exercises introduced by Lord Kitchener in 1900. However, in a Memorandum on Army Training in India 1910-11, Lieutenant General Douglas Haig wrote:

> Reports show that in too many cases (cavalry) regiments arrive at brigade concentrations or manoeuvres insufficiently grounded in the first elements of cavalry evolutions. The faults have been pointed out regularly year after year, but, except in the case of a few regiments, insufficient steps have been taken to correct them.[40]

The training carried out by the Bannu Brigade in 1908 was a very well-planned exercise, including infantry and artillery as well as two cavalry regiments.[41] A mock 'village' with targets was built so that live firing could be carried out. The setting for the exercise was, however, based upon tribal warfare on the frontier. The report on the training makes no specific reference to the performance of the Indian officers. Valuable training also took place during the First World War as exemplified by Captain Grimshaw's note:

> Saturday 12 December. Reconnaissance scheme with squadron. Most useful for teaching the men to work in a foreign country. All the Indian officers told me on their return that the scheme was full of instructional value.[42]

The study of successive Army Lists enables a comparison of the qualifications of Indian officers at various dates. For instance, in the Poona Horse in 1903 the seventeen Indian officers held only five Musketry Certificate between them. By 1914 the same number of officers in the same regiment held thirteen Musketry Certificates, nine of them were qualified in MG plus three at extra or distinguished level and six held Equitation Certificates. This is clearly a significant increase in the level of training. However, Colonel Maunsell, who commanded the Scinde Horse between the World Wars, was scathing in his criticism of the Indian cavalry immediately prior to the First World War:

> As a result of inadequate training nearly the whole of the NCOs were quite incapable of imparting instruction, and a number of the Indian officers as well. The

---

39    See Shahid Hamid, *So They Rode and Fought*, p. 41.
40    Gen Sir D. Haig, Memorandum on Army Training in India, 1910-11, p. 4, OIOC, L/MIL/17/5/2198.
41    See Report on Brigade Training, Bannu Brigade. (Allalabad: Pioneer Press, 1908), NAM.
42    Grimshaw, *Indian Cavalry Officer*, p. 52.

proportion of either who could read a map was very small. There were numbers of Indian ranks who were too soft or too old to stand the strain of active service, and who, moreover, did not want to go when their chance came. It was a matter of the greatest difficulty to get rid of an incapable Indian officer owing to lack of support from higher authority. [43]

Maunsell also commented on the requirement to give 'Indian officers and NCOs a thorough grounding in elementary recruit instruction, particularly in making the men work smartly.'[44]

The need to offer Indian officers better training and more responsibility and to take more care in their selection had been made before the War; Captain Barrett pointed out that:

The requirements of modern war, and the great width of front which armies now occupy, in comparison to what they formerly did, tend to throw more and more responsibility on the native officers and call for increased initiative, self-reliance and skill on their part. They may find themselves far removed from any possibility of consulting with their British officers, and the decisions they then arrive at may seriously affect the whole course of operations. It becomes therefore continually more and more necessary that they should be thoroughly well grounded in the science of their profession. The material is excellent, it only remains to make the best of it.[45]

Another British officer wrote that:

Responsibility and initiative are not subjects that can be taught at a college but are abstract qualities that are bred in a man. To bring these qualities forward in sufficient prominence, the only method is to give frequent opportunities and ample encouragement to the young native officer to practise himself in the exercise of them.[46]

Both these writers deprecated the practice whereby the young inexperienced British officer inevitably took precedence over his older and more experienced Indian counterpart.

After the Great War and with the change in organisation of infantry companies from two half-companies to four platoons, the argument regarding the need for a

---

43 Col Maunsell, *The Scinde Horse* (Published by a Regimental Committee, 1926) p p. 45-46.
44 Ibid., p. 208.
45 Captain A.L.Barrett, 'The appointment of Native Officers in the Indian Army', *JUSII*, Vol XXXVI, No 167 April 1907, p. 177.
46 'Verb Sap' 'Our Native Officers', *JUSII*, Vol XXXVI, 1908, pp. 209-210.

College to train Indian officers re-surfaced. The new system required the platoon commanders to operate much more independently in battle and rendered central control by the company commander more difficult. Captain Bonham-Carter of the 40th Pathans who had commanded a District Platoon Commander's School wrote a long article in the *Journal of the Indian United Services Institution* in 1922. He argued that: 'Indian officers had been given very little responsibility under the old system of half-companies and had been restricted to passing on the orders of their British officers. They had little opportunity of using their own initiative and possessed no sense of command.'[47]

Selection for promotion to Viceroy's Commissioned Officer was on a regimental basis but no special training was offered to the NCO prior to his appointment. As Brigadier Dennison recounted: 'Viceroy's Commissioned Officers were selected within a unit from the best and most experienced havildars, keeping a balance of the races within the unit.'[48] Captain Bonham-Carter contrasted the training which the Indian officers received compared with that their British counterparts who emerged from Sandhurst at the end of an eighteen-month course:

> In the Indian Army, the training that a candidate receives as an NCO, and the examination which he now has to pass for promotion are considered sufficient, and the platoon commander is created at the stroke of a pen. He has no special training, no school to go through to help him understand the duties and responsibilities of his new position. He is merely created a platoon commander and left to work out his own salvation.[49]

Right up to the end of the Second World War, the VCOs were still battalion appointments.[50] Lt-Col Montagu, who commanded the 2nd/2nd Punjab Regiment, commented that:

> The VCO, was selected at battalion level because he already possessed military skills, had a grounding of literacy and was able to read and write Urdu. He knew his men – and their families – down to the last detail. However, they received no special training on promotion though they might later attend specialist courses, for instance on the 3" mortar or machine gun.[51]

A confidential handwritten note prepared by Major Owen of the Bombay Grenadiers in 1947 for the incoming battalion commander, Lt-Col Tighe, gives

---

47   Captain B. H. Bonham-Carter. 'The training of Infantry Platoon Commanders', *JUSII*, Vol LII, No 229, Oct 1922, p. 370.
48   Brigadier G.E. Dennison, 7th Battalion, 2nd Punjab Regiment, telephone interview.
49   Bonham-Carter, 'The training of Infantry Platoon Commanders', p. 370.
50   Lt Col Montagu, 2nd Battalion, 2nd Punjab Regiment, telephone interview.
51   Ibid.

an idea of the type of NCO likely to be selected for promotion. For instance, one havildar is described as 'A good reliable, capable NCO with guts and stamina. Will make a good VCO.' On the other hand, another man is described as 'Well educated but with no powers of command at all. Will never make a VCO and is not worth his salt as an NCO.'[52] In a class-company regiment, the issue of maintaining the balance of classes within a regiment when considering promotions could be especially important. In the same memo, Major Owen refers to the 'Balance of Power' within the unit. Apparently there had already been trouble and jealousy between different groups within the battalion. Major Owen ascribes this partly to the fact that there were few VCOs who were Jats from Rajputana compared to those Jats from the Punjab, leaving the former group discontented. A very strong bloc of Rangars in one company had victimised their Khaimkani and Khanzada comrades. Only Rangars were pushed forward for promotion at the expense of the other groups.[53] Major Owen therefore suggested that, as far as possible, a balance should be kept between the racial groups when appointing NCOs and VCOs. On the other hand, a promising officer might find his way upwards blocked because there were many candidates of his own class. Jemadar Jamyat Singh joined the 2nd Punjab Cavalry in 1853 and served with it for 25 years. He was promoted to Jemadar in 1859 and advanced to the 1st Class of the Order of Merit in 1862, following the campaign in Afghanistan. However, in 1878 he transferred to the 5th Punjab Cavalry as a rissaldar as an excess of officers of his rank and class meant that further advancement in the 2nd was unlikely.[54]

The appointment of the subedar-major was especially crucial, given the vital importance of his position within a regiment. Gordon Corrigan, who served with the Gurkhas and was therefore writing from experience, wrote that:

> The senior Indian officer combined many of the functions of the Second-in-Command, the RSM, the Chaplain, the Adjutant and the Station Families Officer in a British unit as well as being prophet, soothsayer, unofficial justice of the peace, marriage broker, historian and a spare company commander when needed! He was the custodian of all that made the regiment what it was. He had enormous power and prestige.[55]

According to Corrigan: 'The subedar-major was selected from the very best of the subedars. Those subedars who had been senior to him, but had failed to be selected themselves, were sent on pension.'[56] Brigadier Dennison pointed out that: 'The

---

52  Hand-written notes prepared for Lt-Col Tighe by Major Owen, Bombay Grenadiers, 1947, The Tighe Papers, NAM, B206/83-21.
53  Ibid.
54  Bengal Army List for 1877.
55  Corrigan, *Sepoys in the Trenches*, p. 10.
56  Ibid.

subedar-major, as the commanding officer's right hand man, set the tone of the regiment and ensured the highest standards throughout the unit.'[57]

The Indian Army of 1914 had concentrated on training for fighting the tribes on the North-West Frontier. Amar Singh described the training as including:

> Camps, transport, marches, convoys advanced guards, rear guards, attacks, piquets and retirements. Because the tribal groups now had modern weapons, piquets had to be positioned over 1600 yards from the main body. The necessity of greater tactical dispersion … and increasing initiative, self-reliance, skill and intelligence was evident.[58]

Regiments of the Punjab Frontier Force who spent the majority of their service on the Frontier quickly became experts in this type of warfare. In many ways the Frontier was an excellent training ground against a most skilful enemy using live ammunition. Any mistake or lapse in concentration was sure to be punished by the loss of a rifle or worse. Although experience of this type of warfare was no preparation for the conditions which the Indians were to experience in France in 1914.

However, change was coming and training improved. The Annual Report on Indian State Forces for 1926-27 contains an Appendix that details of a course held at Gwalior in 1927 between January and March for senior officers of the State Forces.[59] Lectures from the course commandant and his second-in-command covered topics such as Map Reading, Training of NCOs, Use of Sand Models, Attack, Defence, Reconnaissance, Night operations, Rearguards and Retirement and Mountain Warfare. The tactics were being taught at company and squadron level. Demonstrations, carried out by the 4th Gwalior Infantry and 3rd Gwalior Lancers included the company as an advanced guard to a battalion, intercommunication in the field, the personnel of a battalion in attack, a squadron as an advanced guard, the company in the attack, an out-post Company etc, together with a demonstration by the Royal Engineers and another on the Lewis Gun. Schemes were linked to the lectures and demonstrations and there were more specialised lectures on topics such as camouflage, armoured cars, machine guns and supply in the field.

As we have seen, following defeat by the Japanese and the retreat from Burma in 1942 there was a dramatic re-assessment of the Indian Army's training. There had not been enough time for the basic training of the infantry units and there had been a lack of experienced leaders, partly due to the vigorous 'milking' which had taken place. The Infantry Committee's Report of 1943 stressed the need for a simple, consistent and

---

57    Brigadier G.E. Dennison, 7th Battalion, 2nd Punjab Regiment, telephone interview.
58    Amar Singh diary, 28. 10. 19.
59    See Annual Report on State Forces 1926/7, OIOC, L/P and S/13/268/Col2/4.

recognised jungle warfare doctrine.[60] Units were taken out of the line for systematic retraining. Pamphlets were produced for circulation in order to draw out the lessons learnt in battle and to share best practice. Fighting in the jungle meant that the key elements were the infantry sections and platoons and the significance of well-trained NCOs and VCOs was therefore all the greater.

Lack of even an elementary education was to be a problem for recruits to the Indian Army throughout the nineteenth century and into the twentieth. In the British Army the officers came in the main from the educated upper class whereas the Indian officers were promoted from the ranks. The establishment of regimental schools and the insistence on NCOs ( and thus eventually Indian officers) being in possession of educational certificates went at least some way towards remedying this deficiency. Much more serious was the total lack of specific training for VCOs. They received no special training either prior to, or on, appointment and had only their considerable experience on which to rely.

60   See Report of the Infantry Committee, India, June 1-14 1943, OIOC, L/WS/1/1371, quoted in Marston, *Phoenix from the Ashes*, pp. 96-97.

# 11

## The Changing Perception of the Role of the Indian Officer

---

Two vignettes, separated by almost exactly one hundred years, illustrate the professional competence of the Indian officer. In 1853, General Robertson inspected the Scinde Horse. His report included the following comments:

> On separate mornings, I caused the regiments to parade singly under the personal command of the senior native officers, Risaldars Shaik Abdool Nabbee and Mohbut Khan Bahadoor. The words of command were given in the most excellent English and repeated by squadron officers and troop commanders in a most perfect manner. Both regiments worked under these native officers in a most creditable style and all praise is due to Major Jacob and his officers for the manner in which they have taught those under their command to conduct themselves in every situation.[1]

The second incident, which took place towards the end of the Second World War, is reported by John Masters, a British officer who had served with the Gurkhas and who at that time was commanding a Brigade. The Indian Army had not been allowed to possess any field artillery from the time of the Mutiny until just before the Second World War. Now, the Indian (artillery) colonel, bending close to an English colonel over a map, straightened and said with a smile, 'OK George. Thanks, I've got it. We'll take over all tasks (ie predetermined artillery targets) at 1800. What about a beer?[2]

Sadly, in the intervening ninety years between 1857 and 1947, many Indian officers were to be denied opportunities to demonstrate their leadership qualities. The degree of responsibility allowed to Indian officers varied considerably throughout this period. Initially, Indian officers had a considerable amount of autonomy, especially in the

---

1  Record Book of the Scinde Irregular Horse, Vol II, 3rd October 1851 to 13th June 1855, p. 81.
2  John Masters, *The Road past Mandalay* (London: Michael Joseph, 1981), p. 313.

so-called 'irregular' regiments. This degree of freedom was to decline during the first half of the nineteenth century as the numbers of British officers in regiments increased. The Mutiny gave rise to a re-appraisal and throughout the second half of the century there was an on-going debate between those who argued for better training and more responsibility for the Indian officers and those who wished to restrict their role. Unfortunately it was the latter group who won the argument with the result that when the Indian Army went to war in 1914, the Indian officers were unused to responsibility and some were unable to use their initiative when their British officers became casualties. After the Great War, King's Commissions were offered to a small number of Indians and the 'Indian Sandhurst' was set up at Dehra Dun in 1932 and a programme of 'Indianisation' introduced. This was envisaged as leading – eventually – to all officers in the Indian Army being Indians though it was to be a very gradual process. A side effect, foreseen or otherwise, was to downgrade the position of the jemadars and risaldars who had gained their Viceroy's Commissions through service in the ranks and who, in many cases, came to be seen as glorified NCOs.

The debate about the proper role and responsibility of Indian officers within the Indian Army began immediately after the Mutiny. Enlightened officers such as John Jacob and George Chesney argued that not only ought Indian officers to be given more responsibility but that change was inevitable. It was an argument that was to continue throughout the second half of the nineteenth century and into the twentieth. It took the Second World War to bring about the large-scale commissioning of Indian officers on the same basis as their British counterparts. Nor was there always any clear definition of the part which Indian officers were expected to play within the regiment. As early as 1826 Captain W Badenach pointed out, when discussing the posting of British sergeants and sergeant-majors to each Indian infantry battalion, that:

> Strange as it may appear, up to the present period, the most important point connected with their (Indian officers) duty has never been sufficiently defined. This has sometimes been productive of very serious consequences and created discontent among the native officers.[3]

Opinion among the British officers regarding the ability of the Indian officers to take greater responsibility and to act independently was divided. Some British officers argued strongly in favour of Indian officers and their capability. Lord Napier stated that:

> His personal knowledge satisfied his Excellency of their (Indian officers) general efficiency and of their ability to command their troops and companies and to perform their duties when on detached command and removed from the immediate control of British officers. He particularly noticed the intelligence and

---

3   Quoted in Menezes, *The Indian Army*, p. 105.

comparatively superior education of many of the Native commissioned officers and non-commissioned officers of the Bombay army. The Native officers of the Bengal Army showed during the famine a very high standard of intelligence, administrative ability and integrity.[4]

General Jacob in an Appendix to the same memorandum, wrote that: 'the Native officers under a proper organisation would be the very nerve of the whole body, of which the sepoys formed the bones and muscles and the European gentlemen the brains.'[5] Jacob was a strong supporter of the Indian officer and argued, on the basis of his experience as a commander of irregular cavalry regiments (the 1st and 2nd Scinde Horse), that there should be the absolute minimum of hand-picked British officers. In 1826 for instance, the Hyderabad cavalry regiments had only three British officers (one of whom was the surgeon) together with nine Indian officers.[6] Philip Mason quotes Jacob as saying that if there were too many British officers: 'the native officer finds himself of no importance and the sepoy becomes a lifeless automaton.'[7] Jacob believed that Indian officers, picked for their energy and efficiency, should be trusted and given real responsibility. He went so far as to suggest that Indian officers were better than junior British officers as commanders of isolated outposts. However, as Mason points out, one of the difficulties with the arrangement proposed by Jacob was, that with such a small number of British officers in a unit, they were on duty virtually all the time and it was unclear what would happen if they all became casualties. He questions whether the Scinde Horse would be able to function when their three officers were dead as: 'Their Indian officers had no experience of commanding anything more than a squadron.'[8]

Sir George Chesney, Military Member of the Supreme Council, wrote in 1888 regarding the military education of Indians:

> I venture to suggest that the time has come when, on grounds of justice no less than of policy, it is right and proper to open a military career to the higher classes of the Native subjects of the Queen, including the Native soldiers already in the army who are deserving of advancement. The present status of a Native officer is very suitable for the class which in the main has hitherto filled it – the ignorant peasant promoted from the ranks. But there have always been serving

---

4    Lord Napier: Response to a letter from the Military Department to the Adjutant General in India, the Governors of Madras and Bombay and the Lt Governor of the Punjab, OIOC, L/MIL/7/7240.

5    Gen J. Jacob, Appendix to the Memorandum which includes comments from a number of eminent British officers, OIOC, L/MIL/7/7240.

6    See Major E.A.W. Stotherd, *History of the Thirtieth Lancers (Gordon's Horse)* (Aldershot: Gale and Polden, 1911), pp. 18-19.

7    Mason, *A Matter of Honour*, p. 323.

8    Ibid., p. 325.

in the cavalry many Native gentlemen of a much higher class, although they too are most of them illiterate, and, although good soldiers, uneducated ones. The class of Native officers in all branches is now, however, rapidly improving and selection from the ranks is now made on merit rather than on seniority and in the infantry as well as in the cavalry, direct commissions are frequently given to men of good family.[9]

He drew attention to the opportunities for advancement which were opening up for Indians in the Civil administration, while at the same time there were no similar opportunities for Indians serving with the Army: 'The class which remains loyal and silent, and which asks for nothing, gets nothing.' He believed that it was impossible to maintain the status quo and that it was far more dangerous to stand still than to advance and to enter 'a policy of trust.' The increasing pressure of public opinion would inevitably lead to change in the military system. He suggested that enhancing the status and role of Indian officers would have not only a practical but also a pecuniary advantage. Giving the Indian officers increased power and responsibilities would help to overcome a potential shortage of British officers. Indian officers should be educated 'in modern military requirements,' so that they could, when necessary, take the place of the British officers when they was absent.[10]

Unfortunately, these progressive ideas were not taken up and the traditional view of the Indian officer and his abilities was maintained. The conservative view was based largely on racial prejudice. As Major Young wrote at the time:

> Be the native officer ever so capable, ever so zealous, ever so trustworthy, ever so plucky, the sepoy does not believe in him, nor will he attempt, under his native officer, feats which he will both attempt and succeed in under a British one.[11]

Lord Roberts, Commander in Chief in India, 1885-1893, was a strong advocate of the Indian Army and very popular with the sepoys. However, he was probably expressing the views of typical British officer when he wrote:

> Native officers can never take the place of British officers ... Eastern races, however brave and accustomed to war, do not possess the qualities that go to make good leaders of men ... I have known many natives whose gallantry and devotion could not be surpassed but I have never known one who would not have looked to the youngest British officer for support in time of difficulty or danger.[12]

---

9    Sir G. Chesney, Military Education for Natives of India, 1888. OIOC, L/MIL/17/5/2202.
10   Ibid
11   Major G.F.Young, 'The Efficiency of our Native Regiments with a view to their preparation to meet an European Army', *JUSII*, Vol. 9, 1885, p. 128.
12   Quoted in Mason, *A Matter of Honour*, p. 347.

However, as Philip Mason points out, the Indian officers were taught to turn to the British officers – they were subordinates who might well be blamed if they did not.

> Progressively, as the (nineteenth) century wore on to the Mutiny, the native officer became less of an ally and more of a foreman. The new native officer was a subordinate, if an honoured one. He was emphatically much closer to the men than to the British officers.[13]

Mason suggests that the growth of the idea that the sepoys must be commanded by: 'gentlemen, men of education and understanding' is due, in part at least, to the change in the English class system which followed the French Revolution and which created a deeper division between the classes. He wrote that 'In the later days of Queen Victoria the English, without much consciousness of what they were doing, were building up an imperial ruling class of public-school boys, trained on the classics, cold baths and bodily exercise.'[14]

The Indian officer, who had not had the benefit, if it may be so termed, of an English public school education, if indeed he had received any education at all, came increasingly to be seen as a second-class citizen when compared to his English counterpart. Respected and trusted he might be, but there was certainly no possibility of him being promoted to command a battalion. Sir George Chesney stated that:

> For the ordinary Native officer as he is found at present, the question of educating him to a higher standard practically does not arise. The Native officers whose merits have brought them to notice as deserving of further advancement are practically illiterate and middle-aged men, who cannot now be sent to school, and they all, I believe, labour under the disadvantage of not knowing English. Some of the best of them have had little or no education of any kind, even to the extent of being able to read and write in their own language.[15]

Because in the early days of the Indian Army the British officers did not speak the language of their men nor understand their customs, they needed intermediaries – the Indian officers – in the command structure to interpret their orders to their men. As recently as 1965, Brigadier Grant in an article entitled '*Carry on Subedar*' could suggest that;

> The Indian officer's main job was to interpret to the men the thought process of the British officer by suitably translating it into the Indian pattern of thinking

---

13   Ibid., p. 174.
14   Ibid., p. 328.
15   Sir G. Chesney, Military Education for the Natives of India, 1888. OIOC, L/MIL/17/5/2202.

and execution. His second task was to relieve the British officer of the strain and stress of direct command, and to take the first shock of any indiscipline or mismanagement.[16]

Major John Jacob, then commanding the Scinde Irregular Horse wrote to the Assistant Adjutant General (who dealt with appointments and promotions) of the Scinde Division in 1849 asking for appointment of a Risaldar-Major.

The Risaldar-Major completes the connection between the European Commandant and the Native soldiers on all manner of subjects, not always directly connected with the ordinary routine of military duty but on which the excellence of the Native soldier very greatly depend. In fact, in a Native regiment, an officer in the position of Risaldar-Major, by whatever name called, is required to ensure a perfect understanding and mutual confidence between the Englishman and the Asiatic The appointment is one of great repute and respectability and is something to look forward to as a reward for long and meritorious service.[17]

The view of the function of the Indian officer as an intermediary continued until the end of the Raj. Brigadier Grant quotes the Commander-in-Chief's Instructions of 1945 which define the duties of the senior VCO who is seen as occupying the position of confidential adviser to the commanding officer and who is supposed to reflect the pulse of the unit to him.[18] The best Indian officers were in close touch with the sepoys or sowars and could pass on grievances to their commanding officers. When the relatively minor mutinies of the period 1858 to 1947 occurred, it was often because this system had broken down, for whatever reason. Brigadier Dennison, who served through the Second World War in the 7th Battalion 2nd Punjab Regiment, indicated that the VCOs provided the close link between British officers and their Indian soldiers whose different nationality, religion and customs, it was considered, made this necessary. Whatever the origins, it provided an excellent working relationship that fostered friendship, loyalty and superb team spirit. The British officers and jawans accepted the VCOs for what they were, reliable, dedicated, able officers who had the Army's interests as their prime concern. The VCOs were perceived by the soldiers as wise elders, authoritative and gallant soldiers; they were seen by the British officers as experienced, wise, reliable soldiers who were entirely trustworthy – an excellent link in the chain of command.[19]

16   Brigadier N. B.Grant, 'Carry on Subedar' in *JUSII,* July/Sept 1965, p. 317.
17   Gen J. Jacob, Letter to the Assistant Adjutant General in *Record Book of the Scinde Irregular Horse,* OIOC, L/MIL/7/7240.
18   See Grant, 'Carry on Subedar', p 138.
19   Brigadier G.E.Dennison, 7th Battalion, 2nd Punjab Regiment. Private Communication.

Brigadier Dennison's comments are echoed by Lt Col Montagu of the 2nd Battalion, 2nd Punjab Regt who agreed that Indian officers were given rather more respect by the British officers than they would give to British NCOs. In his view, there was a strong and deep link between the British officers and the Indian officers encompassing mutual respect, loyalty and affection. The Indian officers were a necessary and very effective strata of command and they were selected because they already possessed military skills, had a grounding of literacy and were able to read and write Urdu.[20] In many regiments the newly promoted VCO was brought to British officer's mess for a drink by Risaldar-Major and his Squadron Risaldar; this was an important occasion and all British officers were expected to be present.[21]

However, not all British officers were happy with the Indian officer as an intermediary. Major Young wrote in 1885 that:

> The idea that a native officer is necessary as a 'link' between the British officer and the sepoy is, I believe, a fallacy – at all events as far as the Punjab sepoy is concerned. Over and over again I have felt that the native officer stood like an impenetrable wall between me and the men. Only now and then, out shooting perhaps with one or two, does one get any insight into their real character and ways of thought; once in the presence of, or near, a native officer the sepoy becomes a thing of wood and without any idea other than what he knows his native officer intends him to have. And the native officer, as a rule, prefers he should be blind, and deaf and dumb.[22]

British sergeant-majors were not unknown to have wished the same of a British private soldier.

Indian officers enjoyed a position of considerable importance and status within their regiments. Even though the oldest and most senior of them were subordinate to the most newly joined British subaltern, they carried swords, were saluted by other ranks and were addressed as 'sahib'. According to Charles Allen:

> Although the most senior Native Officer was nominally junior to the lowliest British subaltern, no junior British officer worth his salt would do other than confer with and defer to his Native officers, many of whom were twice or even three times his age.[23]

---

20    Lt-Col Montagu, 2nd Battalion, 2nd Punjab Regiment. Private Communication.
21    Captain Keown., Probyn's Horse. Private Communication.
22    Major G.F. Young, 'The Efficiency of our Native Regiments', *JUSII*, Vol 9, 1885, p. 130.
23    Charles Allen, *Soldier Sahibs: The Men who made the North-West Frontier* (London: John Murray, 2000) p. x.

Byron Farwell supports this view:

> The senior Indian officer enjoyed enormous prestige. For the young soldier he served as the village patriarch; for the commanding officer he was an adviser on Indian customs and personnel matters. He was treated with respect by the junior British officers, who took care not to offend him.[24]

Captain Guest of the 8th Cavalry confirms the importance of the Indian officers:

> The real stability of an Indian Cavalry regiment undoubtedly lay in the reliable hands of the senior Indian officers. These wonderful men with their long periods of service – many of them serving for thirty years or more – were the mainstay of any regiment. With their great experience they were always ready to advise and guide any young British officer through the many problems which confronted him from time to time.[25]

The VCOs were the middlemen, 'God's own gentlemen' who stood at the elbow of every inexperienced British subaltern.[26] Chenevix Trench in his study of the Indian Army includes a story related by a young British officer serving in the 45th (Rattray's) Sikhs. The young man having been selected to attend a young officers' rifle course at Pachmarhi was practising his bayonet fighting under the best instructor in the regiment, watched by the Subedar Major. The officer thought that he was doing well but was taken aside by the Subedar Major who said:

> Huzoor, I hope you will forgive me mentioning it, but your bayonet fighting leaves more than a little to be desired. I hope that you will put in considerably more practice before you go to Pachmarhi. When you get there, you must never forget that you represent the 45th Sikhs.[27]

Colonel Adrian Hayter describes the assistance which he received from the subedar who was second-in-command of his company when he joined the 2nd Gurkha Rifles as a young officer. The Subedar had years of experience in the regiment and was addressed as 'father' by the young soldiers:

> He guided me through those early years without my fully realising it then. Slowly he built up my morale and self-confidence by leading the discussion of any problem in such a way that the answer became obvious out of my own mind;

---

24   Farwell, *Armies of the Raj* (London: Viking, 1989), p. 28.
25   Captain F. Guest, *Indian Cavalryman* (London: Jarrolds Publishers, 1959), p. 138.
26   Mason, *A Matter of Honour*, p. 321.
27   Chenevix Trench, *The Indian Army and the King's Enemies*, p. 16.

he never directly corrected me to leave my own mind unexercised and with a feeling of inadequacy. He shielded the men from my worst blunders, by his never failing support of me showing an example to them, and so he gradually brought understanding of each other to both.[28]

Major Corrigan, who served with the Gurkha Rifles, wrote that:

The Viceroy's Commissioned Officers were men of great ability, naturally highly intelligent, knowing everything that could be known about low-level soldiering and with a deep knowledge and understanding of their men and the background whence they came. They were brave, outstandingly loyal and impeccably disciplined. The Indian officer saw himself as having a vital role to play ... and as having a vested interest in ensuring that the British officer's ideas were correctly put into practice. To function properly an Indian regiment needed both British and Indian officers and neither was capable of doing the job of the other except for short periods.[29]

Corrigan is one of the few British writers seriously to examine the role of Indian officers. He argues that the division between the British and Indian officers was not a matter of racial prejudice but rather a differentiation of roles. 'The Indian Army operated by using the British officer as the instigator and promulgator of policy, while the Indian officer executed it.'[30] The perceived impartiality of the British officer in matters of caste etc was another important factor.

However, the greater the number of British officers in a unit, the lower the status of the Indian officers and the less their authority. Racial prejudice made the thought of placing Indian officers in command of British troops, and especially of British officers, quite unacceptable. Sir Charles Egerton stated that in his view:

It is not only impolitic but practically impossible to place European officers or soldiers in any position of subordination to Natives of India. How can we encourage an increase in the self-reliance and importance of the native officer without weakening or diminishing that almost unconscious assumption of authority over indigenous races on the part of junior British officers, which however open to condemnation theoretically, is an essential characteristic of our nationality?

He suggested that the status of Indian officers could be enhanced by their more honourable recognition by the Civil Authorities. Their commissions should be signed by the Sovereign himself (as those of British officers were) and there

---

28   Col A. Hayter, *The Second Step* (London: Hodder and Stoughton, 1962), p. 50.
29   Corrigan, *Sepoys in the Trenches*, p. 12.
30   Ibid., p. 11.

should be positions of Honorary rank for specially selected officers: 'Only men of undoubted social position and influence should be selected with whom the Imperial Cadets could associate on equal terms.'[31] There is a note on Egerton's paper by 'AE' who sounds a warning: 'There seems to be a danger that we shall be treating the Native officer like the possessor of the one talent and 'take away even that which he seemeth to have.'[32]

An officer who identified himself only under the pseudonym 'Verb Sap' wished to see the Indian officers given more responsibility and greater status and wrote in the *Journal of the Indian United Services Institution* in 1908: 'The British officer is made to dwarf the native officer out of existence. What is wanted is for the native officer to be taken seriously. He is an officer and must receive an officer's treatment.' He realised that the system then current did not encourage the Indian officers to take responsibility or to use their initiative, writing:

> Responsibility and initiative are not subjects that can be taught at a college but are abstract qualities that are bred in a man. To bring these qualities forward in sufficient prominence, the only method is to give frequent opportunities and ample encouragement to the young native officer to practise himself in the exercise of them.[33]

Nor were Indian officers always accorded the respect due to them. On his way home from France, Amar Singh's boat stopped at Malta where they celebrated Christmas. The British officers treated the Indian officers (all but one of them Gurkhas) to drinks and cigarettes. Amar Singh appreciated being invited to the event and was deeply touched talking to the Indian officers. He wrote: 'These brave but simple men had some very bad experiences of warfare and were excellent men. I felt very proud of them.' Amar Singh was quick to defend the status of Indian officers, believing as he did that they should be saluted by British troops. When a British Quarter-Master Sergeant mistreated and insulted a Gurkha jemadar on board the ship, the sergeant was quickly reprimanded by his Colonel and Amar Singh translated the reprimand for the Gurkha officer.[34] Captain Roly Grimshaw of the Poona Horse recounts a similar incident when a R.A.M.C. officer wished to move Indian officers out of a first-class compartment on a train in order to provide accommodation for British warrant officers.[35]

The Character Roll of Native Officers and NCOs of the 1st Battalion, 2nd King's Edward's Own Gurkha Rifles contains comments written annually probably by their

---

31   Sir C. Egerton, Military Education for the Natives of India, OIOC, L/MIL/17/5/2202.
32   Ibid
33   'Verb Sap', 'Our Native Officers' *JUSII*, Vol XXXVI, p. 208/209.
34   Amar Singh's Diary, 7. 3. 16.
35   See Grimshaw, *Indian Cavalry Officer 1914-15*, p. 28.

company commanders, or possibly by the adjutant.[36] These offer us a valuable insight into the qualities of the Gurkha officers as perceived by their British officers. For instance the comment written on Subedar Motilal Lama in 1913 states that he is 'Thoroughly straightforward and reliable. A Gurkha officer with lots of presence and a natural aptitude for command.' He subsequently rose to the rank of subedar-major. The comment of the same date on his colleague Subedar Sarahjih Gurung states that he is 'Smart, intelligent, reliable and very hard working. Well satisfied with him in every way.' Both of these officers were later awarded the Order of British India, 2nd Class.[37]

Comments written thirty years later on their successors stress the same qualities. Jemadar Ganesh Gurung was a awarded a Military Cross during the Malayan Emergency of 1948 to 1960: 'He is a really first class Gurkha officer, intelligent, clever, well-qualified and not afraid to use his initiative. Well above the average Gurkha officer.'[38] Jemadar Jakul Pun, who also won the Military Cross in Malaya, is described as 'A good platoon commander with plenty of personality. He is keen and steady and has a good command of his men.'[39] Comments on Subedar-Major Gaganing Rana include the following:

> I have only known this officer for two months. During that time he has given me every possible assistance and has been loyal to a degree. An excellent disciplinarian who is respected by all those serving under him.[40]

Jemadar Panchsube Gurung of the 1st/2nd King Edward's Own Gurkha Rifles was awarded an immediate Military Cross following his leadership in a successful ambush in Waziristan. The Digest of Service commented: 'The complete calmness displayed by him during and after the fight and his methodical, yet exceptional, surprise tactics were most notable.'[41] These comments, and many other similar remarks on their comrades, show that these men possessed all of the attributes necessary in order to command in battle and indeed did from time to time exercise such command. Loyal to their British officers, they were firm disciplinarians but had the respect of their men. They had grown up in the regiment and would often have come from the same area in Nepal as their men. This meant that there was a mutual understanding between them and the men that they commanded. As Sir Charles Egerton pointed out 'The whole history of the Native army teems with instances of skill and courage shown by Native officers when thrown upon their own resources.'[42]

36   The Character Roll is now in the Gurkha Museum, Winchester.
37   Ibid.
38   Ibid., comment dated 1949.
39   Ibid., comment dated 1947.
40   Ibid., comment dated 1947.
41   Digest of Service 1/2 KEO Gurkha Rifles in the Gurkha Museum, Winchester.
42   Sir Charles Egerton, Note on the Status of Indian Officers, OIOC, L/MIL/7/7152.

At the start of the nineteenth century, Indian officers could be given consider-able responsibility. An article by Sir John Malcolm recounts how, in 1799,during the Fourth Mysore War, Subedar Cawder Beg, of the 3rd Regiment of Native Cavalry in the Madras Army, was given command of a force of 2000 men. This force consisted of infantry from the 11th (Madras) Regiment and cavalry provided by the Nizam of Hyderabad and its purpose was to prevent bandits attacking the supply trains of the main army. Sir John wrote:

> Scarcely a load of grain was lost, hardly a day passed that the activity and strat-egies of Cawder Beg did not delude some of the enemy's plunderers to their destruction. Personal courage was the least quality of Cawder Beg. His talents eminently fitted him for the exercise of military command.[43]

Recognising the many virtues of the Indian officer, in spite of their lack of a formal education, Sir Charles Egerton wrote:

> Though their education may be deficient according to our standards, they possess a natural shrewdness, combined with a gift of observation, and a power of adapting themselves to circumstances, that go far to make up that deficiency. They are keen judges of character and of course understand the idiosyncrasies of their fellow countrymen as no European can ever hope to do.[44]

Byron Farwell comments that:

> The VCOs were men of great ability, naturally highly intelligent, knowing everything that could be known about low-level soldiering and with a deep knowledge and understanding of their men and the background from whence they came – a background they shared. They were brave, outstandingly loyal and impeccably disciplined. They were not, however, educated men. They had little knowledge of, and less interest in, the Army outside their own immediate regimental family.[45]

From the earliest days, Indian soldiers who did well in battle were rewarded with money, promotion, presentation swords – even loot. The Indian Order of Merit was established (the latter with a small stipend of 2 rupees a day) as an incentive in 1837. The IOM was issued in three classes and the soldier had to be awarded the bronze

---

43   Sir J. Malcolm,. An article in the *Quarterly Review* for January 1818, quoted in Lt Col W.J. Wilson, *The Historical Records of the 4th PWO Madras Light Cavalry* (Madras: Foster and Co., 1877).
44   Sir Charles Egerton, Note on the Status of Indian Officers, OIOC, L/MIL/7/7152.
45   Farwell, *Armies of the Raj*, p. 30.

and silver medals before being entitled to consideration for the gold medal. The gold medal was abolished when Indian soldiers became eligible for the Victoria Cross in 1911. Between 1911 and 1947, some 40 Indian soldiers were awarded the VC. Indian officers on retirement were occasionally given honorary commissions as lieutenant or captains. This was not only an honour but it doubled the officer's pension which in 1900 was only about 10 rupees a month. Sometimes pensions included land grants. After the Great War, all those soldiers who had received decorations or rendered distinguished service were given titles and allotted large areas of fertile land so that they could live in comfort in their old age. 420,000 acres of land were distributed among the 5,902 VCOs and other ranking Indian officers. Specially selected VCOs received grants of land and pensions and some two hundred of them were granted honorary King's Commissions which entitled them to higher pensions.

The rank of subedar-major was initially instituted in 1818 in order to increase the prospects for Indian officers. Sir Henry Russell, Resident of Hyderabad, stated in evidence in 1832 to the Parliamentary Select Committee on the Affairs of the East India Company that:

> The chief cause of discontent of native officers is that once they have attained the rank of Subedar, they have nothing more to look to; having got all that they can get, they have no further inducement to exert themselves; they first become indolent, then dissatisfied. There ought to be some higher object kept in their view to which by diligence and fidelity they may still attain. There was a native officer of the Madras establishment of the name of Mohammed Yusuf, who was entrusted in the early British operations with a considerable independent command, of which he discharged the duties with judgement and fidelity.[46]

In 1844, Sir Henry Lawrence pointed out that despite the sop of the creation of the ranks of subedar-major and risaldar-major

> There are many commandants in the Maratta and Seikh service, who were privates in our army. Is it not absurd that the ranks of subedar-major and risaldar-major are the highest that a native can attain in a native army of nearly three hundred thousand men, in a land that above all others has been accustomed to see its military merit rewarded and to witness the successive rise of families from the lowest conditions, owing to gallantry in the field.[47]

The Indian officer was normally promoted from within the non-commissioned ranks of his own unit, although there were instances right up to the end of the nineteenth century of officers of higher social standing being awarded direct commissions,

---

46   Quoted in Menezes *The Indian Army*, p. 23.
47   Ibid., p. 25.

especially in the cavalry. Given their general lack of education and low social background, coupled with the high degree of racial and social prejudice within the British community at this time, it is not surprising that the position of the Indian officer was always anomalous. Those far-sighted British officers who argued for change and for enhanced status for their Indian colleagues were always in the minority, right up to the Second World War. Indian officers might be rewarded with medals, pensions and grants of land but the perception during the nineteenth century and the first half of the twentieth century was that they could never be the equal of the public school educated and Sandhurst-trained British officer. The commonly held view was that, when the crunch came, the sepoy, and indeed the Indian officer, would always turn to the British officer for leadership. It was this failure to recognise that, given the education and training of his British counter-part, the Indian officer was at least his equal, that led, in part at least, to the difficulties experienced by the Indian Corps in France in 1914-15.

# Conclusion

Can it be believed that the countries which produced the armies of Hyder Ali and Tippoo cannot now give so many as two men out of a hundred possessed of courage and intellect enough to command a troop or company under every circumstance? History and practical experience are opposed to such an opinion.[1]

The British owe an enormous debt to the Indian Army. They were with us in the First World War, they were at Gallipoli, they were with us in the Second World War. The British had the benefit of a wonderful Army which they used in many places.[2]

The Indian Army has a proud record stretching back to the time of the Great Mughals and beyond and the army of the British Raj was but a brief spell in that long history. The Raj gave India a railway system, cricket and a common language – English. It also bequeathed an army, an army which would cherish its enhanced traditions gained under British rule, and which would become highly professional and as effective as that of the Mughals or Mahrattas. Indian soldiers fought bravely in two World Wars as well as in many minor campaigns. Because the Indian infantry left France in 1915, their exploits have been largely forgotten and overshadowed by those of the Australians, Canadians and New Zealanders who followed them. But the Indians were the first of the troops from the Empire in the field and their contribution to the First Battle of Ypres was vital. It is just possible that, without their presence, the Germans might have broken though. Though the Indian cavalry had little opportunity to show their mettle in France, they achieved great success in Palestine. The Indian Army of the Second World War was the largest ever volunteer army ever assembled which carried out the longest retreat in the history of the British Army before giving the Japanese Army its greatest ever defeat on land.

In India soldiering was always been seen as an honourable profession in a way in which it never has in Great Britain. For a Hindu, to bear arms was a profession

---

1   Lord Napier, Memorandum 1875, para 22, IOIOC, L/MIL/7/7240.
2   A British Officer speaking on Radio 4 *Stand at East*, a programme on the Indian Army, transmitted 04/06/05.

second only to the priesthood while it was the highest possible calling for a Muslim. To be a soldier in India was to enjoy respect in one's community in a manner to which the average British soldier was quite unaccustomed. The concept of *izzat*, of honour which made sepoys ready to risk their lives, was another potent factor in determining the effectiveness of the Indian soldier. British officers, when writing their regimental histories argued that their soldiers had given their lives for 'the honour of the Regiment' which they regarded as their 'mother and father'. They died for *izzat*, the idea of not letting down one's family, village or regiment and upholding its values and traditions. Major General Rafiuddin Ahmad and Major Rifat Nadeem Ahmad, the regimental historians of the 8th Punjab Regiment put it thus: 'It was honour that kept them true to their oath and led them to such extraordinary feats of bravery and self-sacrifice; and made the British Indian Army envy of the world.'[3]

Although an artificial concept imported from Europe and strongly linked to the martial race theory, regimental loyalty, closely linked to *izzat*, was an important factor in the organisation and effectiveness of the Indian Army.[4] In a less innocent and more materialistic world the almost mystical reverence shown by the Indian soldiers towards the King-Emperor, a figure whom many of them would have never seen or at best glimpsed in the distance at some review or durbar, seems hard to understand. The closeness of the 'regimental family' is a key aspect in determining the efficiency and effectiveness of a unit. Through the martial race system, Indian regiments recruited from specific localities in a way in which British regiments generally did not. When the British recruiting officer went out into the villages he was met by pensioners eager to hear news of the Regiment and their old comrades. Family ties took on a quite literal meaning when son, and in time his son, followed father into the regiment so that successive generations served in the same regiment often eventually rising to the same senior ranks

Linked to the concept of honour was the Indian's rather more fatalistic approach to death. Balwant Singh, of the Jodhpur Lancers wrote home in September 1917: 'It is the special duty of a Kshastriya to give his life for his King on the battlefield.'[5] The Indian officers of the Raj were just as capable as their British counterparts, in spite of the latter's superior education, and that the part which they played in the maintenance of high standards within their units was crucial. The Indian officers were 'ordinary' men from the villages of India; the equivalent, perhaps, of Gray's 'village Hampdens and Cromwells'[6] They may have been uneducated but they were brave – almost foolhardy at times, proud, incredibly loyal and often deeply religious. They offered unstinting support to their British officers, many of whom were much less

---

3   Major General Rafiuddin Ahmad and Major Rifat Nadeem Ahmad, *Unfaded Glory: The 8th Punjab Regiment* (Uckfield: Naval and Military Press, 2006) p. 348.
4   See Roy, *Brown Warriors of the Raj*, p. 190 et seq.
5   Report of the Chief Censor, OIOC, L/MIL/5/827.
6   Thomas Gray, *Elegy Written in a Country Churchyard* (1751).

experienced than themselves. Their letters home reveal that their concerns were those of ordinary men. Yet they were capable, when given the opportunity, of providing inspirational leadership.

There was a symbiotic relationship between the British government in India and the Indian Army. Though the army was just part of the framework of collaboration upon which the British depended in order to govern India, they needed the Army in particular in order, in the last resort, to take over from the police and to control the country. In order to secure their loyalty the British saw to it that the troops were relatively well paid and could retire on good pensions often with grants of land in addition. This made soldiering an attractive career, especially to those races with a martial background. Some Indian nationalists saw the sepoys as mercenaries fighting for a foreign power and made, generally unsuccessful, attempts to suborn them, as for instance with the so-called Indian National Army formed by the Japanese. As Independence drew near, however, the nationalists realised that that they, too, would depend upon a loyal and professional Army just as much as the British had before them.

Although symbiotic, the relationship was not seen, by the British at least, as an arrangement between *equal* partners. Imperialism appears to be almost inevitably linked to feelings of condescension and of superiority; the conqueror always tends to look down upon the conquered – their customs, culture and their abilities. The British in India often treated the Indians with an appalling lack of good manners. Lord Napier wrote that:

> I confess that the Native officers (in Bengal) did not appear to me to be treated generally as Native Officers are treated on this side of India (i.e. Madras); that is, with the courtesy and consideration due to gentlemen holding commissions. I may have been misled by appearances but such was my impression.[7]

Though there were a few honourable exceptions to the general pattern, the sheer racial prejudice and snobbery of the majority of British officers and their wives was one of the main reasons why Indian officers were not permitted to advance to the higher ranks of command before the Second World War. Philip Mason argued that, on the whole, this was due to ignorance and that this tendency increased during the nineteenth century. This may be perhaps because the position of the British in India was growing ever stronger – the English were becoming intoxicated with power.[8] Lord Macaulay writing in the 1830s stated that he, 'Looked forward to the proudest day in English history when a grateful India would set up on her own as a free country.'[9] This more liberal notion of trusteeship was by no means widely held among the British especially among the less well-educated. There was resentment and jealousy of the

7    Lord Napier, Memorandum, L/MIL/17/5/1674.
8    See Mason, *A Matter of Honour*, p. 197.
9    Quoted in Menezes, *The Indian Army*, p. 403.

increasing education and employment opportunities for Indians and a consequent fear that Indians would take over jobs hitherto held by British men. The view that Indians were second class citizens and to be treated as such was, if not endemic, certainly widespread in both civil and military circles

The social gulf between British and Indians – even high class Indians – was very real and very deep and the attitude of British women was particularly significant. The majority of British wives never entirely integrated with the Indian people and this was very significant as far as the whole ethos of the Raj was concerned. The men, who worked closely with Indians on a day-to-day basis, were inevitably much more closely integrated than their wives who kept themselves aloof. The events of 1857 undoubtedly had a major impact on the attitude of the British women in India. Field-Marshal Auchinleck commented that:

> So far as the men were concerned, the Mutiny meant nothing to them. But the Englishwomen remembered the Mutiny and they influenced to a certain extent the behaviour and feelings of their menfolk. I think that they were very largely responsible for the break-up of relations between the British and the Indians.[10]

Over the two hundred years of the Raj from the founding of the Indian Army in the 1750s until Independence for India in 1947, the status of the Indian officer waxed and waned. Although always a key figure in providing an essential link between the British officer and the sepoys, the degree of responsibility and freedom given to an Indian officer varied. At times the Indian officers might almost be considered as de facto commissioned officers on a par with their British counterparts, at other times, especially in the first half of the nineteenth century, they were perceived as little more than glorified non-commissioned officers. It was the Second World War which provided the impetus to train and commission large numbers of Indian officers and provided them with opportunities to reach the higher levels of command. Without this opportunity, the Armies of India and Pakistan would have been in some considerable difficulty as their British officers left for the last time in 1947.

The Indian Army, was unique in having two sets of officers, one British and one Indian. These two very disparate groups of officers managed to function effectively together in order to produce a highly professional army, an army in which regimental tradition and the bond between British and Indians enabled the soldiers to overcome often appalling conditions and to achieve victory. Indian officers made a considerable contribution to the well-being of their regiments, particularly through their family traditions, and the undoubted leadership displayed by many of those officers. The professionalism displayed by the modern Indian Army is a tribute to the contribution made by their forebears.

---

10   Field Marshal Lord Auchinleck, quoted in Mason, *A Matter of Honour*, p. 251.

Fear of a repetition of the awful events of 1857 underpinned some of the prejudice against Indians as officers and the determination to keep them in subordinate positions. If Indian officers were trained and given experience of command might they not one day rise up and lead their men against the British? The fact that the Indian artillery was restricted to mountain guns was certainly one practical example of concern about a possible uprising in the future. Although it was accepted that Indian officers might well be able to assume command, even in difficult circumstances, they were thought of as lacking the moral and financial integrity of a British officer. In particular there was a fear, not always entirely unjustified, that Indian officers would favour members of their own caste or clan unduly. A further concern was the perceived difficulty which might arise if an officer of one class was asked to lead men of another.

It does not seem possible to seriously to doubt the courage and leadership potential of the Indian officers and many instances of this have already been given, Sir Charles Egerton commented in 1908 that:

> They (Indian officers) have frequently shown marvellous courage, resource and readiness to assume command and responsibility under extremely difficult and trying circumstances. Subedar Naranger Singh of the 1st Sikh Infantry at Maizan in June 1897 carried out a steady and orderly retirement over 9 miles of difficult country – no British officer could better have displayed greater skill in extricating the troops from their position.[11]

It was the intransigence of men like Roberts and their refusal to accept that Indians were perfectly capable of command which prevented the implementation of full Indianisation much earlier.

There were British officers who recognised the abilities of Indian officers and who wished to see those abilities put to better use. Sir Charles Egerton writing in his report of 1908 made suggestions as to how the status of Indian officers might be improved. Though they were less well educated than the British, the Indian officers were seen to possess personal qualities such as shrewdness and the ability to adapt themselves to circumstances which went some way to make up that deficiency. Integrity and the ability to deal equal-handedly with all classes within the regiment without giving preference to his own was seen as an important quality in an Indian officer

Apart from the attitude of the British towards them, another important reason which hindered Indian officers was their lack of basic education even down, in many cases, to their inability to read and write. This is not to say that they were incompetent or that they lacked ability or military skills. Lord Ismay wrote in his autobiography published in 1980: 'Our senior Indian officer could not even sign his name. For all his illiteracy, there was no better troop leader in frontier warfare in any army in the

---

11   Sir Charles Egerton, The Status of Indian officers in the Native Army and suggestions for its improvement, 1908, OIOC, L/MIL/7/7152.

world.'[12] This lack of education reflected the overall lack of educational opportunities for most Indians during the nineteenth century and well into the twentieth.

In spite of the difficulties in their path, it is clear that many, if not all, Indian officers made a vital contribution to their regiments and to the army as a whole and many British officers were quick to recognise this contribution. The Indian officers were a crucial link between the British officers and the soldiers. Promotion to jemadar offered an opportunity for advancement to the able and ambitious sepoy. The subedar-major, in particular, was a very significant figure in the regiment. He acted as a father figure to the younger sepoys and adviser to the British subalterns. Stephen Cohen points out that he might well have entered the regiment at the same time as the Colonel:

> They often formed bonds of friendship and military brotherhood that were unbreakable under stress. The experienced VCO was vitally needed in the peasant army, and the combination of VCO, sepoy and British officer formed a stronger whole than the sum of the individual components.[13]

In spite of this recognition of the qualities and abilities of the Indian VCOs, no attempt was made to fit them for higher command. The process of Indianisation was painfully slow and had barely begun at the start of the Second World War. As weapons and tactics became increasingly more sophisticated, the lack of education and experience on the part of the majority of Indian officers became ever more of a handicap. It was the events of 1939-45 and the vast increase in the size of the Indian Army which provided the spur which finally brought about real Indianisation. It was the Second World War which brought about real changes in the attitudes of the British towards the notion of Indian officers and finally speeded up the process of Indianisation. The young British men who were being commissioned at that time had not acquired the prejudices of their older colleagues. Daniel Marston, who interviewed a significant sample of British and Indian officers who had served in the campaign in Burma, found at that time that little racial prejudice was experienced by the newly-commissioned Indians.[14] Many British and Indians realised that there was a job to be done and they worked harmoniously together in order to achieve their goal.

Leadership is crucial in determining the effectiveness of any military unit. It is a truism that there are no bad soldiers, only bad officers. Mason suggests that the best British officers of Victorian times were like schoolmasters, devoting themselves to the instruction and encouragement of young men.[15] Their dedication inspired a corresponding allegiance and devotion from their men. Men like Jacob and Lawrence were able to identify and bring out the best qualities in the Indian troops and at the

---

12   Lord Ismay, *Memoirs of Lord Ismay* (London, Heinemann, 1960), p. 10.
13   Cohen, *The Indian Army*, p. 44.
14   See Marston, *Phoenix from the Ashes*, p. 227.
15   See Mason, *A Matter of Honour*, pp. 530/1.

same time recognized that Indians could be just as capable leaders as they themselves were. The Indian officers provided experience and continuity; they were the bedrock on which a regiment depended. Unfortunately, only gradually, and often unwillingly, did the British as a whole come to recognise the truth of this. Indianisation proceeded very much more slowly in the army than it did in the civil administration. Queen Victoria's proclamation of a career open to all Indians was more honoured in the breach than in the observance, at least as far as the army was concerned. The demand for Indianisation of the army raised serious questions about British policy and British stereotypes. It seemed unthinkable to many British officers that Indians could perform as well as they themselves did. If they accepted this then their own secure positions in the military hierarchy were at risk. It took the Second World War and the vast increase in numbers required in the army to expose the myth of the so-called martial races. Thus a valuable resource was wasted. What, for instance, might have been the impact of two well- trained, fully equipped Indian Corps coming into the line at the first Battle of Ypres?

The modern Indian Army is built upon the great traditions of its predecessors. An anonymous leader writer in *The Times* discussed the misconduct of some of the soldiers of the multi-national UN Force operating at that time in the Congo. He paid tribute to the discipline and professionalism of the Indian forces involved:

> Peace-keeping forces should be drawn from as wide a pool as possible, in practice few armies have the necessary discipline, training and combat experience. British, French (with occasional exceptions) and Indian troops have all performed effectively in harsh, unfamiliar conditions.[16]

The American historian Roger Beaumont wrote:

> The Indian Army may yet appear to be an imperfect and flawed but brilliant jewel in the now-fallen crown of empire. If there is any significance in the Indian Army it is that, like life itself, in spite of all the reasons why it should not have been at all, it grew, and it endures.[17]

Field Marshal Earl Wavell, Viceroy and Commander in Chief in India wrote of the 4th Indian Division which fought in Africa and Italy that it would go down in history as one of the great fighting formations of all time; to be compared with The Tenth Legion, The Light Division in Spain and Napoleon's Old Guard.[18] In his Notes on the Bengal Army, Brigadier General Brownlow wrote in 1875: 'The key note of my observation, and my belief is, that you cannot have a good Indian regiment without good

---

16    *The Times*, 21 December 2004.
17    Beaumont., *The Sword of the Raj*, p. 196.
18    Quoted in Bristow, *Memories of the British Raj*, p. 204.

Indian officers.'[19] Throughout the two hundred year history of the British Raj Indian officers made a vital contribution to the success and achievements of the Indian Army. Initially they were a crucial link between the, often inexperienced, British officer and the sepoys. Their long experience and commitment to their regiments combined to build esprit-de-corps. Without their contribution the army would have been but a pale shadow of what it became and what it still is in today's India. They could have done more but the fact that they were not permitted to do so was not their fault. Their swords of were indeed glittering, but they were kept trembling in their scabbards for far too long.

19   Brigadier C. H. Brownlow, *Notes on the Indian Army of Bengal*, L/MIL/17/2/468, quoted in Kaushik Roy, *Brown Soldiers of the Raj*, p. 250.

# Bibliography

## PRIMARY SOURCES

(I) ORIGINAL RECORDS, DIARIES AND LETTERS.

### Documents in the Oriental and India Office Collection, the British Library, London. (OIOC)

Abstract of Confidential Reports of Native regiments as to the efficiency of Native officers, 1876, L/MIL/7/7240.

Annual Report on Indian State Forces, 1924/5, 1926/7, 1927/8, 1930/31 and 1931/32, Calcutta, L/P and S//13/268 Col 2/4.

Appendix V to the Papers relating to the Organisation of the Native Army, published by the India Office Military Department in 1876, L/MIL/7/7240.

Appendix to the Viceroy's Note by C in C India: L/MIL/7/19006.

Appendix to the Viceroy's Note by the Governor-General North-West Frontier Province, L/MIL/7/19006.

Appendix to the Viceroy's Note by the Lt-Governor of Burma, L/MIL/7/19006.

Blood, Sir B., Memorandum dated 30 December 1914 L/MIL/7/19006.

Chesney Sir G., 23rd January 1888, Military education for Natives of India, L/MIL/5/2202.

Departmental Minute No 438 of 1876, submitted to the Secretary of State 20. 5. 1876. L/MIL/7/7240.

Despatch from the Government of India dated 24 November 1916, L/MIL/7/19006.

E.G.B., Minute signed and dated 20 March 1917, L/MIL/7/19006.

Egerton, Gen Sir C. 1908, Note on the status of Native officers of the Indian Army and suggestions for improvement, L/MIL/7/7152.

Haig, Sir D., Memorandum on Army training in India, 1910-11, L/MIL/17/5/2198.

Jacob, Major J., commanding Scinde Irregular Horse. Letter to the Assistant Adj Gen Scinde Div, 6.8.1849, L/MIL/7/7240.

Jacob, Gen J., The Appendix to the Memorandum which includes comments from a number of eminent British officers, L/MIL/7/7240.

Kitchener, Lord, 1908, Memorandum on the Future of Native Officers, L/MIL/17/5/1746.

Letter from the Viceroy to India Office dated 17 April 1917, L/MIL/7/19006.

Letter from the War Office to the India Office dated 5 July 1917, L/MIL/7/19006.

Military Secretary, Minute dated 28 September 1914, L/MIL/7/19006.

Memorandum submitted to the Secretary of State for India 1876, L/MIL/7/7240.

Napier, Lord, Memorandum 1875, L/MIL/7/7240.

Napier Lord, Response to the letter was sent from the Military Department in 1875 to the Adjutant General in India, the Governors of Madras and Bombay and the Lt Governor of the Punjab, L/MIL/7/7240.

Norman Sir H.W., 1875, Note on the organisation of the Indian Army, L/MIL/7/7240.

Norman, Sir H.W., 5th July 1878, Note on officering the Indian army, L/MIL/17/5/1686.

Note by Viceroy on the granting of commissions to Indians, October 1915, L/MIL/7/19006.

Reports of the Chief Censor: Letters to and from Indian soldiers in The Great War. L/MIL/5/ 825, 826 and 827.

Report of the Indian Sandhurst Committee, L/MIL/17/5/1783.

Report of the Indian Sandhurst Committee; evidence of Lt Col Maynard, 4/6th, Rajputana Rifles, L/MIL/17/5/1785.

Report of the Indian Sandhurst Committee; evidence of Col Walshe, commanding RA, Eastern and Western Command, L/MIL/17/5/1785.

Report of the Indian Sandhurst Committee, evidence from Risaldar Sardar Khan, Indian Adjutant and QM RIMC, Dehra Dun, L/MIL/17/5/1785.

Secret Memo from the Secretary of State for India to the Cabinet, 20 July 1917, L/MIL/7/19006.

The Secretary of State for India to the Governor General on the 10th of August 1876, L/MIL/7/7240.

**Kanota, Jaipur**

The diaries of Kanwar Amar Singh, typescript copies kept together with the original at Kanota, Jaipur quoted by kind permission of the late Mohan Singhji of Kanota and his sons, Man Singh and Prithvi Singh. Extracts from these diaries have been published in two books:

Rudolph S.H. and Rudolph L.I., with Mohan Singh (Eds), *Reversing the Gaze* (New Delhi: Oxford University Press, 2000) covers Amar Singh's diaries for the period 1898-1905

DeWitt C. Ellinwood, Jr, *Between Two Worlds: A Rajput officer in the Indian Army 1905-1921* (Lanham, Maryland: Hamilton Books, 2005).

**National Army Museum, London (NAM).**

Maxwell, Captain (later Lt-Colonel) E.L., Letters, 7402-34.
Regimental Order Book of the Scinde Irregular Horse, Two volumes.
Regimental Order book, Sam Browne's Cavalry, Handwritten, 1898.
*War Narrative of 9th Hodson's Horse,* anonymous typescript.

**Gurkha Museum, Winchester**

The Gibbs Papers. A collection of material on different aspects of regimental life of
    the 6th Gurkha Rifles, collected and compiled by Lt-Col H.R.K. Gibbs, 6th
    Gurkha Rifles.
Regimental Letter Book for the nineteenth century, 1st Gurkha Rifles.
The Character Roll of Native officers and NCOs, 1914-1948, 1st Bn, 2nd KEO
    Gurkha Rifles.

**National Archives of India**

Private Papers of Field Marshall K.M. Cariappa.
Record Book, 28th Regiment Bombay Infantry.
The Tighe Papers, relating to service in the Bombay Grenadiers, 8206/83.
Typescript notes on the History of the 2nd Punjab Cavalry, 6910-11-2(a).

**The National Archives, Kew**

War Diary of the Jodhpur IS Lancers Aug 1914–Dec 18.

**(ii) Printed Sources**

**Diaries, Correspondence and Speeches**

*Lord Curzon in India: A Selection of Speeches 1898-1905* (London: Macmillan, 1906).
Robson, B. (ed), *Roberts in India: The military papers of Field Marshal Lord Roberts
    1876-1893* (Stroud: Alan Sutton for the Army Records Society. 1993).

**Autobiographies**

Bristow, Brig. R.C.B., *Memories of the British Raj* (London: Johnson, 1974).
Creagh, Sir O'Moore, *Autobiography* (London: Hutchinson and Co, 1925).
Grimshaw, Captain R., *Indian Cavalry Officer 1914-15* (Tunbridge Wells: D J Costello
    Ltd., 1986).
Guest, Captain F., *Indian Cavalryman* (London: Jarrolds Publishers, 1959).
Hayter, Col A., *The Second Step* (London: Hodder and Stoughton. 1962).

Ismay, Lord, *Memoirs of Lord Ismay* (London: Heinemann, 1960).
Lunt, J. (Ed), *From Sepoy to Subedar: the Life and Adventures of Sita Ram* (London: The Military Book Society, 1970).
Masters, J., *Bugles and a Tiger* (London: Michael Joseph, 1956).
Masters, J., *The Road past Mandalay* (London: Michael Joseph, 1961).
Willcocks, General Sir J, *With the Indians in France* (London: Constable, 1930).

**India Army Lists**

The Bengal Army List, January 1877
India Army List, July 1914
Indian State Forces Army List, July 1924

**Articles in the *Journal of the United Services Institution of India (JUSII)***

Barrett, Captain A.L., 'The appointment of Native Officers in the Indian Army', Vol. XXXVI, No. 167, April 1907, p. 177.
Bonham-Carter, Captain B.H., 'The Training of Indian Platoon Commanders', Vol. LII, No. 229, October 1922.
Cadell, Col Sir P., 'From Sepoy to Subedar – Fact or Fiction?', No. 327, April 1947, pp. 265-272.
Elsmic, Major A.M.S., '56th Punjab Rifles FF. Native officers of the Indian Army', Vol. XXXVI, No. 167, April 1907, p. 45 et seq.
Grant, Brig N.B., 'Carry on Subedar Sahib', July/September 1965, pp. 136 et seq.
Hennill, Captain R., 'Bombay Army. Soldiers' Institutes for the Native Army of India'; Vol. 5, 1876.
J McD B., 'The Higher Training of Infantry Native Officers', Vol. 14, 1892.
Laing, Major F.C., '12th Pioneers, Education in the Native Army', Vol. XXXVIII, 1909, pp 287 et seq.
Morton, Captain S., '24th Punjabis Recruits and Recruiting in the Indian Army', Vol. XXXVI, No. 166, January 1907, p. 53.
Radcliffe, Major A.W.T., '14th Sikhs, Increase of British officers for the Native infantry', Vol. XXXVI, No. 127. 1896.
'Verb Sap Our Native Officers', Vol. XXXVI, No. 167, April, 1907, p. 209 et seq.
Yadav, Brig H.S., 'Tips from the Subedar Major', October/December 1965, pp 249–252.
Young, Major G.F. AQMG, 'The efficiency of our Native regiments with a view to their preparation to meet an European Army'. Vol. 9, 1885.

(III) TELEPHONE INTERVIEWS WITH BRITISH OFFICERS WHO HAD SERVED IN THE INDIAN ARMY PRIOR TO **1947**

The following were interviewed:-
Dennison, Brig G.E., 7th Battalion, 2nd Punjab Regiment.

Francis, Major P.W., Machinegun Battalion, 9th Jat Regiment
Keown, Captain, Probyn's Horse
Leslie-Jones, Colonel R.E., served with Royal Bombay Sappers and Miners
Montagu, Lt Col. 2nd Battalion, 2nd Punjab Regiment

## SECONDARY SOURCES

### Regimental and Unit Histories

Ahmad, Major General Rafiuddin and Ahmad, Major Rifat Nadeem, *Unfaded Glory: The 8th Punjab Regiment* (Uckfield: Naval and Military Press, 2006).

Anon, *History of the Second Panjáb* (sic) *Cavalry from 1849 to 1866.* (London: Kegan, Paul, Trench and Co, 1888).

Anon, *Historical Records of the 20th (Duke of Cambridge's Own) Infantry 1908–1922* (London: Butler and Tanner, 1923).

Anon, *History of the 5th Royal Gurkha Rifles (Frontier Force)* (Aldershot: Gale and Polden, c. 1928).

Birdwood, Col F.T., *The Sikh Regiment in the Second World War* (Norwich: Jarrold and Sons, n.d).

Bolt, D., *Gurkhas* (London: Weidenfield and Nicolson, 1967).

Cardew, Major F.G., *Hodson's Horse.* (London: Blackwood, 1928).

Condon, Brig W.E.H., *The Frontier Force Rifles* (Aldershot: Gale and Polden, 1953).

Cooper, G. and Alexander, D. (eds), *Bengal Sappers 1803-2003 An Anthology* (Chatham: Insitution of Royal Engineers, 2003).

Drake-Brockman, D.H., *With the Royal Garwhal Rifles in the Great War 1914-1917* (Originally published 1934 but no further details, reprint Uckfield, Naval and Military Press, 2006)

Duncan, Maj-Gen R.C., *History of the Jodhpur State Forces in the War 1939-45* (Jodhpur: Jodhpur Government Press, 1946)

Haig, Major A.B., *War Records of the 24th Punjabis 1914-20* (Aldershot: Gale and Polden, 1934).

*History of the 15th (IS) Cavalry during the Great War 1914-18* (London: HMSO, undated).

Hanut Singh, Maj-Gen, *'Fakhr-E-Hind' The Story of the Poona Horse* (Dehra Dun: Agrim Publishers, 1993).

Hogg, Major G.C. and Erskine, Major C.M., *Historical Records of the Poona Horse* (Bombay: Education Society Press, c. 1882).

James, Lt-Col F.H., *History of the 1st Bn, 6th Rajputana Rifles* (Aldershot: Gale and Polden, 1938).

Lawford, J., *30th Punjabis* (Oxford: Osprey Publishing, 1972).

Maunsell, Col E.B., *The Scinde Horse 1839-1922* (London: Butler and Tanner, 1926).

Merewether, Lt-Col J.W.B., CIE and Smith, Rt Hon Sir F., *The Indian Corps in France* (London: John Murray, 1917).

*Report on Brigade Training, Bannu Brigade* (Pioneer Press: Allalabad 1908).

Ogle, Colonel N. and Johnston, Colonel H.W., *History of the 1st Battalion, 2nd Punjab Regiment* (London: W. Straker Ltd, c. 1923).

Pigot, G., *History of the 1st Battalion, 14th Punjab Regiment* (New Delhi: Roxy Printing Press, 1946).

Smith, E.D., *'Valour' A History of the Gurkhas* (Stroud: Spellmount, 2007).

Stevens, Lt-Col G.R. OBE, *Fourth Indian Division* (Toronto: McLaren and Son Ltd., nd).

Tennant, Lt-Col E., *The Deccan Horse in the Great War* (Aldershot: Gale and Polden, 1939).

Tugwell, Col W.G.P., *History of the Bombay Pioneers 1777–1933* (Bedford: The Sydney Press, 1938).

Watson, Maj-Gen W.A., *KGO Central India Horse: The Story of a Local Corps.* (Edinburgh: Blackwood, 1930).

Wylly, Col. C.B., *The Poona Horse (17th QVO Cavalry)* (London: RUSI, 1933).

## General Histories relating to the Indian Army

Alavi, S., *The Sepoy and the Company: Tradition and Transition in Northern India 1770–1830.* (Delhi: Oxford University Press, 1998).

Allen, C., *Soldier Sahibs: The Men Who Made the North-West Frontier.* (London: John Murray, 2000).

Anon, *The Army in India and its Evolution* (Calcutta: Government Printing Press, 1924).

Barat, A., *The Bengal Native Infantry: its organisation and discipline 1796–1852.* (Calcutta: Firma K. L. Mukhopadhway, 1990).

Barua, P., *The Army Officer Corps and Military Modernisation in Later Colonial India* (Hull: University of Hull Press, 1999).

Barthorp, M., *Indian Infantry Regiments 1860-1914* (Oxford: Osprey Publishing, 1979).

Beaumont, R., *The Sword of the Raj: The British Army in India 1747-1947* (Indianapolis: The Bobbs-Merrill Company Inc, 1977).

Boyden, P. and Guy, A. (eds), *Soldiers of the Raj* (London: NAM, 1997).

Carman, W.J., *Indian Army Uniforms (Cavalry)* (London: Leonard Hill Books, 1961).

Chenevix Trench, C., *The Indian Army and the King's Enemies 1900–1947* (London: Thames and Hudson, 1988).

Cohen, S.P., *The Indian Army: It's Contribution to the Development of a Nation.* (Delhi: Oxford University Press, 1990).

Corrigan, G., *Sepoys in the Trenches: The Indian Corps on the Western Front 1914-15.* (Staplehurst: Spellmount Ltd. 1999).

David, S., *The Indian Mutiny 1857* (London: Viking, 2002).

Falls, Capt. C. and Becke, Major A.F., *Military Operations in Egypt and Palestine from June 1917 to the end of the War* (London: HMSO, 1930).

Farwell, B, *Armies of the Raj From the Mutiny to Independence 1858 to 1947* (London: Viking, 1989).

Gaylor, J., *Sons of John Company: The Indian and Pakistan Armies 1903–1991.* (Tunbridge Wells: Spellmount Ltd., 1992).

Glover, M., *An Assemblage of Indian Soldiers and Uniforms* (London: Perpetua Press, 1973).

Harris, J., *The Indian Mutiny* (London: Book Club Associates, 1973).

Heathcote, T.A., *The Indian Army: The Garrison of British Imperial India 1822-1922* (London: David and Charles, 1974).

Hibbert, C., *The Great Mutiny* (London: Penguin Publishers, 1976).

Jackson, Major D., *India's Army.* (London: Sampson, Low, Marston & Co., c. 1940).

Jacob, Brig-Gen J., *Tracts on the Native Army of India; its organisation and discipline.* (London: Smith and Elder, 1857).

James, L., *Raj: The Making and Unmaking of British India* (London: Little, Brown and Company, 1997).

Kaye, J.W., *The Sepoy War in India* (London: W H Allen 1870-76), two volumes.

Lawrence, Sir H., *Essays Military and Political* (London: Henry Colborn, 1959).

MacMunn, Lt-Gen Sir G., *The Armies Of India* (London: A and C Black, 1911).

MacMunn, Lt-Gen Sir G., *Martial Races of India* (London: Sampson Low, Marston and Co., n.d.).

Marston, Daniel P., *Phoenix from the Ashes; The Indian Army in the Burma Campaign* (Westport, Conneticut: Praeger, 2003).

Mason, P., *A Matter of Honour* (London: Jonathan Cape, 1974).

Mason, P., *The Men who ruled India* (New Delhi: Rupa Press, 1985).

Menezes, Lt-Gen S.L., *Fidelity and Honour: The Indian Army from the Seventeenth to the Twenty-first Century* (New Delhi: Penguin Books, 1993).

Menpes, M. and D., *The Durbar* (London: Adam and Charles Black, 1904).

Narinder Singh Desri, *Sikh Soldier, Vol III, Policing the Empire* (Uckfield: Naval and Military Press, undated).

Rajendra Nath, Maj-Gen, *Military Leadership in India: The Vedic Period to the Indo-Pak wars.* (New Delhi: Lancer Books, 1990).

Omissi, D., *The Sepoy and the Raj: The Indian Army 1860–1940* (London: Macmillan, 1994).

Reid, S., *Armies of the East India Company 1750-1850* (Oxford: Osprey Publishing, 2009).

Roy, K., *Brown Warriors of the Raj* (New Delhi: Manohar Publishers Ltd,2008),

Shahid Hamid, Maj-Gen S., *So they Rode and Fought* (Tunbridge Wells: Midas Books, 1983).

Sharma, Lt-Col G., *The Nationalisation of the Indian Army 1885-1947* (New Delhi: Allied Publishers Ltd, 1996).

Singh Sandhu, Major General G., *The Indian Cavalry: The History of the Indian Armoured Corps until 1940*. (New Delhi: Vision Books, 1981).

Summer, Ian, *The Indian Army 1914-1947* (Oxford: Osprey Publishing, 2001).

**Biographies**

Arthur, Sir G., *Life of Lord Kitchener* (London: Macmillan and Co, 1920) two volumes.

Thomas, Lt-Gen T. and Jasrit Mansingh, *Lt-Gen P S Bhagat PVSM VC*. (New Delhi: Lancer International, 1994).

Van Wart, R.B., OBE, *The Life of Lt-Gen HH Sir Pratap Singh* (London: Oxford University Press, 1926).

**Other Books**

Bond, B., *The Victorian Army and the Staff College 1854 -1914* (London: Eyre Methuen 1972).

Briggs, Col. J., *Letters to a Young Person in India* (Oxford: Oxford University Press, 1922).

Dalrymple, W., *White Mughals* (London: Harper Collins, 2002).

Keay, J., *India: A History from the Earliest Civilisations to the Boom of the Twenty First Century* (updated edition, London, Harper Press, 2010).

Gitanjali Kolanand, *Culture Shock India* (London: Kuperand, 1994).

Mockler-Ferryman, Major A.F., *Annals of Sandhurst: A Chronicle of the Royal Military College* (London: Heinemann, 1990).

Parkes, F., *Begums, Thugs and White Mughals* (London: Sickle and Moon Books, 2002).

Street, H., *Martial Races: The military, race and masculinity in British Imperial culture 1857-1914* (Manchester: Manchester University Press, 2004).

Yardley, M., *Sandhurst: A Documentary* (London: Harrap, 1987).

**Unpublished PhD Theses**

Jarboe, A.T., 'Soldiers of Empire, Indian Sepoys in and beyond the Imperial Metropole during the First World War'. Northeastern University, Boston, Massachusetts, 2013.

Chandar Sundaram, 'A Grudging Concession: The Origins of the Indianization of the Indian Army's Officer Corps, 1817-1917'. McGill University, Montreal, Canada, 1996.

**Articles**

Callahan, R., 'Servants of the Raj: The Jacob family in India 1817-1926' *Journal of the Society for Army Historical Research*, Vol. 56, No. 225, Spring 1978, pp. 4–24.

Chibber, Lt Gen M.L., 'Regimental System and Esprit-de-Corps in the Indian Army', *Indo-British Review*, 16 (1984), pp. 139-150.

Chhina, R. and McClenaghan, T., 'The VCO: Origin and Development', *Journal of the Indian Military Historical Society*, Vol 28, No 3, Autumn 2011.

Jack, George M., 'The Indian Army on the Western Front, 1914-15: A Portrait of Collaboration' in *War in History*, 2006, Vol. 13, No. 3, pp. 329-362.

Mclain, R A, 'The Indian Corps on the Western Front: A Reconsideration' in Wiest and Jensin (eds) *Warfare in the Age of Technology* (New York: NYU Press, 2002).

Greenhut, J., 'The Imperial Reserve: The Indian Corps on the Western Front', *Journal of Imperial and Commonwealth History*, XII, pp. 54-73, 1983.

Sharpe, A., 'The Indianisation of the Indian Army' *History Today* Volume 36 March 1986'.

Sundaram, Chandar, 'Reviving a 'Dead Letter': Military Indianisation and the Ideology of Anglo-India 1885-91' in Partha Gupta and Antrudh Deshpande (eds) *The British Raj and Its Indian Armed Forces 1857-1939* (New Delhi: Oxford University Press, 2002).

Sundaram, Chandar, 'The Imperial Cadet Corps and the Indianisation of the Indian Army's Officer Corps, 1897-1923. A Brief Survey' *'Durbar', the Journal of the Indian Military Historical Society* Vol 27 No 2 Summer v2010 pp 53-62.

Sundaram, Chandar, 'Treated with Scant Attention', *Journal of Military History*, Vol. 77, No. 1, January 2013.

# Index

## Index of People

## Index of Places

## Index of Military Formations & Units

# Index of Miscellaneous Terms

Lightning Source UK Ltd.
Milton Keynes UK
UKOW06n1919060315

247413UK00005B/28/P